A GUIDE TO
MILITARY ART

—

THE YEOMANRY AND VOLUNTEERS OF 1794-1808

A GUIDE TO MILITARY ART

—

THE YEOMANRY AND VOLUNTEERS OF 1794-1808

RAY WESTLAKE

The Naval & Military Press

Published by

The Naval & Military Press Ltd
Unit 5 Riverside
Bellbrook Industrial Estate
Uckfield, East Sussex
TN22 1QQ
England

Tel: +44 (0) 1825 749494

www.naval-military-press.com

ACKNOWLEDGEMENTS

A book of this type would not have been possible without the kindness and generous help of the Anne SK Brown Military Collection held at Brown University, Providence, RI, USA and its curator Peter Harrington. And of course my wonderful wife Claire who, in addition to being an essential source of encouragement, has had the thankless task of checking my spelling, grammar and punctuation. Finally, my thanks to Chris and Gary Buckland of the Naval & Military Press for their continuing faith in this 'Guide' project.

INTRODUCTION

This 'Guide' is not intended to be in any shape or form a history of the many hundreds of yeomanry and volunteers corps that were raised between 1794 and 1808 due to the threats of invasion from France—the so called 'Napoleonic Volunteers.'

It was film producer and pioneer of the American animation industry Walt Disney who said, 'Of all of our inventions for mass communication, pictures still speak the most universally understood language.' And, of course, we must not forget the wider use of 'A picture is worth a thousand words.' Certainly, if we set out to make a study of uniform, we can learn much from looking at pictures. But, as that superb reference work published by the Army Museums Ogilby Trust in 1972, Index To British Military Costume Prints 1500-1914, points out, '...it must not be supposed that a contemporary artist, however celebrated, does not make mistakes in drawing what he thought he had seen.' To this we could add, 'or what he thought might look good'—artistic licence, in fact. Here, as an example, I bring to mind a comment made by no less that Richard Caton Woodville who, after the end of the Great War, was given a commission by the London Scottish to paint a picture recalling that regiment's brave stand at Messines Ridge at the end of October 1914. Up in the Mess went the finished article. Those that were there pointed out recognisable faces and features of the battle and in general were pleased at what they saw. But up stepped one veteran who, with finger pointing, exclaimed, 'They're wearing sporrans. We never had them on the Ridge. They were left behind at our billets.' This point was raised with the artist who remarked without hesitation, 'Yes, I'm quite aware of this. I included them as I thought the men looked quite empty without them.'

At this point the serious student of military dress may well abandon the idea of including prints and pictures in his study of the subject, and instead content him or herself with official publications such as Dress or Clothing Regulations. 'But, before the critic condemns an artist for depicting a uniform that was never approved under the regulations' (Index to British Military Costume Prints again), 'let him remember that the British officer has long been noted for his independence from Dress Regulations.'

With all that said, let us now set about enjoying what talented people have placed on paper and canvas for centuries. How wonderful it must have been to have called into Rudolph Ackermann's shop at 96 Strand, London in the 1790s to purchase something from his vast stock of military or sporting prints. And equally in more recent times, the Parker Gallery at 2 Albemarle Street, Piccadilly where you could treat yourself to something of the old regiment to go up above the living room fireplace. Here, then, is a selection of prints and pictures to enjoy.

INDEX

1 – LIGHT INFANTRY VOLUNTEERS ON A MARCH

Hand-coloured etching with caption 'Light Infantry Volunteers On A March'. Below this, in a rough hand, the line 'Published by R [Rudolph] Ackermann June 8 1804 n' 101 Strand. Signed and dated 'Rowlandson [Thomas] 1804'.

As a straggler tries to keep up with a party of volunteers making their way up a steep hill, three overweight infantryman take time out to rest within the shade of a tree. One man, his wig having been given a temporary location on the muzzle of a musket, mops his brow with a white handkerchief as he enjoys a pipe. A helmet with tall green feather plume by his side, the exhausted part-time soldier wears a red coat with blue collar, cuffs and turnbacks, a white bulging waistcoat and white breeches. Still with helmet and wig in situ, a second man sleeps peacefully on the hard ground, his red, rolled cloak with blue lining doing good duty as a temporary pillow. (*Image courtesy of the Anne SK Brown Military Collection, Brown University Library*)

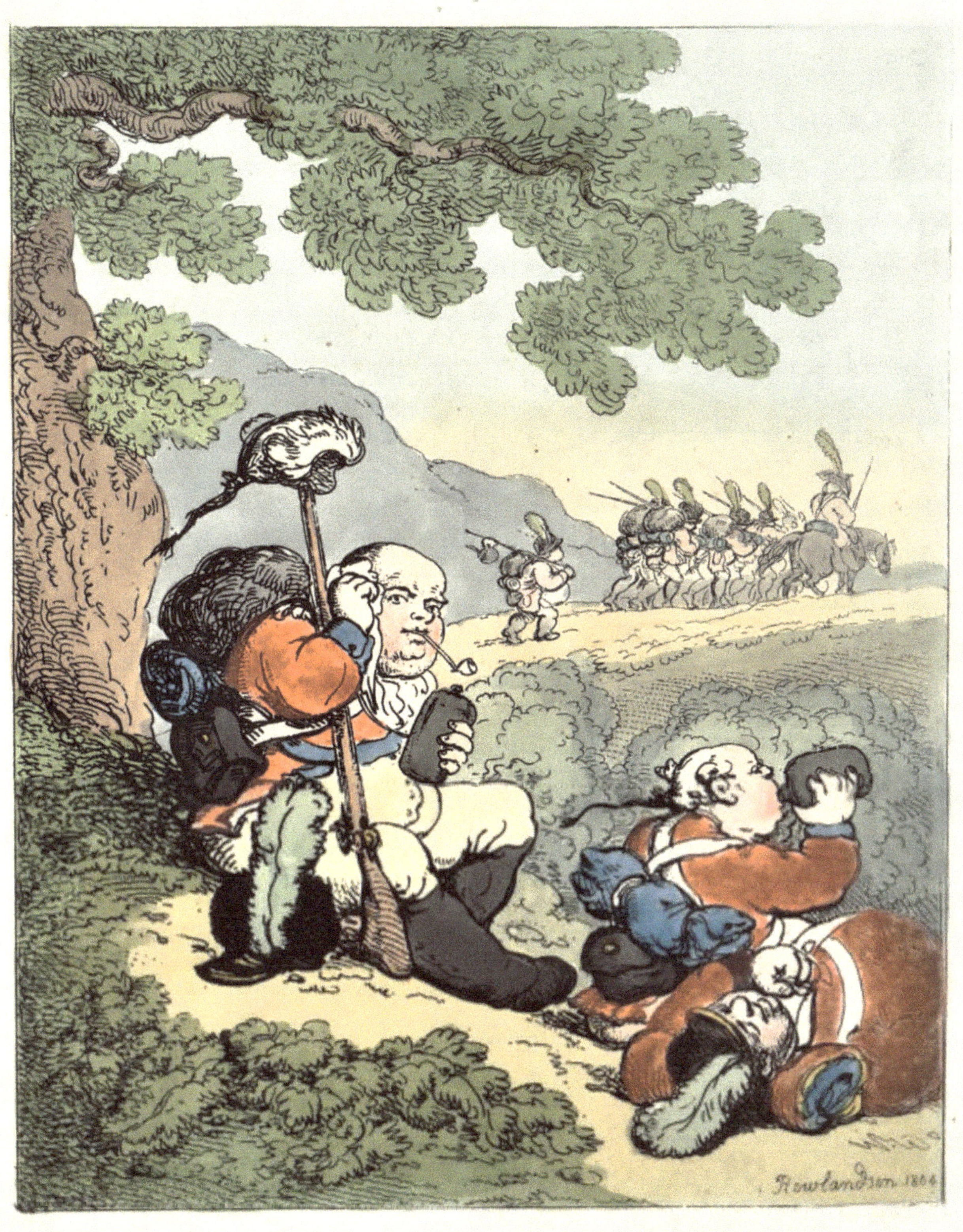

LIGHT INFANTRY VOLUNTEERS ON A MARCH.

Publish'd by R. Ackermann June 1 1804 No. 101 Strand

2 – PRIVATE CADER IDRIS, EDEYRNION AND PENLLYN VOLUNTEERS, 1803-1809

Colour frontispiece after Captain Herbert Oakes-Jones to Merioneth Volunteers and Local Militia During the Napoleonic Wars (1795-1816) by Hugh J Owen and published in Dolgelley by Hughes Bros, 1935.

A single figure, standing at ease with a musket at his side, wears the universal infantry pattern uniform of the time which includes the shako introduced to the Army in 1800 and worn until 1812. The brass plate is again of the general type with its royal cypher, garter, trophies of arms and lion of England. White shoulder-belts are worn with an oval brass plate which would have displayed the Prince of Wales's coronet and plumes. The coat is scarlet with dark blue collar, cuffs and shoulder straps which end in white worsted tufts. The collar is edged all round with white braid, the same material being used for the buttonholes and cuff decoration. Black buttoned gaiters are being worn which rise up to just below the knees.

The North Wales county of Merionethshire also included a volunteer corps raised at Barmouth during the Napoleonic wars which, notes Hugh Owen, had the same uniform but the colour of the breeches was blue instead of white.

The Cader Idris Volunteer Infantry took its name from the Cader Idris mountain (2,927 feet) situated at the southern end of the Snowdonia National Park close to the town of Dolgelley, and it was here that the corps was raised by Sir Robert Williams Vaughan Bart towards the end of 1803. Sir Robert of Nannau, who represented Merionethshire in Parliament from 1792-1836 prior to becoming high sheriff in the following year, became its first lieutenant-colonel commandant.

The corps was divided into six companies under the command of Captains Edward Owen (No 1), Edward Price Anwyl (No 2), Humphrey Williams (No 3), Thomas Richards (No 4), William Williams (No 5) and William Lloyd (No 6). Hugh Owen's book makes the interesting point regarding Privates Nos 54 to 89 who were mentioned in a return with the remark 'Clothes in store and not given out on account of Harvest time.' 'No doubt', he remarks, 'these men were engaged in agriculture and were therefore excused attendances.'

The Vale of Edeyrnion lies between Corwen and Pont Calettwr in the north east of the county, a distance of about eight miles. Permission to raise a corps in the area was granted to Sir Watkin Williams Wynn after his letter to the War Office dated 27 November 1803. In the following December he was able to report that an enrolled strength of 204 had been obtained and that the Edeyrnion Volunteers had been organised into three companies with headquarters at Cowen and the following officers: Major Edward Lloyd Edwards, Captains Hugh Davies, William Davies and Thomas Davies, Lieutenants Walter Jones, Henry Maesmawr, Ensign Robert White, Quartermaster Robert Jones and Surgeon Robert Davies.

The Penllyn Volunteer Infantry had its headquarters at Bala under the command of Lieutenant-colonel commandant Richard Watkin Price. There were four companies, these originally commanded by Captains David Anwyl, Griffith Richards, John Jones and Gabriel Davies.

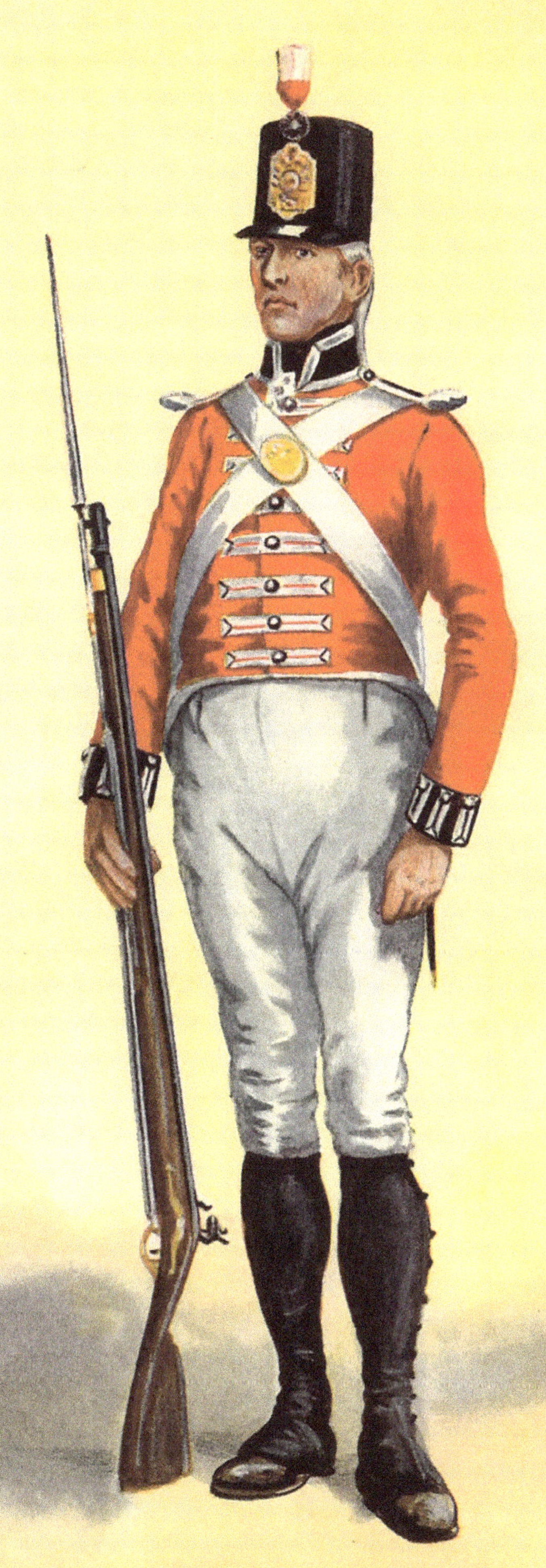

3 – GUILDHALL LIGHT INFANTRY VOLUNTEERS, 1798

Watercolour by Charles Lyall showing a member of the Guildhall Volunteer Association in the second 'Prime and Load' position—being the weapon held in the left hand while the right hand opens the cartouche box to draw out a cartridge.

The volunteer wears a scarlet coat which has wide blue lapels with yellow metal buttons, a deep blue collar, blue cuffs and turnbacks. The shoulder straps are blue with yellow edgings and fringes. The black leather helmet has black fur rising across the top from front to back, a blue and yellow turban and tall green feather plume. Yellow buttons can be seen on the white waistcoat and breeches, the artist being careful to include these on the essential front flap of the latter.

The current City of London Guildhall dates from 1411 and for many years acted as a court, those coming before its bench including Henry Garnet, for his part in the Gunpowder Plot, Thomas Cranmer, who Mary I had put on trial for treason and heresy, and the so-called 'Nine Days Queen', Lady Jane Grey. Come forward a few centuries and it would be here that the Guildhall Volunteer Association was formed in May 1798 under the command of Major Commandant Jasper Atkinson.

Rudolph Ackermann's series of prints published c1797-8 records that as well as the Light Infantry Company, the corps also included a battalion of Grenadiers. Colours were presented from the hand of Mr Atkinson on 10 October 1798 at Pentonville on the then northern fringe of the City of London.

Interestingly, Lyall's painting is clearly based on the Rowlandson image produced for Ackermann. The turban, however, is described and shown as being of leopard skin. The same notes also tell us that the oval cross-belt plate in the picture (detail unrecorded) was engraved with a representation of the Guildhall within wreaths of laurel and with the words 'Guildhall Volunteer Association'. The buttons had a crown with the letters GVA below.

1798.

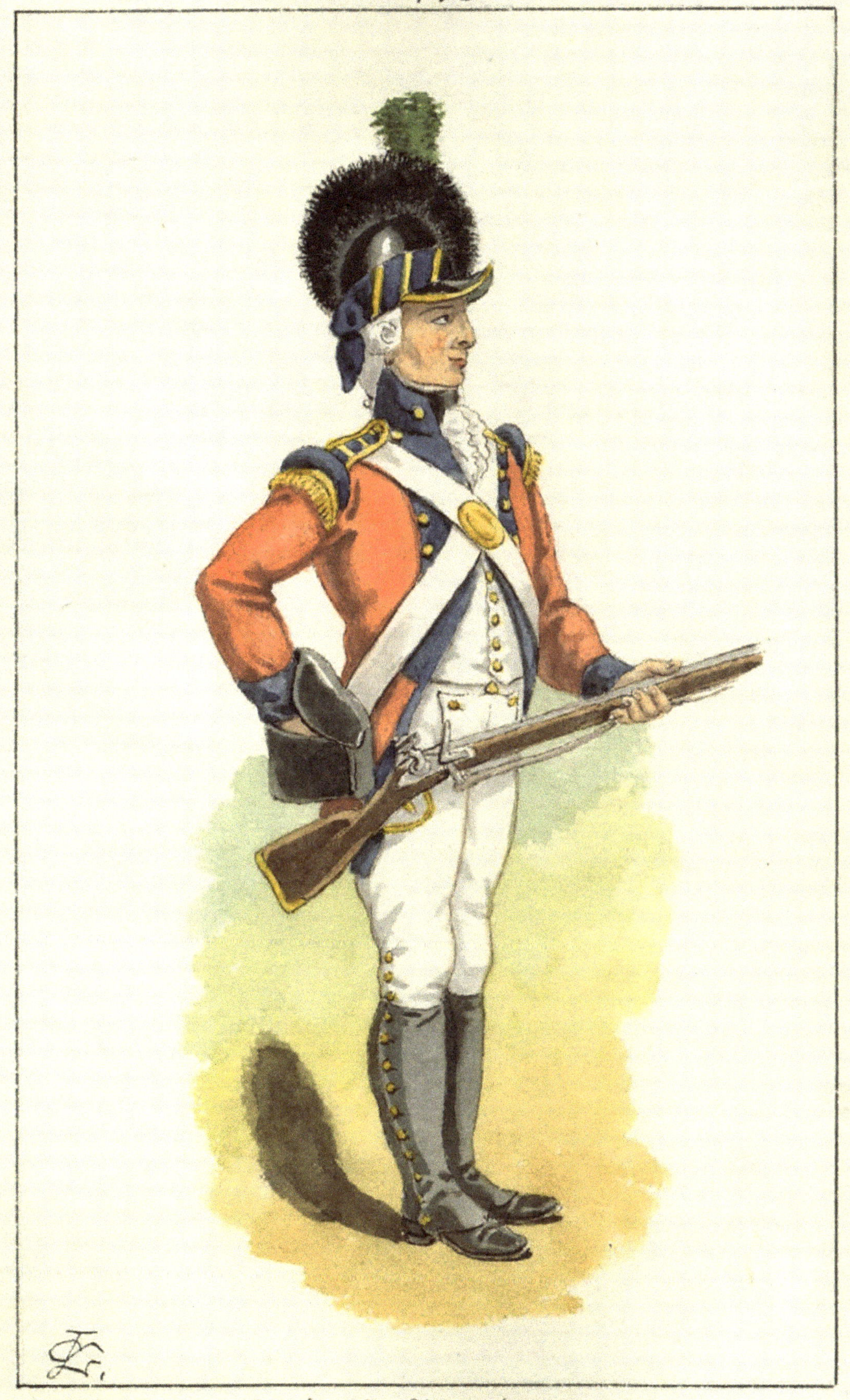

Guildhall Light Infantry.
Volunteers.

4 – OXFORD LOYAL VOLUNTEER

Hand-coloured stipple engraving published on 1 January 1799 by T Taylor of High Street, Oxford showing a single figure in the process of fixing or un-fixing his bayonet. He wears a dark blue coat with red collar, cuffs and piping, the latter forming an edging to the shoulder straps and wide lapels. The buttons are of white metal. A white waistcoat is worn with white breeches, and the white metal oval cross-belt plate is engraved with a crown over the letters OLV. The headdress is a black Tarleton helmet which has a black fur crest rising from front to back and a tall white feather plume.

An unmounted example of this image (purchase price £300) recently came up for sale by Sanders of Oxford Antique Prints & Maps who mentioned in their catalogue listing how Oxford had responded well to the call for volunteers, with great local support coming from the direction of both the university and city. Colours were presented by Lady Mackworth on Friday 27 July 1798 and the corps was present at the King George III Birthday Parade which took place at Hyde Park, London on 4 June 1799. *(Image courtesy of the Anne SK Brown Military Collection, Brown University)*

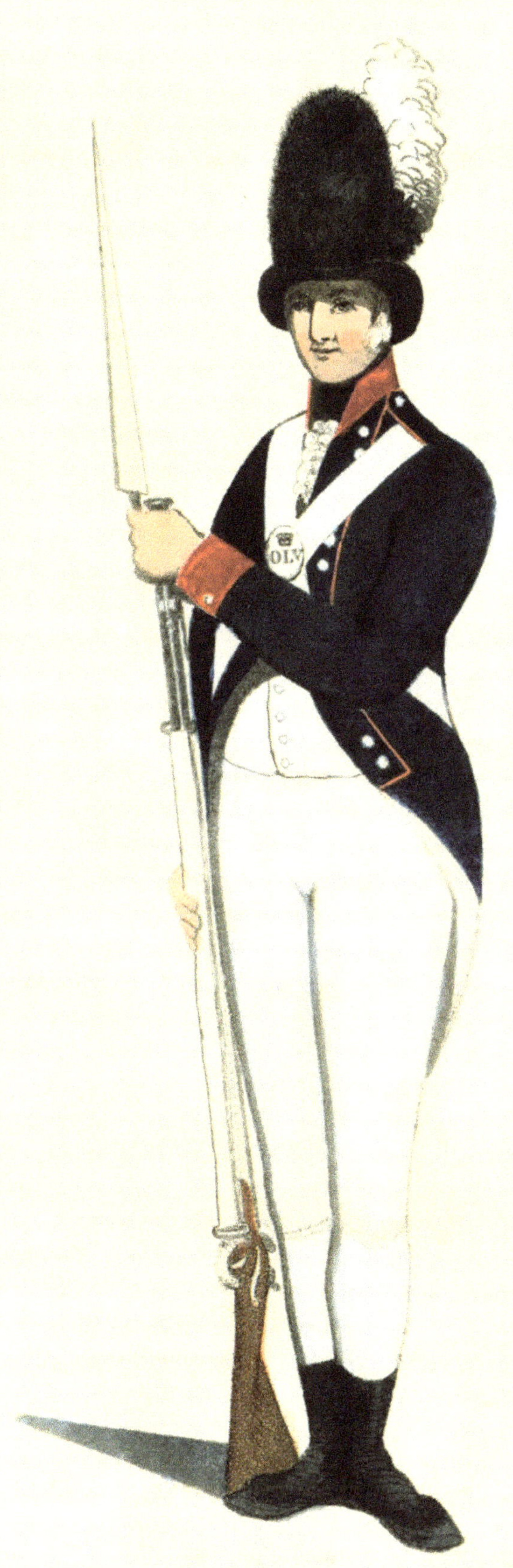

OXFORD LOYAL VOLUNTEER.

Published Jan 1. 1799, by T. Taylor, High Street, Oxford.

5 – OFFICER, HUDDERSFIELD VOLUNTEERS, 1794

Coloured lithograph after PW Reynolds facing page 70 of *A History of the Formation and Development of The Volunteer Infantry From The Earliest Times, Illustrated by the Local Records of Huddersfield and its Vicinity From 1794 to 1874* by Robert Potter Berry and published in 1903 by Simpkin, Marshall, Hamilton, Kent & Co, Ltd of 4 Stationers' Hall Court, EC London and in Huddersfield by J Broadbent & Co, High Street and Albion Street.

The image shows an officer holding a sword. He wears a scarlet coat with dark blue collar, cuffs and lapels, gold buttons and white turnbacks, the waistcoat and breeches being white. The officer has a gold-fringed epaulette on the right shoulder, a gold gorget and oval cross-belt plate. A crimson sash is worn around the waist and tied on the left side. The black hat has gold tassels on each side and is worn with white-over-red plume.

A proposal to raise a corps of volunteers in Huddersfield was put forward at meeting presided over by Sir George Armytage, Bt held at the George Inn on 28 June 1794. The response by the town's citizens was enthusiastic and as a result it was quickly agreed to raise a force consisting of not more than 200 men. For a title, 'The Huddersfield Corps of Fusilier Volunteers' was settled upon and on 6 December the names of the following appointed officers appeared in the London Gazette for 6 December 1794: Major Commandant Sir George Armytage, Captains Richard H Beaumont, Northend Nichols and Joseph Haigh, First Lieutenants Joseph Scott and William Horsfall and Second Lieutenants Walter Stables, Bramwell Dyson and John Hudson. Their commissions bore the date 18 November 1794.

Details of the officers' uniform decided upon, together with a colour plate after PW Reynolds, are given in Robert Potter Berry's book as follows: 'The uniform of the corps was the cocked hat of the period, worn across the head, coats of red cut away at the hips and faced with blue, white breeches buttoned down the length of the leg and presenting a gaiter-like appearance.' As we can see from PW Reynolds's painting, the hat included a white-over-red plume and has two gold tassels. A gilt gorget is being worn, the buttons also gilt and appearing down each of the lapels, on the cuffs and collar. A crimson sash is worn around the waist and over the waistcoat, and a white leather shoulder-belt displays an oval, gilt, plate.

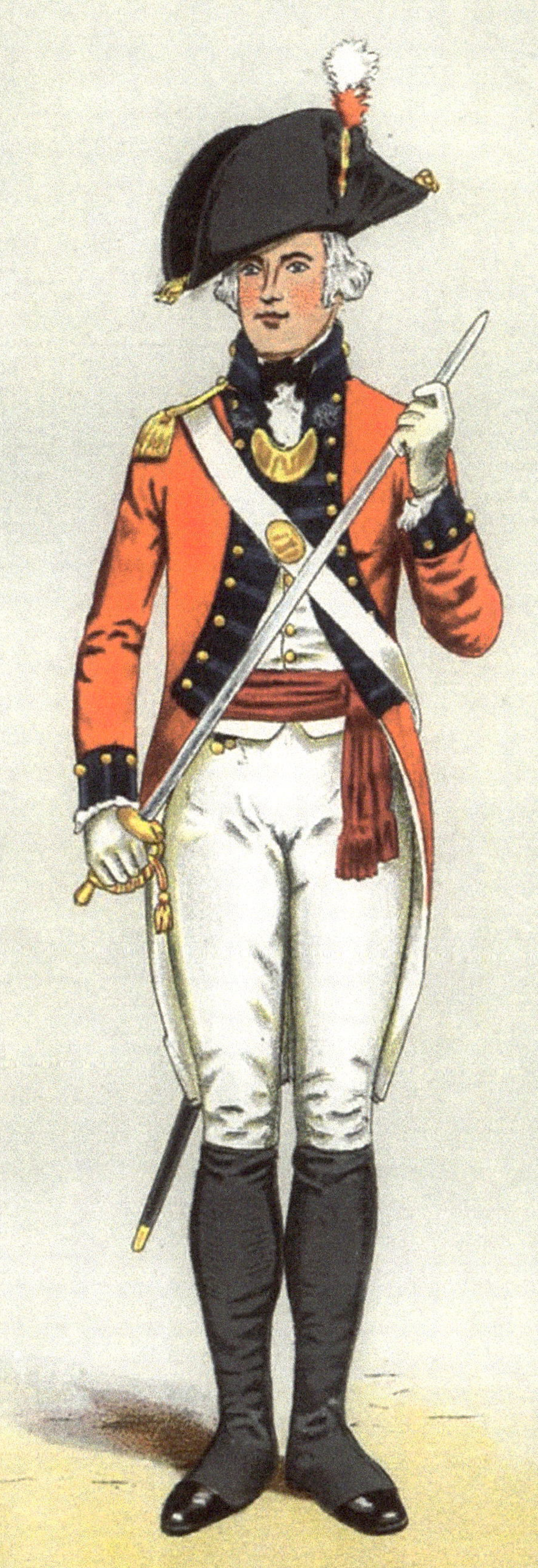

6 – THE VOLUNTEER — 1803

Coloured lithograph by G McCulloch after John Absolon, printed by Day & Sons in 1860 and published by Lloyd Brothers & Co of 96 Gracechurch Street, London being one of a pair produced illustrating a volunteer in conversation with his young sweetheart. The second image featured a sergeant of 1860 in similar circumstances. We see a country scene in which a young girl wearing an orange dress stands on a large rock close to a crude wooden fence and style. Her fan closed in one hand, the other rests on the arm of an infantry volunteer soldier who wears a scarlet coat with white, yellow or buff cuffs. His lapels are of the same colour and decorated with yellow or gold lace. Short black leather gaiters are worn with blue breeches.

Taking into account that Lloyd Brothers was a City of London firm, it may be reasonable to assume that both their 1804 and 1860 subjects are members of a local corps. And with the printing and publishing trade in mind, could it be that in 1860 the company had in mind the 2nd London Rifle Volunteers, a corps raised in 1860 and made up of men employed by the City of London's newspaper and printing industry? However, what we see in the 1803 plate may simply be a case of artistic licence, that oft-encountered departure from historic accuracy by an artist so as to create a more desired effect. As attractive as the black felt shako looks, with its cockade, plaited gilt cords and fine white and red plume, it is indeed unfortunate that the artist responsible for 'The Volunteer – 1803' has made an error in his or her choice for the headdress—the false-fronted shako shown not having been taken into use by the army until 1812. The year 1859 had seen the revival of the volunteer system that was stood down in 1808. Brothers Lloyd soon grasped upon the idea of a pair of romantic prints featuring men from both periods. (*Image courtesy of the Anne SK Brown Military Collection, Brown University Library*)

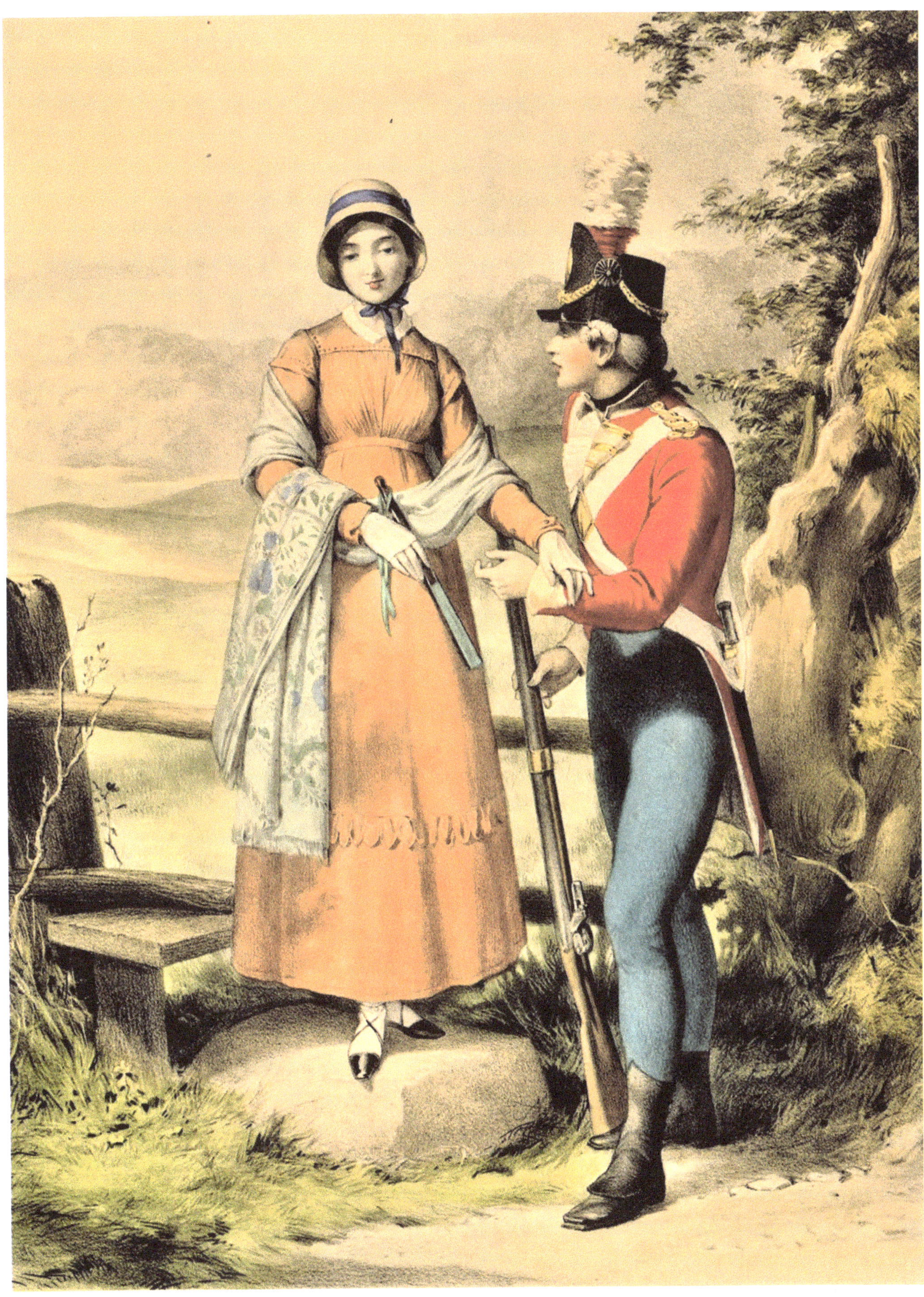

7 – THE AUKWARD SQUAD, OR ENRAGED SERGEANT

Hand-coloured aquatint after Thomas Rowlandson and published in London on 17 July 1798 by Ackermann's Gallery, No101 Strand.

Carrying the caption 'The Aukward Squad or Enraged Sergeant', the image shows a line of seven men shabbily dressed in various types of uniform and headdress. Three are wearing red coats with green collars, cuffs and lapels, two are in blue, one has a white coat with green facings, and another appears in all green. Smart and red faced, a sergeant with blue facings to his red coat waves his stick in the air as if conducting an orchestra. Looking smug with their arms folded and with grins on their faces, two boy drummers dressed in yellow coats with red lace look on. The image, which seemingly shows recruits literally not knowing their right foot from their left, is one of many caricatures produced in Georgian times with a mind to poke fun at Britain's part time amateur soldiers—militia men or volunteers. (*Image courtesy of the Anne SK Brown Military Collection, Brown University Library*)

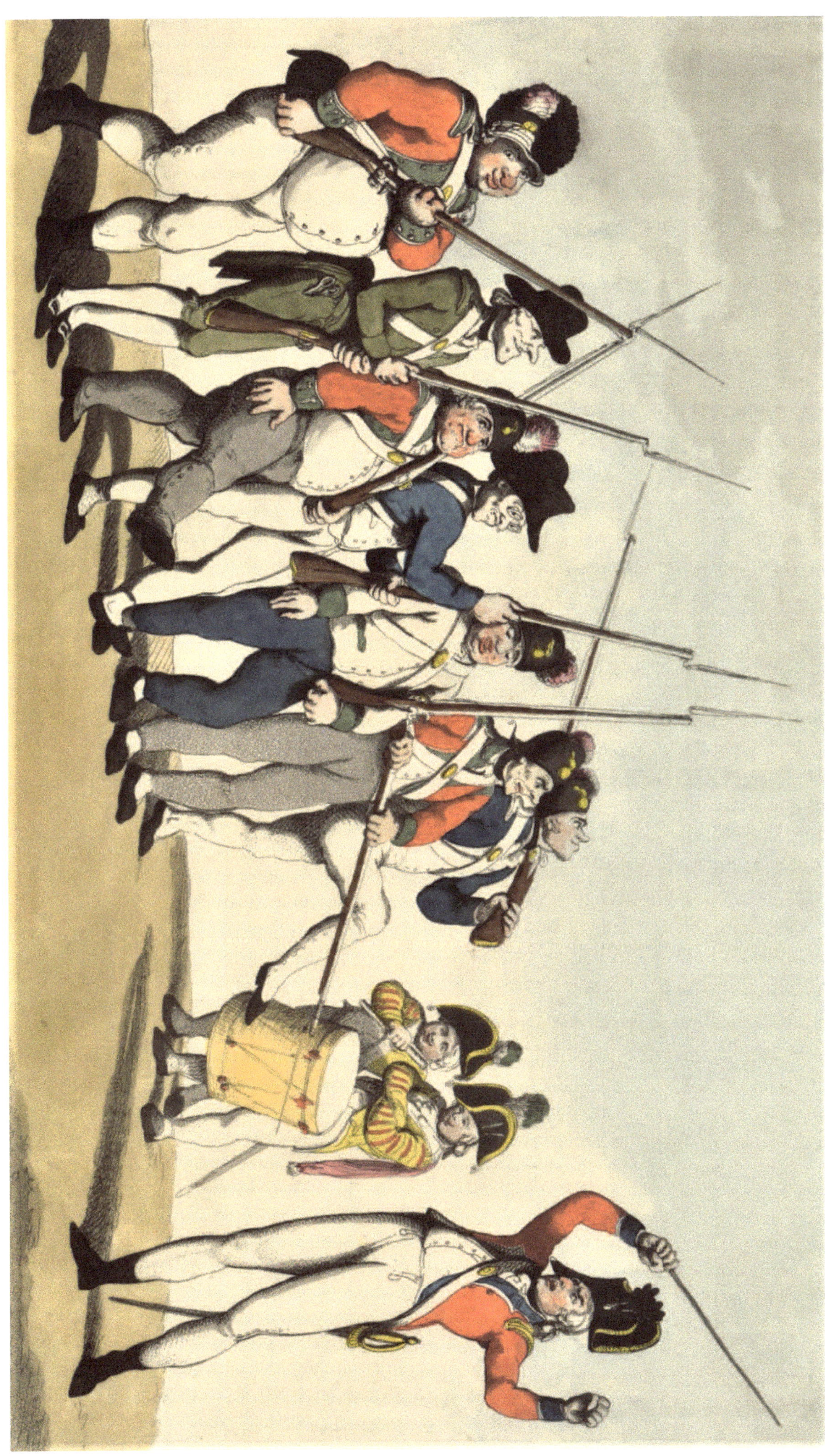

8 – SADLER'S SHARP SHOOTER

Plate No XLVI from *Loyal Volunteers of London and Environs Infantry & Cavalry In Their Respective Uniforms* published by Rudolf Ackermann of 101 Strand, London.

The artwork is by Thomas Rowlandson whose illustration is strong in detail and shows a crested helmet with gilt fittings, a light blue turban and red feather. The jacket is dark blue and the collar scarlet, piped round the top with white. The lapels, cuffs and shoulder wings are also scarlet with white piping, the latter having an additional line of gold lace. Dark blue pantaloons with a narrow strip of red piping down the seams are being worn with black half gaiters. The image is captioned at the top with 'Sadlers Sharp Shooters', and at the bottom 'A Light Infantry Man defending himself with Sadlers Patent Gun & Long Bayonet.' The image carries the date 'Sept. 14 1798'.

No information is to hand regarding the gun, but the bayonet has been described as a weapon that could be used both for slashing and stabbing. The subject of the illustration is one of Sadler's Sharp Shooters. A brief note regarding this corps is set beside the image and informs that Sadler's Sharp Shooters had been partly formed under the direction of Mr Sadler of Pimlico. Now known for its garden squares and Regency architecture (it has more than 350 Grade II listed buildings), Pimlico lies approximately between Chelsea Bridge Road, Ebury Street and Vauxhall Bridge Road. But not always was it the desirable area that we find today. When George III purchased the nearby Buckingham House in 1762, Pimlico was described as being little developed, apart from a brewery (it later became Watney's Stag Brewery) and an inn known as 'Jenny's Whim'. And so it would remain until Thomas Cubitt began his development in the 1830s.

'The Sharp Shooters at present' [August 1, 1799], continues Ackermann's notes, 'are but inconsiderable in number [one source gives 49], but it is intended to extend them to a degree of respectability, and then join with the Westminster Associations. Their excellency is that of certainty in their aim, equal to the Riflemen of America.' The corps at time of writing, Ackermann had been informed, '...was shortly to be officered by the Honourable the Board of Ordnance and at present remains in so imperfect a state as not to admit of illustration satisfactory to the Public.' Indeed, the Sharp Shooters' plate is the only one in the volume that carries no details of officers or uniform.

SADLERS SHARP SHOOTERS. No. 46.

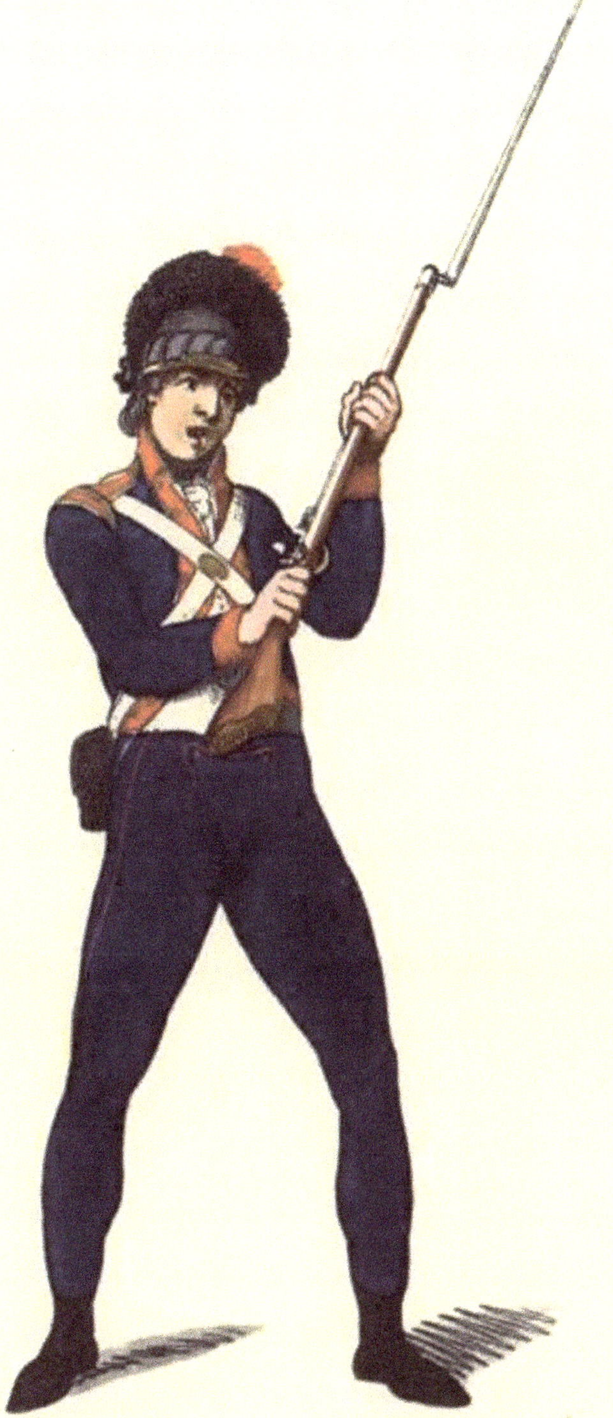

Rowlandson Delin

A Light Infantry Man defending himself with Sadlers Patent Gun & long cutting Bayonet.

London Pub. Sept 14, 1798 at Ackermann's Gallery, 101 Strand.

9 - SADLER'S FLYING ARTILLERY

Colour aquatint after Thomas Rowlandson and published by Rudolph Ackermann showing cavalry and infantry attacking a party of volunteers. A wagon pulled by two horses and with two small wheels at the front and two more than twice their size at the rear, carries a platform mounted high on large springs. On this are two volunteers, one man firing a small cannon, the other in the action of placing a ball into the barrel of another. They, and the driver who is seen urging his pair on with a whip, wear blue coats with red collars, cuffs and lapels, Tarleton helmets and blue breeches. Close behind, and similarly dressed (but they have white breeches) four cavalrymen are about to make a counter charge, three of them firing pistols into the enemy as they gallop forward. To the left of the picture, a gun carriage like that previously mentioned is under fire from a line of infantry and appears to be retreating.

Ackermann's description of Mr Sadler is brief (see Image 8), telling how the man was 'a very ingenious machinist' and 'inventor of the celebrated War Chariot'. The war chariot was described as a vehicle 'in which two persons, advancing or retreating, can manage two Pieces of Ordnance (three pounders) with alacrity, and in safety, so as to do execution at the distance of two furlongs'. Rudolf Ackermann, in fact, would later publish a print after Thomas Rowlandson showing the war chariot, calling it 'Sadler's Flying Artillery', and copies can often be found bound into *Loyal Volunteers of London and Environs*.

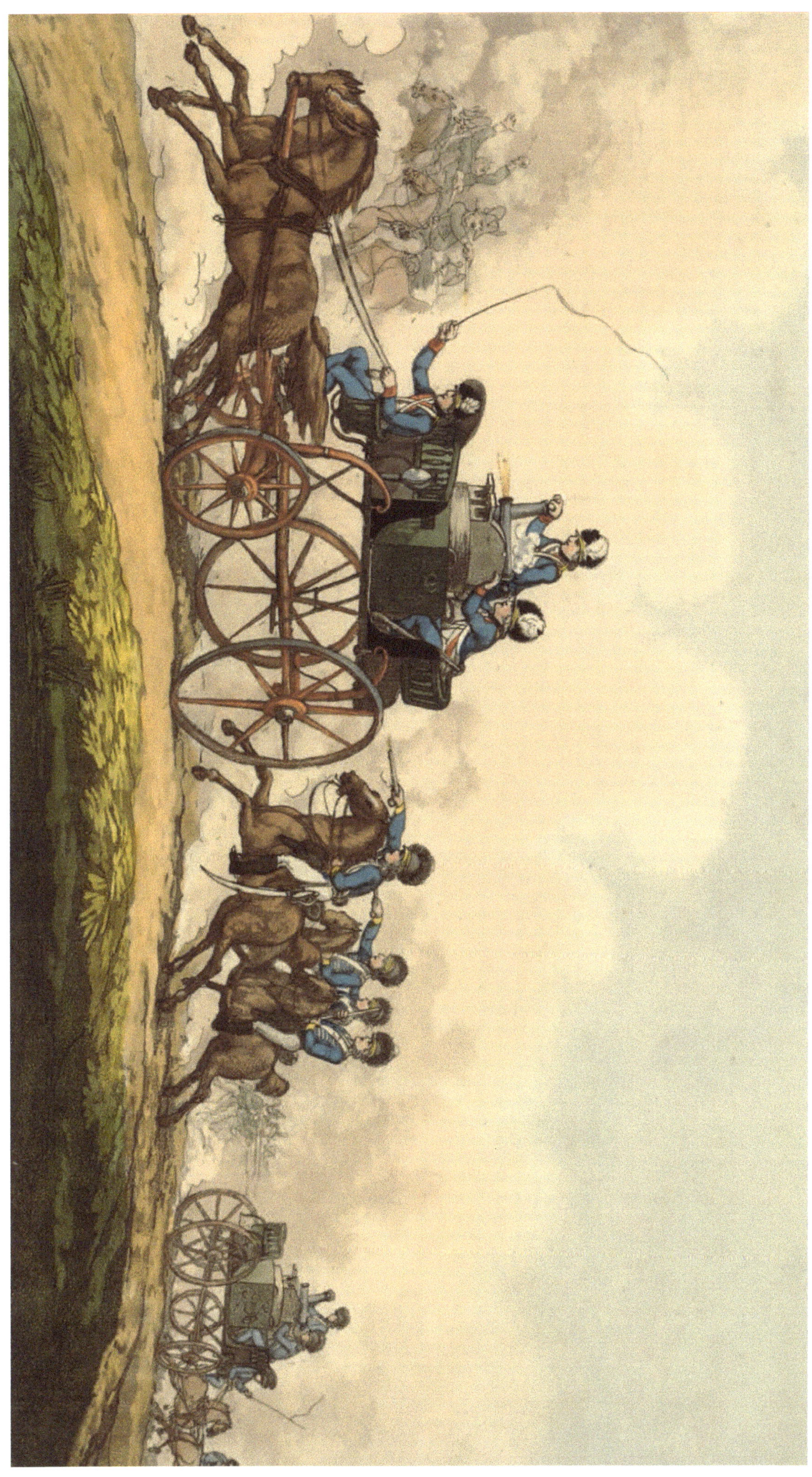

10 – COLONEL HERRIES OF THE LIGHT HORSE VOLUNTEERS OF LONDON & WESTMINSTER

Mezzotint by Charles Turner after John James Halls, published in London 22 May 1817 by Charles Turner of 30 Warren Street, Fitzroy Square and showing a bareheaded half portrait of Colonel Charles Herries in uniform and holding a Tarleton helmet in his right hand. The colonel's jacket is richly decorated across the chest with lace and he wears a pouch-belt over his left shoulder.

Charles Herries died on 3 April 1819 and was subsequently buried in the nave of Westminster Abbey. By the door that leads into the west cloister there is a marble bust of the colonel by Francis Chantrey. Below this an inscription which reads, 'In the nave of this church are deposited the remains of Charles Herries, Esquire, Colonel of the Light Horse Volunteers of London and Westminster....he was a chosen commander of a regiment of gentlemen, who, giving an example of voluntary service, were collected under the standard of loyalty, from the ranks, talents, and property of the Empire, in defence of all that was dear and sacred to men and Britons....The suavity of his manners tempered the strictness of his discipline; respect and love ensured obedience to his authority....The Light Horse Volunteers, regarding him as their father, followed him to the grave with filial reverence and, as a lasting tribute of honour to his memory, have raised this record of his virtues and their affection.'

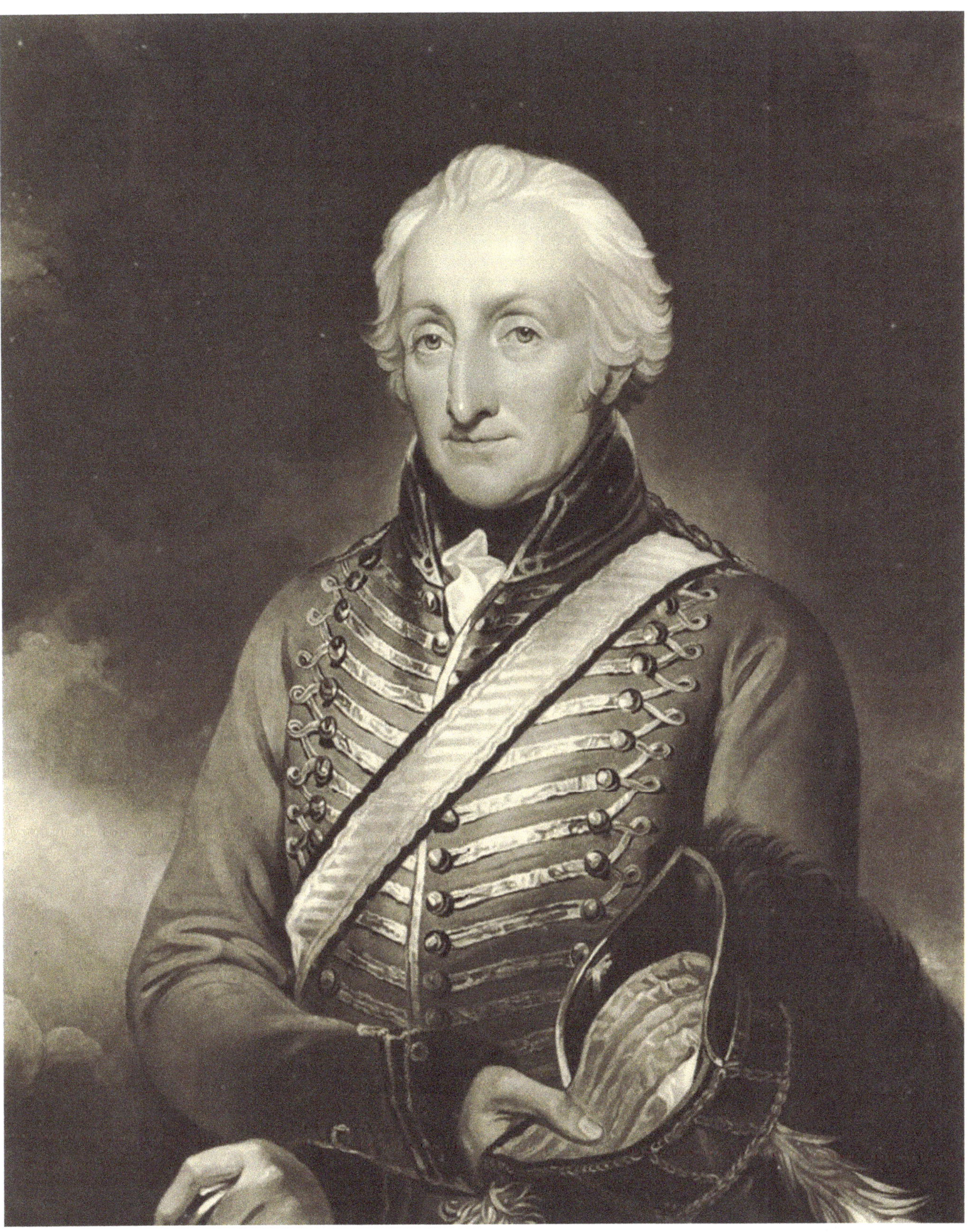

11 – NORWICH RIFLE CORPS

Colour aquatint engraved by Edward Bell after Robert Dixon, published on 15 October 1804 by R Dixon of No 65 St Clement's Church Yard, Norwich.

The image includes the caption, 'To the Officers and Volunteers of the Norwich Rifle Corps this plate of their Uniform is most respectfully Dedicated by their obliged Comrades Robt. Dixon.' Two men wearing green uniforms chat in the foreground. Tall black shakos are being worn with high green feathers, black cockades and green lines that cross the front of the headdress to the top, then fall to the side ending in green tassels. The volunteer on the left wears a black pouch-belt from which hangs a length of silver cord. He also has a wide black waist-belt fastened by a snake-hook clasp and carries his rifle in his right hand. A back view of the second man shows a black pouch, a crimson sash knotted at the back and a short skirt flap with bugle horn device. Most probably an officer, he carries a curved sabre. In the left background, a party of riflemen can be seen firing from the standing and kneeling position, another to the right are marching single file up a hill.

On Sunday 25 December 1803, the *Norfolk Chronicle* reported that, 'This day the Norwich Rifle Corps paraded at St Andrew's Hall, took the oath of allegiance, and attended service at the church of St Peter Mancroft.' (The uniform and appointments of the corps consisted of a dark green jacket, with lace of the same colour, pantaloons, and short black gaiters; hussar cap, with green feather and trimmings; a rifle-carbine, sword bayonet attached to the side by a black waist belt, and a ball pouch and powder horn slung from the left shoulder.' Commanding the corps was editor of the *Norwich Mercury*, Richard Mackenzie Bacon, whose commission as major was dated 6 December 1803. Bacon's fellow officers included Captain John Deere and 1st Lieutenant Samuel Cooke. The quartermaster was James Buttivant and surgeon, James Robinson.

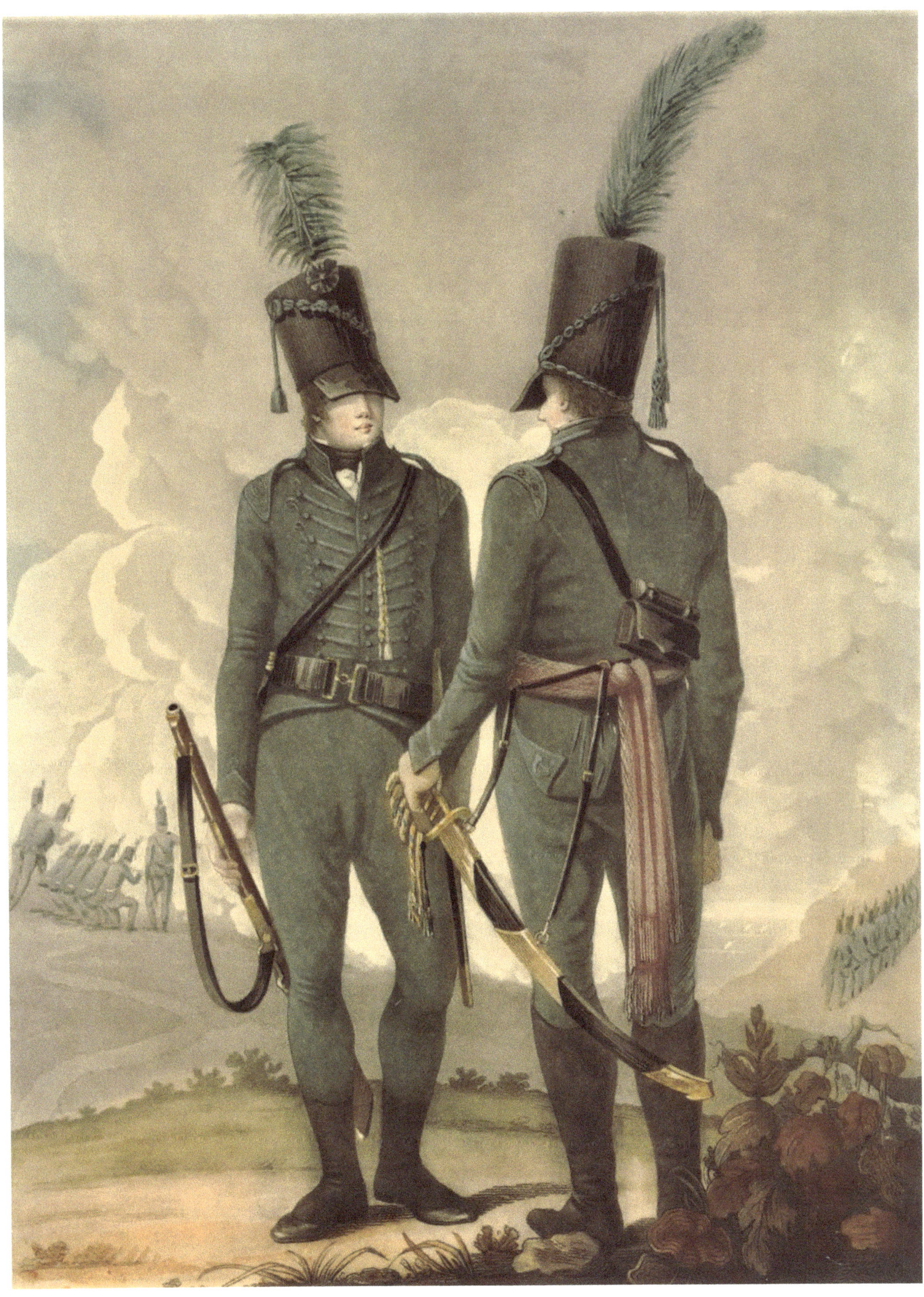

12 – PILE ARMS

Published 20 May 1799 by Rudolph Ackermann of 101 Strand, London after Thomas Rowlandson and showing three figures of volunteer soldiers (numbered as 77, 78 and 79) demonstrating the action of 'Pile Arms', The caption reads: 'At the Command the Front rank (No79) faces to the right about, & at the word Arms, the front & centre ranks (79 & 78) throw their firelocks into the left hand, the front & rear link their ramrods together & the centre ranks lock by passing their ramrods between. All the locks are turned upwards.' The three figures are representatives of the Mile End Volunteers, Shoreditch Volunteers and Trinity Minories Volunteers.

The Mile End volunteer wears a blue coat with red collar, cuffs and lapels, a white waistcoat and white breeches. In the centre, the Shoreditch private has a red coat with blue facings and gold lace. The breeches are white fastened at the knee with four buttons. On the right, a similar uniform is worn by the Trinity Minories volunteer. All three volunteers wear the Tarleton helmet.

The Trinity Minories Volunteer Association of two companies was formed on 7 May 1798 under Captain John Judson. Other officers included First Lieutenant Charles Martin and Second Lieutenant Thomas Hill. The helmet seen in the image had a blue turban with gold lines and a label bearing the name of the corps. The oval silver cross-belt plate being worn was inscribed with the intertwined letter, TMA. The black cartouch box bore the device of a star, the buttons also with TMA.

Formed under John Marshall, Esq in March 1798, the Shoreditch Volunteers (No78) consisted of one company with Captain John Marshall, First Lieutenant Thomas Longbotham and Second Lieutenant Charles Lush. The helmet displayed Shoreditch Volunteers with the Garter and crown on the right side, the brass cross-belt plate having SV in cypher.

At Mile End the corps was formed under John Liptrap, Esq in May1798 with two companies consisting of sixty rank and file each. Captain John Liptrap commanded the first company, a Captain Tompson the second. The oval cross-belt plate seen being worn in Rowlandson's image had the letters MEV in cypher with a crown above. The buttons, the same, but with the letters arranged ME over V.

N° 77.
MILE-END
VOLUNTEER

N° 78.
SHOREDITCH
VOLUNTEER

N° 79.
TRINITY MINORIES
VOLUNTEER

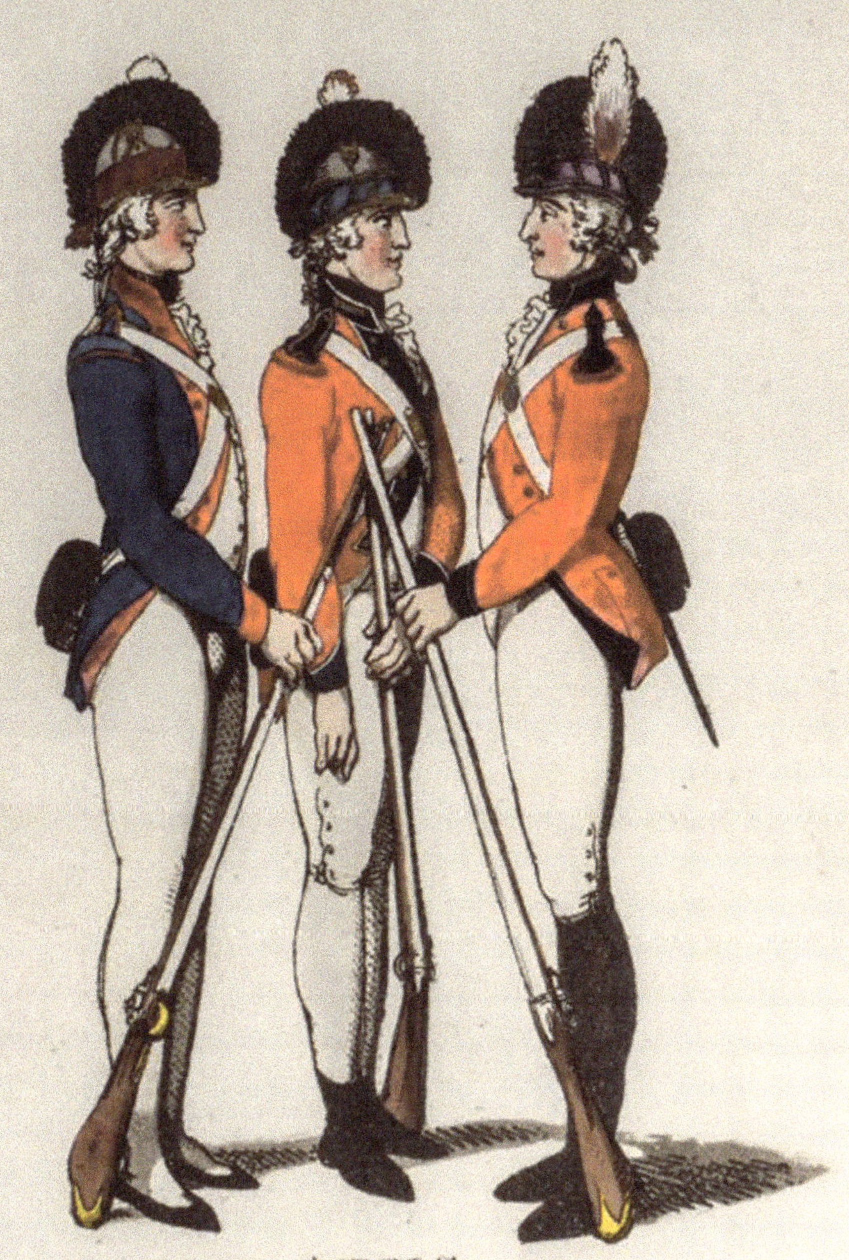

Rowlandson Delin.

PILE ARMS.

At the Command the Front Rank (No. 79) faces to the right about, & at the word Arms, the front & Center Ranks (79 & 78) throw their firelocks into the left hand, the front & Rear link their Ramrods together & the Center Ranks lock by passing their Ramrods between. All the locks are turned upwards.

13 – WARWICKSHIRE YEOMANRY CAVALRY

Colour aquatint engraved by Charles Williams after Edward Rudge and published on 20 April 1801 by Edward Rudge of Birmingham with the following dedication, 'To the Earl of Aylesford Coll, Heneage Legge Esqr Lieut Coll, Major Evelyn Shirley Esq Capt. The other officers and Privates comprising the Four Troops of Warwickshire Yeomanry Cavalry this late is Respectfully Dedicated by their Obedient Humble Servt, E Rudge.'

Against a peaceful background of houses and a church, two mounted yeoman are seen with sabres drawn. One points his at the other who is shown holding a defensive position. The dedication appears at the bottom of the image, the centre of which shows a sketch of a member of the corps relaxing by a tree with one arm resting on a shield charged with the Bear and Ragged Staff of Warwickshire. Close by is another shield, this time bearing the devices of the Earl of Aylesford. On the ground, a spade, sickle and plough representing the agricultural character of the area from which the regiment was drawn.

The uniform worn was red with yellow facings, silver lace and white breeches, James Willson's Chart of 1806 giving the strength as 343. (*Image courtesy of the Anne SK Brown Military Collection, Anne SK Brown University Library*)

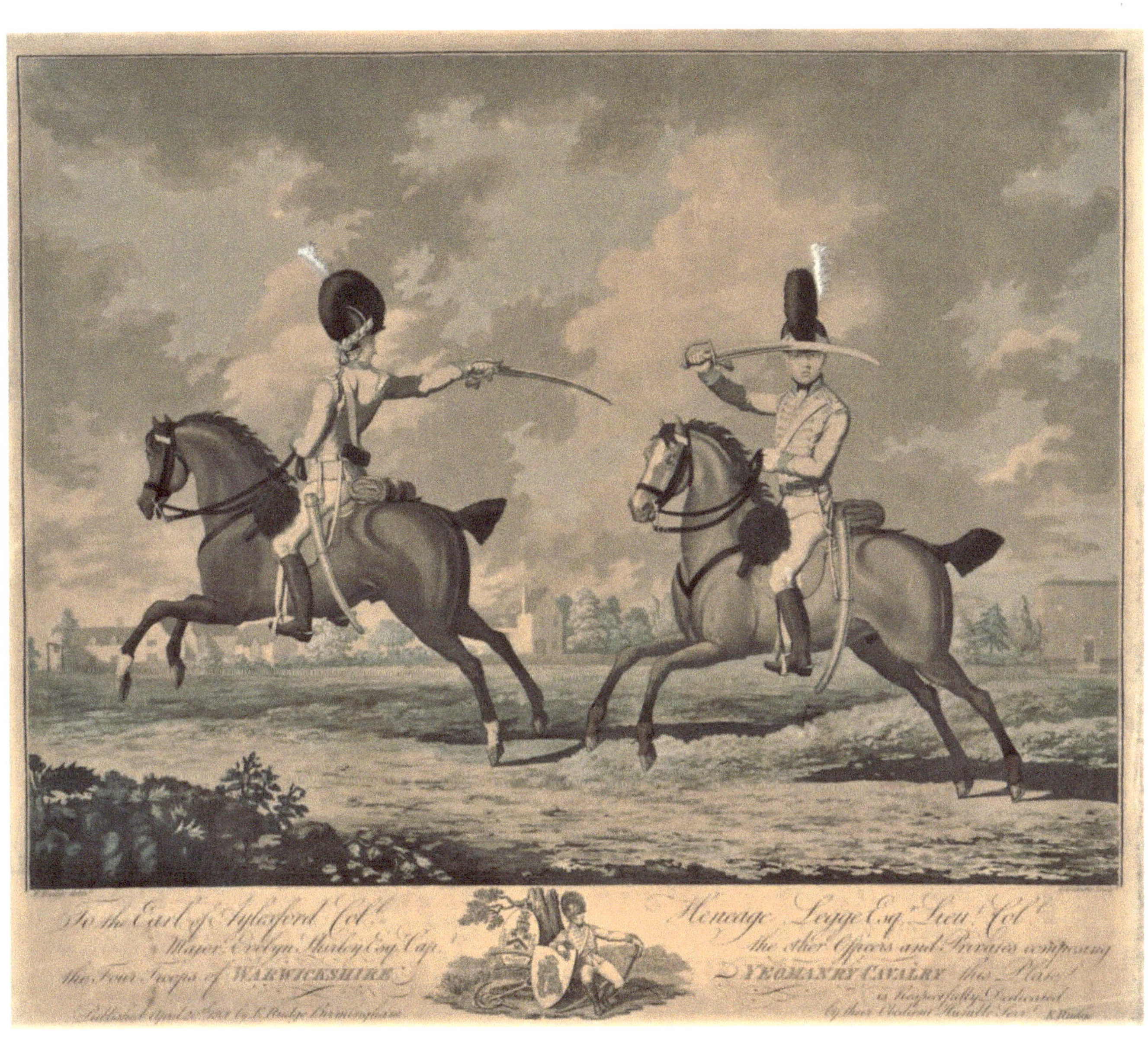
To the Earl of Aylesford Col.
Heneage Legge Esq. Lieu. Col.
Major Evelyn Shirley Esq. Cap.
the other Officers and Privates composing
the Four Troops of WARWICKSHIRE
YEOMANRY CAVALRY this Plate
is Respectfully Dedicated
by their Obedient Humble Serv.

14 – THE VOLUNTEER ARMY OF GREAT BRITAIN, 1806

Stipple engraving by Henry James Richter showing George III with the Princes of Wales to his right and the Duke of York on his left riding along a rough track. With numerous staff behind, the king is at the head of a column of volunteers which falls off to the right, then winds down a hill to the left of the image. The Royal Standard is flying, and many other flags can be seen among the coloum.

The engraving was included at the head of a chart (thirty-nine by twenty-six inches) published by John and Henry Richter of 26 Newman Street, London on 1 March 1807. Compiled by James Willson, the document sets out to record the name of every volunteer corps in existence in 1806, along with details of its uniform (colour of coat, facings, lace and breeches), commanding officer and strength. Lengthy captions appear either side of the engraving. To the left, and below a crown, 'A View of the Volunteer Army of Great Britain in the year 1806 designed to commemorate the great and united spirit of the British People armed for the support of their Ancient Glory and Independence Against the unprincipled ambition of the French Government.' And on the right, this time below the Prince of Wales' plumes, coronet and motto, 'To His Royal Highness George Prince of Wales This Work executed under His illustrious and immediate Patronage Is with His Royal Highness's gracious permission Most respectfully Dedicated by His obedient and faithful Servant Janes Willson.'

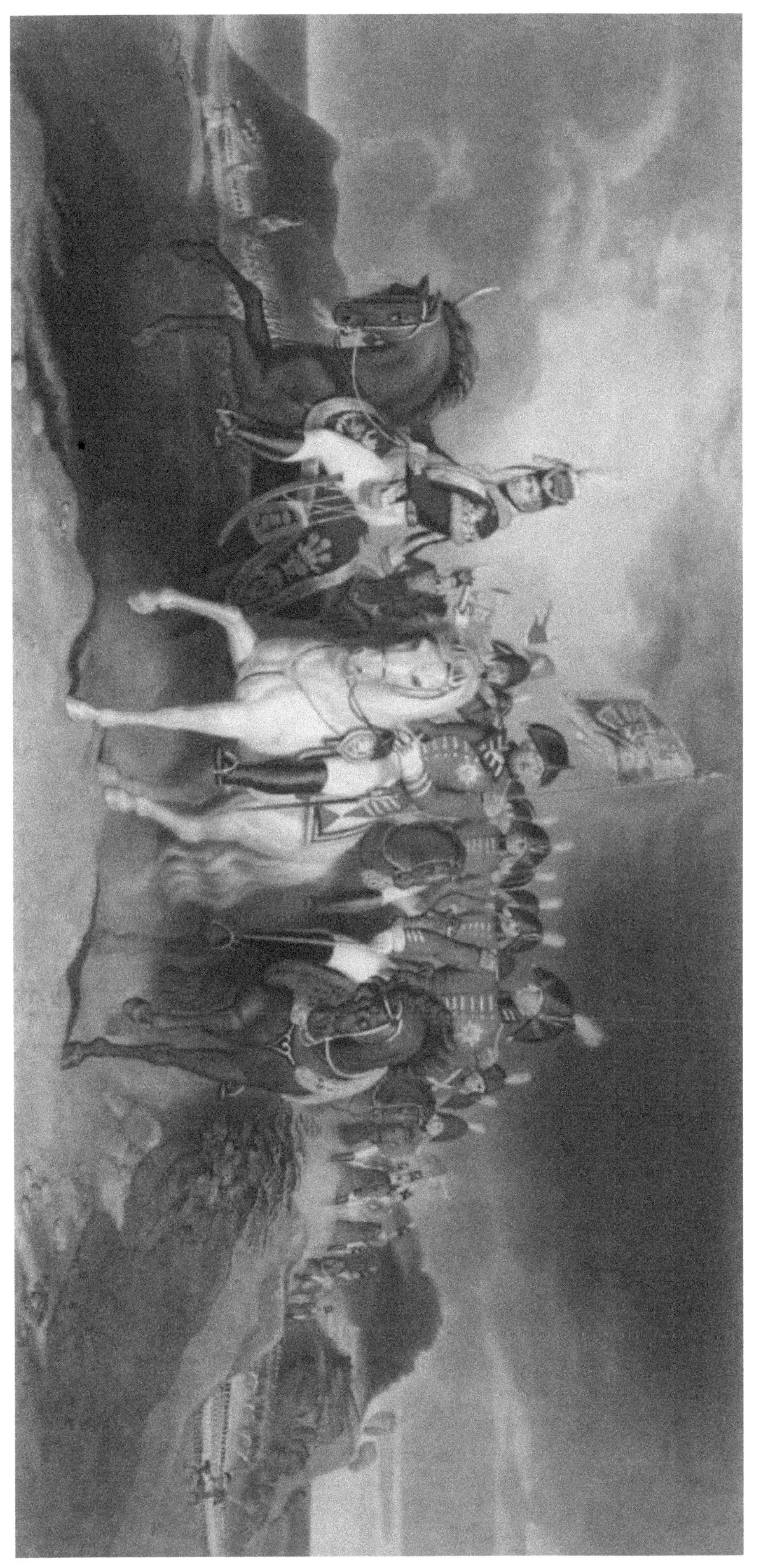

15 – GUARD ROOM TACTICS, BUGS IN DANGER, OR A VOLUNTEER CORPS IN ACTION

Hand-coloured caricature published 23 July 1798 by Samuel William Fores of 50 Piccadilly, London. With muskets and ammunition pouches lodged in racks along the walls, four volunteers dressed in red coats with blue collars, shoulder straps and lapels, white waistcoats and blue breeches are enjoying killing insects. One takes aim exclaiming, 'I'll lodge a bullet in his thorax', another has just fired, 'D…it f I aynt miss'd um all', a third man uses his bayonet to dispatch a bug ('In hum by Goles') while a fourth proudly marches of with his prey calling out, 'There he is a trophy of my victory. I wish we were in Ireland.' *(Image courtesy of the Anne SK Brown Military Collection, Brown University Library)*

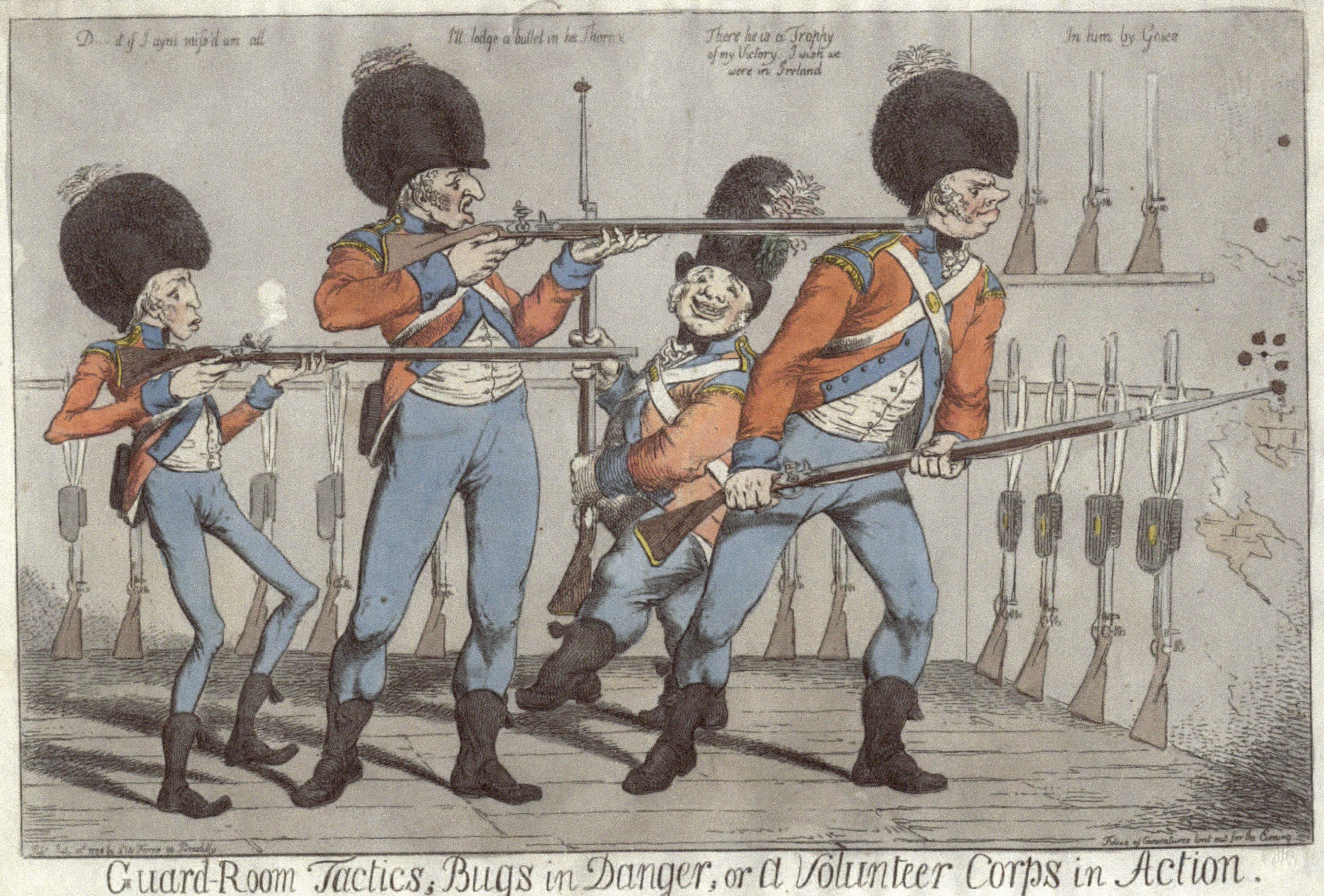

Guard-Room Tactics; Bugs in Danger; or a Volunteer Corps in Action.

16 – St James's Westminster Loyal Volunteer Regiment

Colour aquatint published by I Mease of No 2 Queen Street Soho Square in March 1804. Inscribed upon a rock surrounded by foliage: 'Dedicated to the officers and privates of the St James's Westminster Loyal Volunteer Regiment this plate represents their uniform in the position of the new charge bayonet. Published by I Mease sergeant of the seventh company. No2 Queen Street Soho Square March 1804'. A member of the corps dressed in a scarlet coat with dark blue collar, cuffs and lapels, a white waistcoat and dark blue breeches, peers along the line of a musket which has a bayonet affixed. In the background to the left, smoke rises from the ground high up into the clouds as a number of soldiers look on. To the right, blue-coated artillery move up a narrow pass pulling a gun and limber, the high ground above them having a troops of cavalry advancing towards a hill fortress defended by infantry.

Built of red brick with Portland stone dressing, St James's Church, Westminster is situated on London's Piccadilly. The corps formed in that area was instituted in June 1797, receiving Colours from the hands of the Duchess of York in a field belonging to a Mr Calvert at Somers Town on 5 July of the following year.

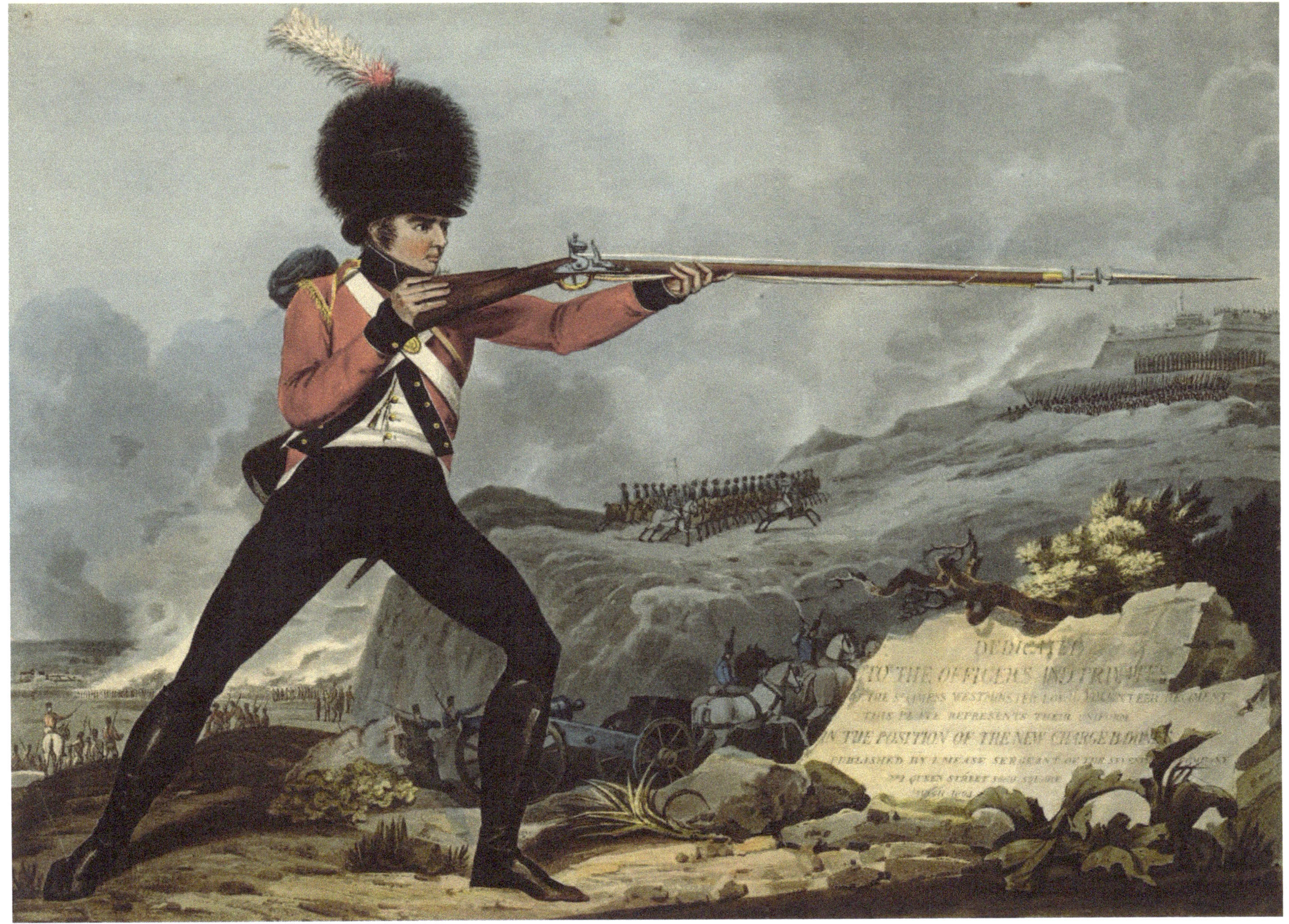
DEDICATED
TO THE OFFICERS AND PRIVATES
THIS PLATE REPRESENTS THEIR UNIFORM
IN THE POSITION OF THE NEW CHARGE

17 – PRESENTATION OF COLOURS TO THE 2ND ROYAL EAST INDIA VOLUNTEERS

Chromolith by and after Henry Mathews published by William Griggs with the caption, 'To The Honourable The Superintending Military Committee of Field Officers of The Royal East – India – Volunteers – This Drawing of their secd Regiment taken on the spot while Receiving the Colours from the hands of Lady Jane Dundas, (in Lord's Cricket Ground, Mary le Bone) on the 27th Day of July, 1797, Is Respectfully presented by their Obedient Humble Servant, Henry Matthews.'

With a background of terraced houses, one of which has a number of people observing from a balcony, three ranks of volunteers dressed in scarlet coats and with their officers before them, parade on a field of grass. To the right, a crowd of men and women watch as an officer receives a King's Colour. Another of blue is close by awaiting presentation. Sergeants with their tall pikes can be seen, and on the far left of the image three drummers. See also Image 18 below.

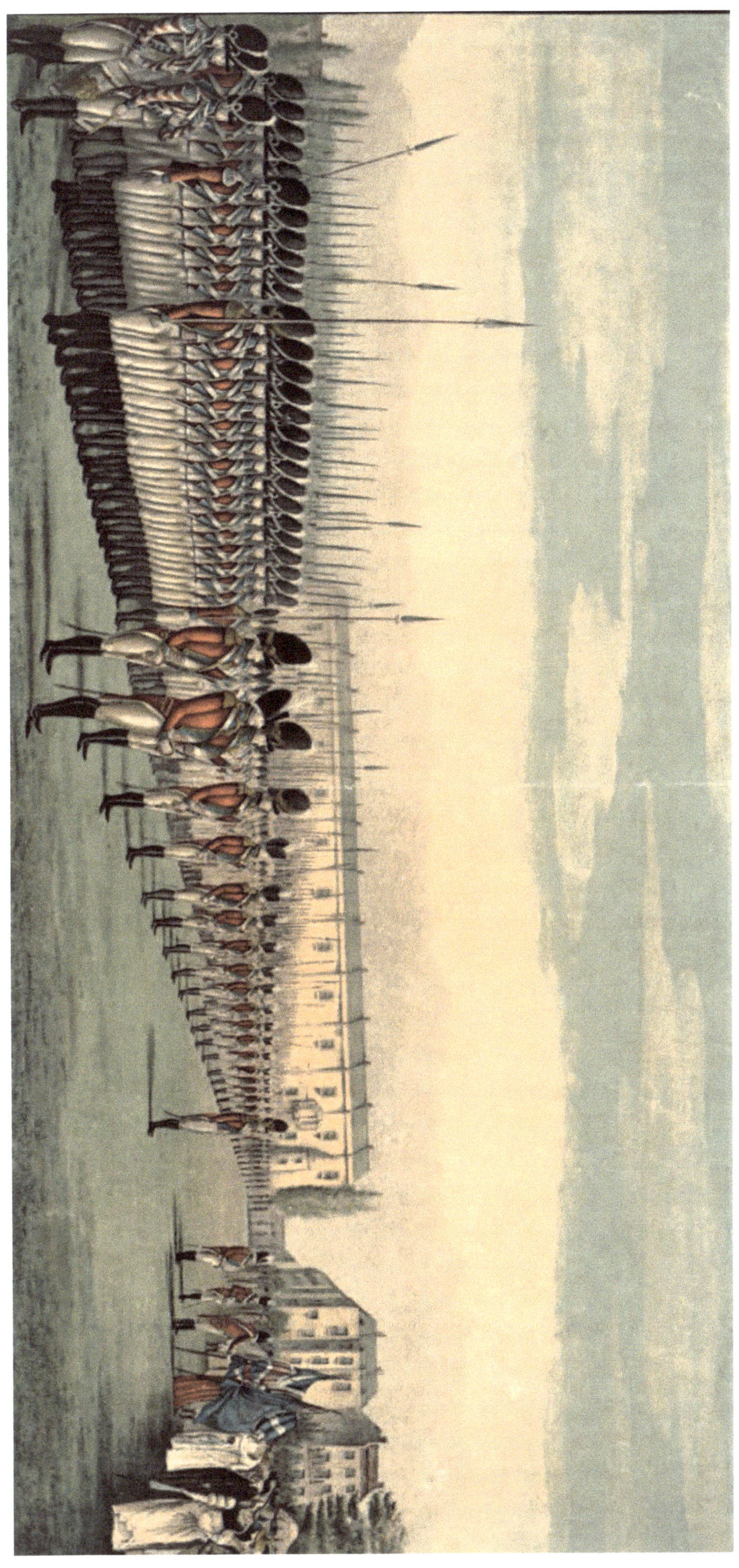

18 – PRESENTATION OF COLOURS TO THE 3RD ROYAL EAST INDIA COMPANY VOLUNTEERS

Photo lithograph by William Griggs of Peckham, SE London carrying the following caption, 'Consecration of the Colours which Lady Jane Dundas presented to the Third Regiment of Royal East India Volunteers on the 29th June, 1799'.

Bareheaded, a senior officer talks to a clergyman dressed in black robes. Behind then, two kneeling junior officers hold King's and Regimental Colours resting in blue belts with gold lace edging. Sergeants, with their long pikes, can be seen in the background, also a trumpeter and drummers. One of them is a black musician holding a pair of cymbals. To the left a stout officer talks to a lady wearing a long red dress standing before a crowd of men, women and young children. Far left, a drummer has caught the attention of a young boy.

For the protection of their London warehouses, the Honourable East India Company raised two regiments in 1796, and a third in 1798. Each consisted of ten companies. The field officers were selected from the company's chairman, deputy chairman and directors, others from India House. NCOs and privates came from the Assistant Elders, Commodores and labourers belonging to the company's warehouses. The Court Minutes of the company dated 24 August 1796 note that the officers uniforms be scarlet with blue facings, buff waistcoats and breeches. Gorgets were worn bearing the HEIC's arms and motto '*Auspicio Regis et Senatus Angliae*' (Under the auspices of the King and Senate of England). The lion crest of the company appeared on the buttons. Colours were presented to the 2nd Regiment on 27 July 1797 (see Image 17 above), and to the 3rd on 29 July 1799. Paintings by Henry Matthews depicting the parades were reproduced in *The Journal of Indian Art*, Volume 4, No 34 of April 1891. That for the 3rd Regiment presentation is illustrated. All three regiments were disbanded in 1814.

An internet item dated 29 March 2019 published by the British Library referes to a four-year project to conserve two Colours belonging to the Royal East India Volunteers. The article also mentions a re-embodiment of the corps during the period 1820 to 1834 and refers to a 'register of labourers' which has survived giving soldiers age, height, home address and reasons for discharge from the corps. Most reasons for the latter are recorded as being due to the man's training clashing with his warehouse duties. One man, Charles Twort, was discharged due to him having 'bad feet and corns.'

Referring to Colours, the internet item shows several images, one depicting Lady Jane Dundas at the 29 June 1799 presentation on Lord's Cricket Ground to the 3rd Regiment. This watercolour is one of those by Henry Matthews mentioned above. Lady Jane, according to the British Library article, seems to have embroidered Colours for all three regiments, the presentation dates being given as April 1797, July 1797 and June 1799.

Cecil CP Lawson in Volume V of his *A History of the Uniforms of the British Army*, makes mention of the drummers belonging to the regiment who wore scarlet coats with blue facings and bearskin caps. There is also a reference to a black bandsman with a white turban and red plume, and a trumpeter with a cocked hat and Hessian boots. His blue trumpet banner is embroidered with the company arms. Both can be seen in Image 18.

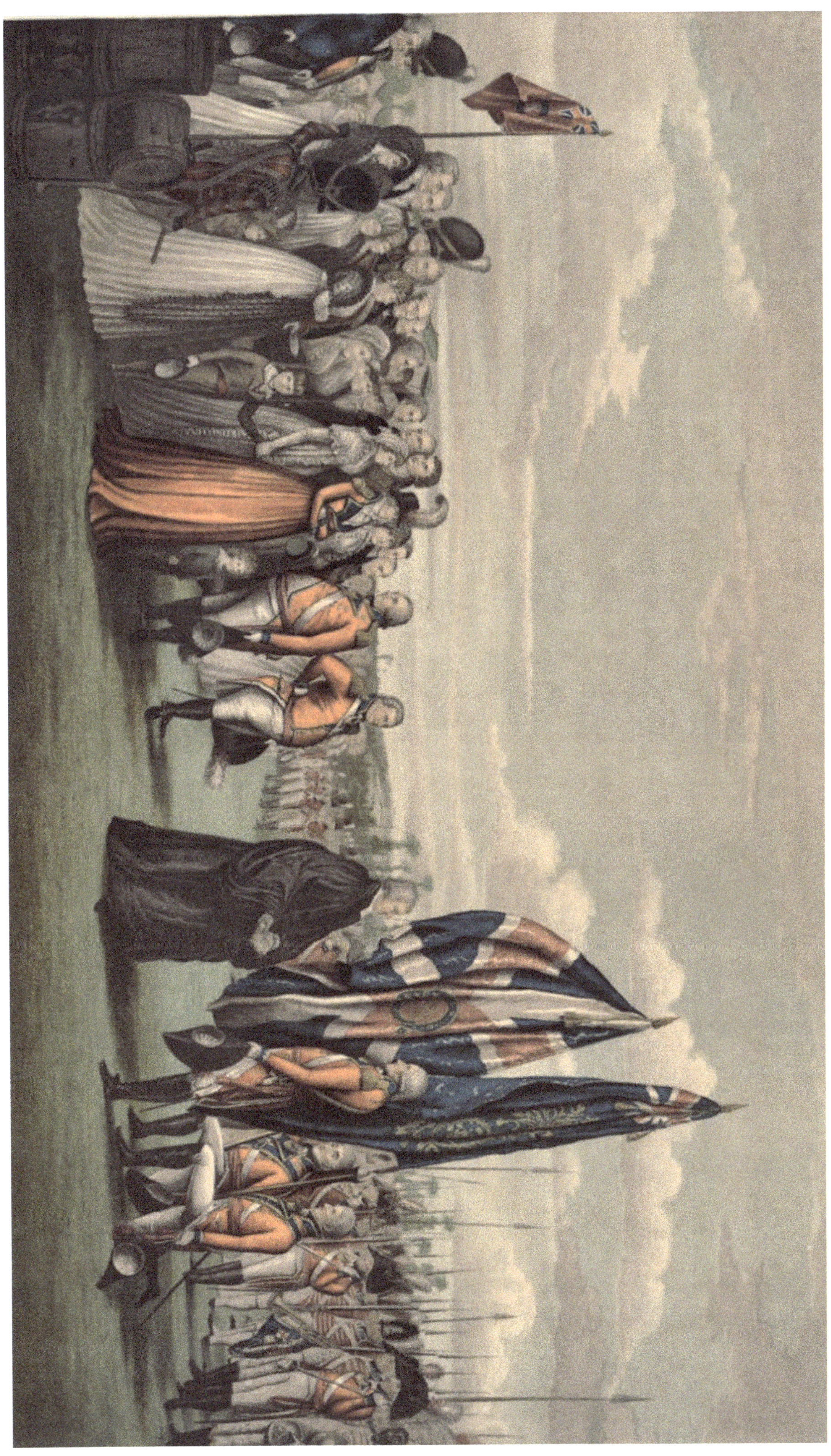

19 – COLOURS, HAMPSTEAD LOYAL VOLUNTEERS

Colour plate from *Records of The Third Middlesex Rifle Volunteers* written and illustrated by ET Evans and published by Simkin, Marshall & Co, London, 1885.

On metal-tipped pikes with cords and tassels, representations of the King's and Regimental Colours of the Loyal Hampstead Volunteers, the former being the Union flag charged with the royal arms. The Regimental Colour is red and shows the badge of the corps, a warrior with sword and shield in the act of defending a women and child. (See Image 22). Above the colours, a rope tension drum, green with yellow wormed hoops. Emblazoned on the drum a crowned shied with the letters HLV on a red ground and within a yellow border.

ET Evans notes how 'Upon the passing of the Defence Act, a general meeting of the Lieutenancy of the County of Middlesex was held on July 18, 1803 at the Guildhall, Westminster, when it was resolved (inter aliâ), that the parishes of St Marylebone, Paddington and Hampstead, do form one division of the County, and that William Brodie, Esq, Aaron Graham, Esq and Nathaniel Conant, Esq be appointed lieutenants of the said Division.' It followed that a general meeting of the inhabitants took place on Hampstead Heath, on 17 August 1803 where some 700 men took the oath. Subsequently, the services of the Hampstead Loyal Volunteers were accepted on12 August 1803. Interestingly, neither of the gentlemen (Brodie, Graham and Conant) appeared in an early list of officers submitted to the War Office. Colonelcy of the corps was given to the British publisher and painter, Josiah Boydell. The Colours were presented by Lady Alvanley at Hampstead parish church on 4 December 1803.

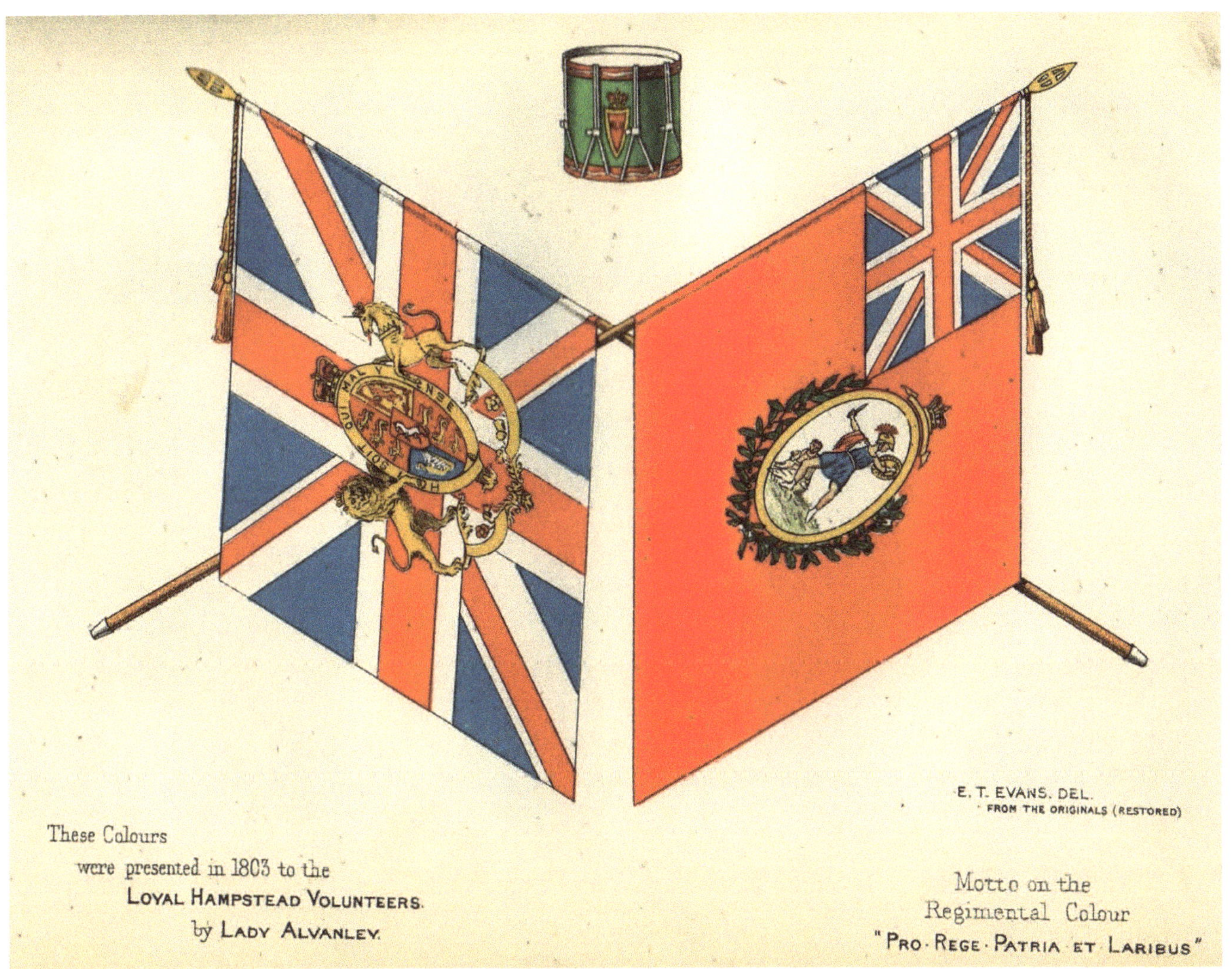
E. T. EVANS. DEL.
FROM THE ORIGINALS (RESTORED)
These Colours
were presented in 1803 to the
LOYAL HAMPSTEAD VOLUNTEERS.
by LADY ALVANLEY.
Motto on the
Regimental Colour
"PRO · REGE · PATRIA ET LARIBUS"

20 – ARMS & ACCOUTREMENTS OF THE HAMPSTEAD LOYAL ASSOCIATION VOLUNTEERS

Colour plate from *Records of The Third Middlesex Rifle Volunteers* written and illustrated by ET Evans and published by Simkin, Marshall & Co, London, 1885. Above crossed muskets, a rope tension drum with red hoops bearing a crowned shield inscribed with the letters HLA and date 1799. Below, and on a hook, a black pouch-belt, the pouch having a yellow metal plate inscribed with the letters LHA in script. On the same hook, another black belt holding a socket bayonet.

ET Evans begins his book with a short account of two earlier volunteer formations within the parish of Hampstead: the Hampstead Loyal Association and Hampstead Loyal Volunteers. He mentions the great review of volunteers that had taken place in Hyde Park on 21 June 1799 and that the Hampstead Loyal Association's name appeared on a list of those taking part. The author gives a good account of the weapons and equipment used by the corps and includes a colour plate (illustrated) by his own hand.

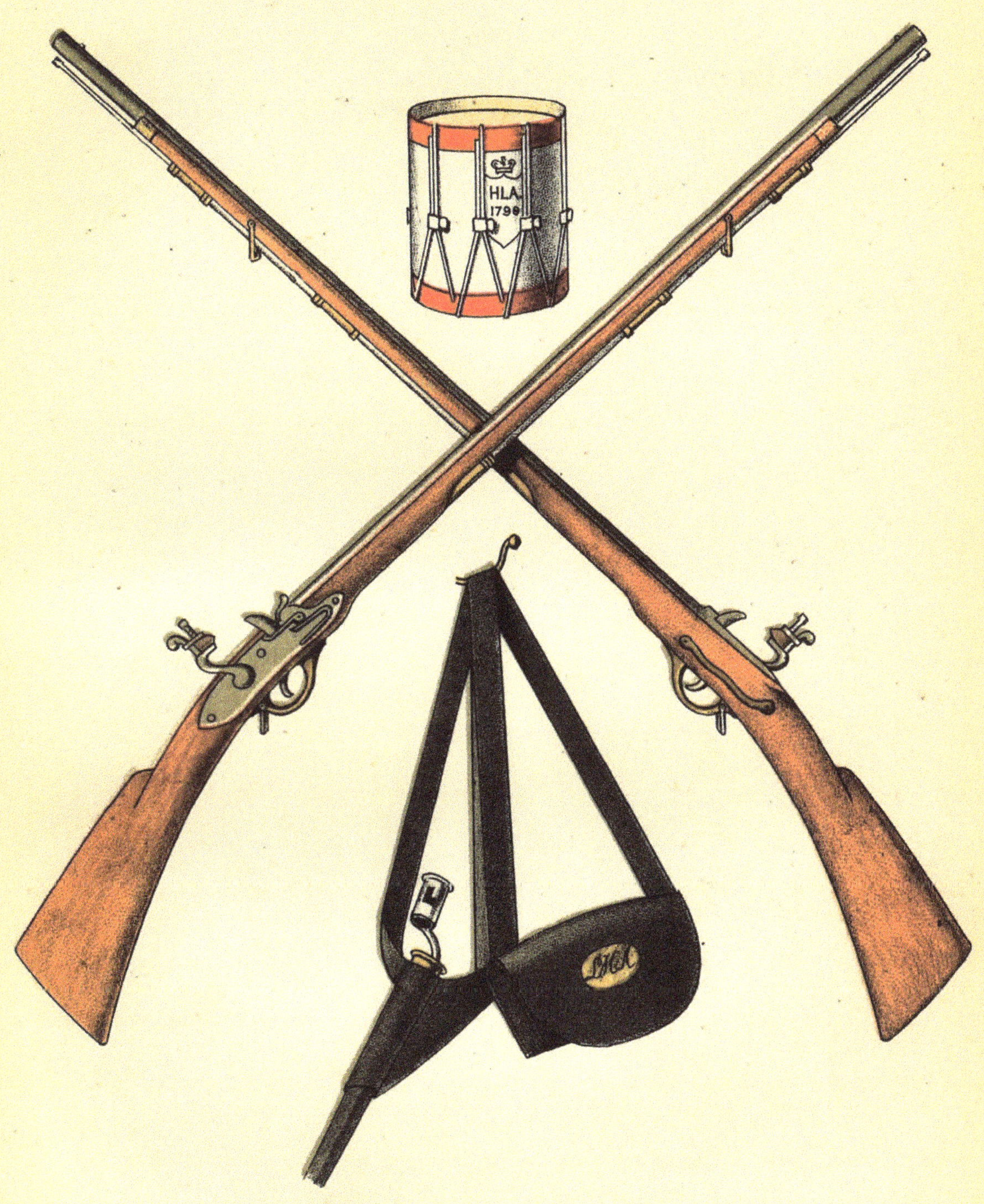

E.T. EVANS, DEL.
FROM THE ORIGINALS.

ARMS & ACCOUTREMENTS
of the
"HAMPSTEAD LOYAL ASSOCIATION."

21 – LIGHT INFANTRY VOLUNTEERS, 1798

Colour plate from *Records of The Third Middlesex Rifle Volunteers* written and illustrated by ET Evans and published by Simkin, Marshall & Co, London, 1885 showing a single figure standing with musket at his side and wearing a scarlet, long-tailed, coat which has a blue collar that continues down as lapels. The shoulder straps and cuffs are of the same colour and the headdress has a tall green feather, black crest and a gold and green turban. Two white belts are being worn, one bearing an oval yellow plate.

ET Evans notes in his book how no information regarding the uniform worn by the Hampstead Loyal Association is on record, but included by him is a delightful image captioned 'Light Infantry Volunteer 1798' which he believes was typical of a London area corps.

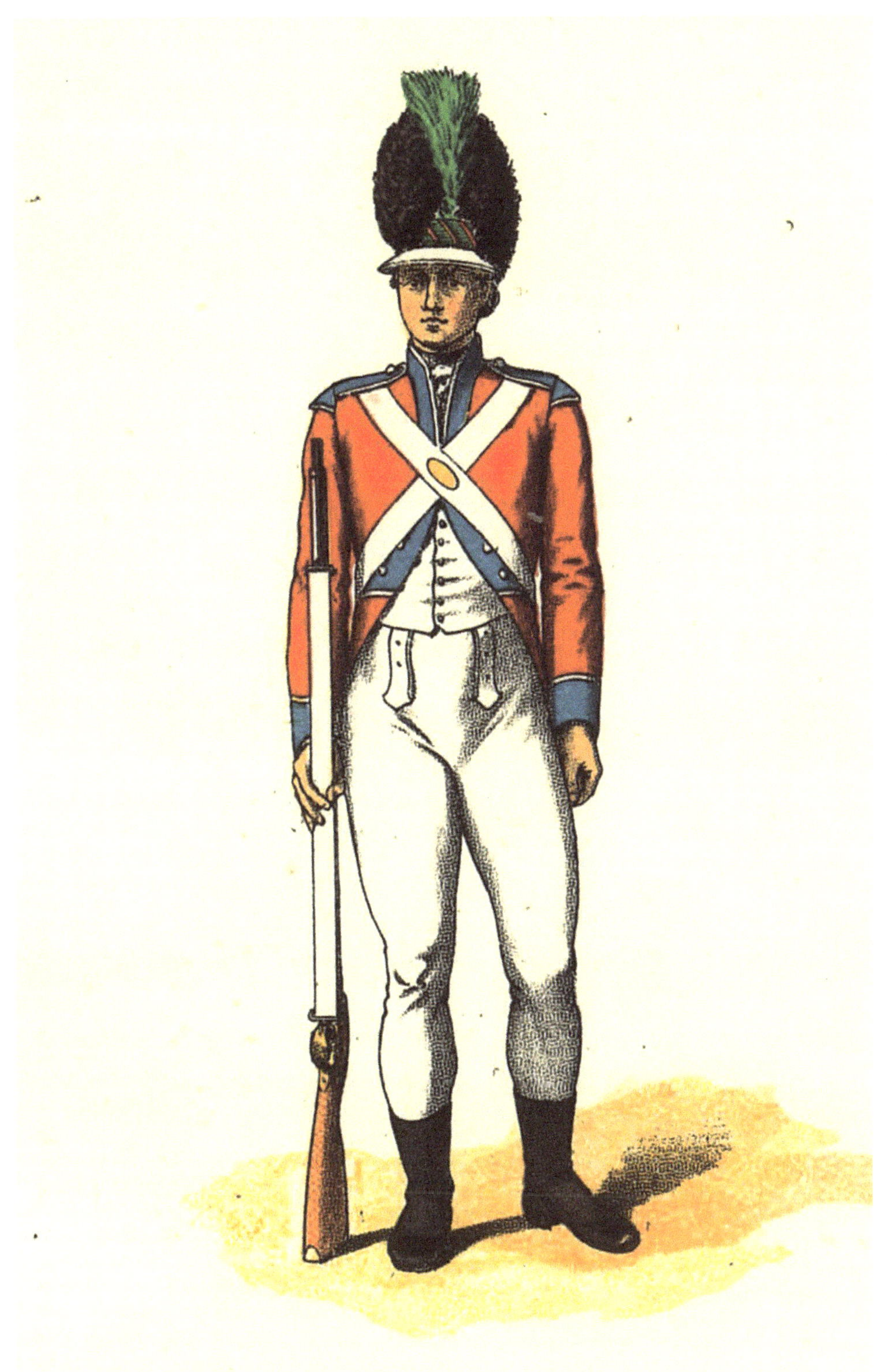

LIGHT INFANTRY VOLUNTEER
1798.

22 – CROSS-BELT PLATE, LOYAL HAMPSTEAD VOLUNTEERS

Engraved plate, signed and dated E Evans 1884, from *Records of The Third Middlesex Rifle Volunteers* written by ET Evans and published by Simkin, Marshall & Co, London, 1885.

The regimental badge of the Loyal Hampstead Volunteers (see also Image 19 above) which shows a helmeted warrior armed with a short sword in his right hand and a shield on the left arm. By his side, a women holding a baby to her breast. Above the image, the motto *Pro rege patria et laribus*, and below, the name Hampstead.

As did many other volunteer corps, the Loyal Hampstead Volunteers chose the Latin motto *Pro rege patria et laribus*—For king and country. The warrior, latterly described as a Roman soldier, was used by the post 1908 Territorial Force battalion, the 7th Duke of Cambridge's Own Middlesex Regiment, as a badge. Headquarters of the battalion's 'A' Company were in Hampstead.

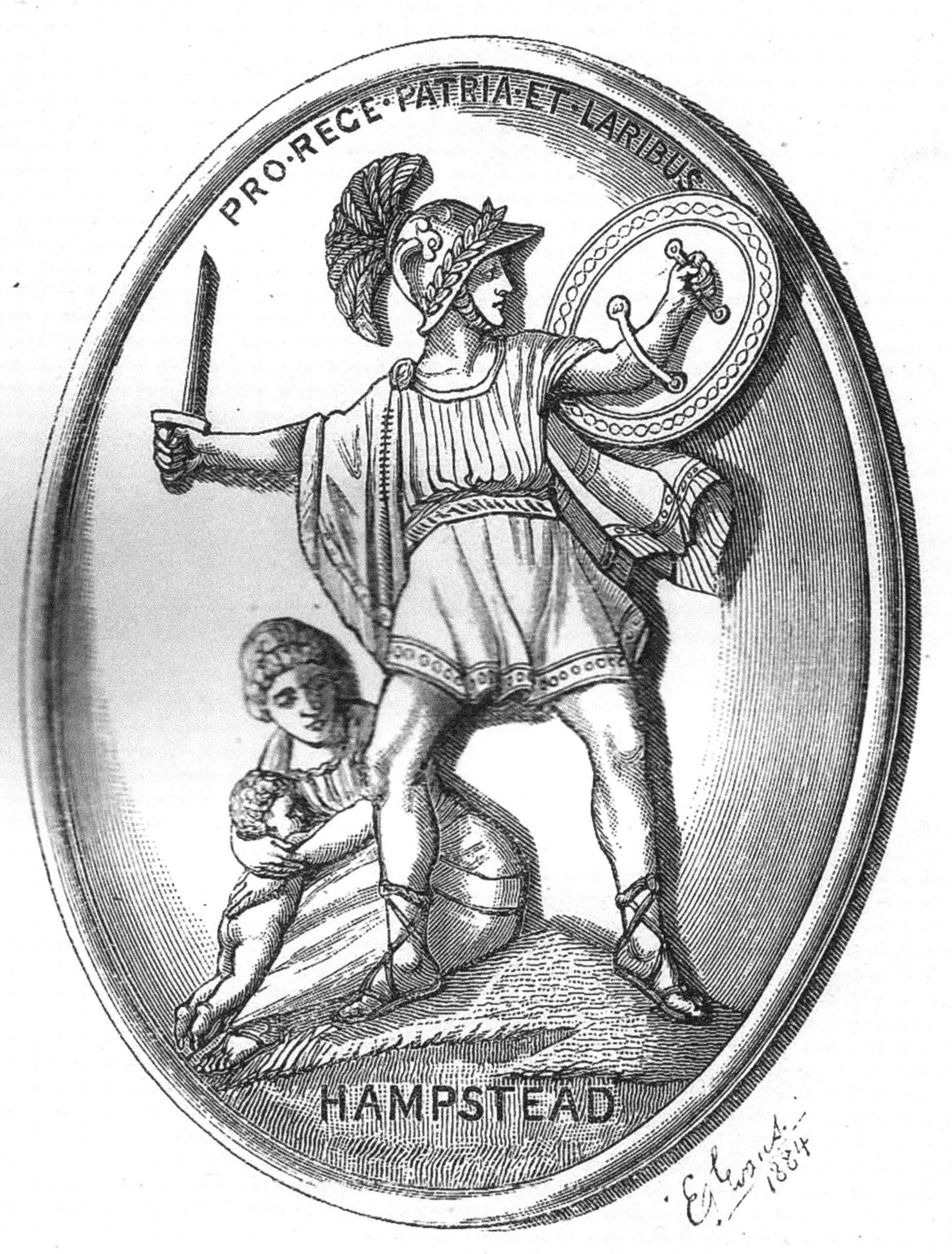
PRO·REGE·PATRIA·ET·LARIBUS
HAMPSTEAD

23 - LOYAL BIRMINGHAM ASSOCIATION VOLUNTEERS

Frontispiece to *The History of the 1st Volunteer Battalion The Royal Warwickshire Regiment and its Predecessors* by Colonel Charles J Hart, VD and published by the Midland Counties Herald Ltd, Birmingham, 1906.

The image was first published on 15 March 1800 by E Rudge of Birmingham, the artist being E Rudge, the engraver SW Fores. Against a country scene, three volunteers in blue coats with red collars, white waistcoats and white breeches stand in a clearing with muskets held in different positions. The plate, which carries the caption 'Birmingham Loyal Association Established May 1797,' identifies them from left to right as being of grenadier, battalion and light infantry companies. The men cast lengthy shadows, but the clouds blanketing the three-storied building in the background suggest that rain might be on its way.

On Tuesday 22 August 1797, the Loyal Birmingham Association Volunteers paraded for the first time at their drill ground in Coleshill Street. They were noted as being in full uniform and presenting a splendid appearance.

Colonel Hart mentions how the 1st Volunteer Battalion was fortunate in as much as it was in possession of many interesting records relating to the old volunteers, and quotes one such document providing the following details of uniform: 'viz., a blue lapelled coat, edged with scarlet, scarlet collar, blue cloth epaulets with gold lace on the edge and small gold fringe at bottom, the skirts lined with white cashmere, turned back with scarlet hearts. Edged with gold lace, gilt buttons with the crown and cypher B.L.A., beneath it; white dimity or cashmere lapelled waistcoat; white cashmere breeches; plain white cotton stockings, and black cloth half gaiters; black stock with white necking; cocked hat, bound, black feather, half silk cockade, and gold button and loop; white belts and gilt plate, with same device as on button; japanned cartouche box.'

As we can see, the colour plate follows closely the description given with the exception that the grenadier (left) wears a white-over-red plume in his cap and the volunteer from the light company (right) has a Tarleton helmet with white-over-red plume and leopard-skin band. Visible, but unclear in the painting, are the grenade and bugle-horn devices worn respectively by grenadier and light infantry troops on the shoulder straps.

Mr E Rudge of Birmingham tells how the Loyal Birmingham Association Volunteers was established in May 1797 composed of master drapers, grocers and other tradesmen, and how the corps was disbanded in 1802. The son of a cloth merchant, Samuel Fores was born in 1761 and made a living publishing and selling illustrations from premises in Piccadilly, London. He died in February 1838 and was buried in his family vault at St James Church, Piccadilly not far from his shop.

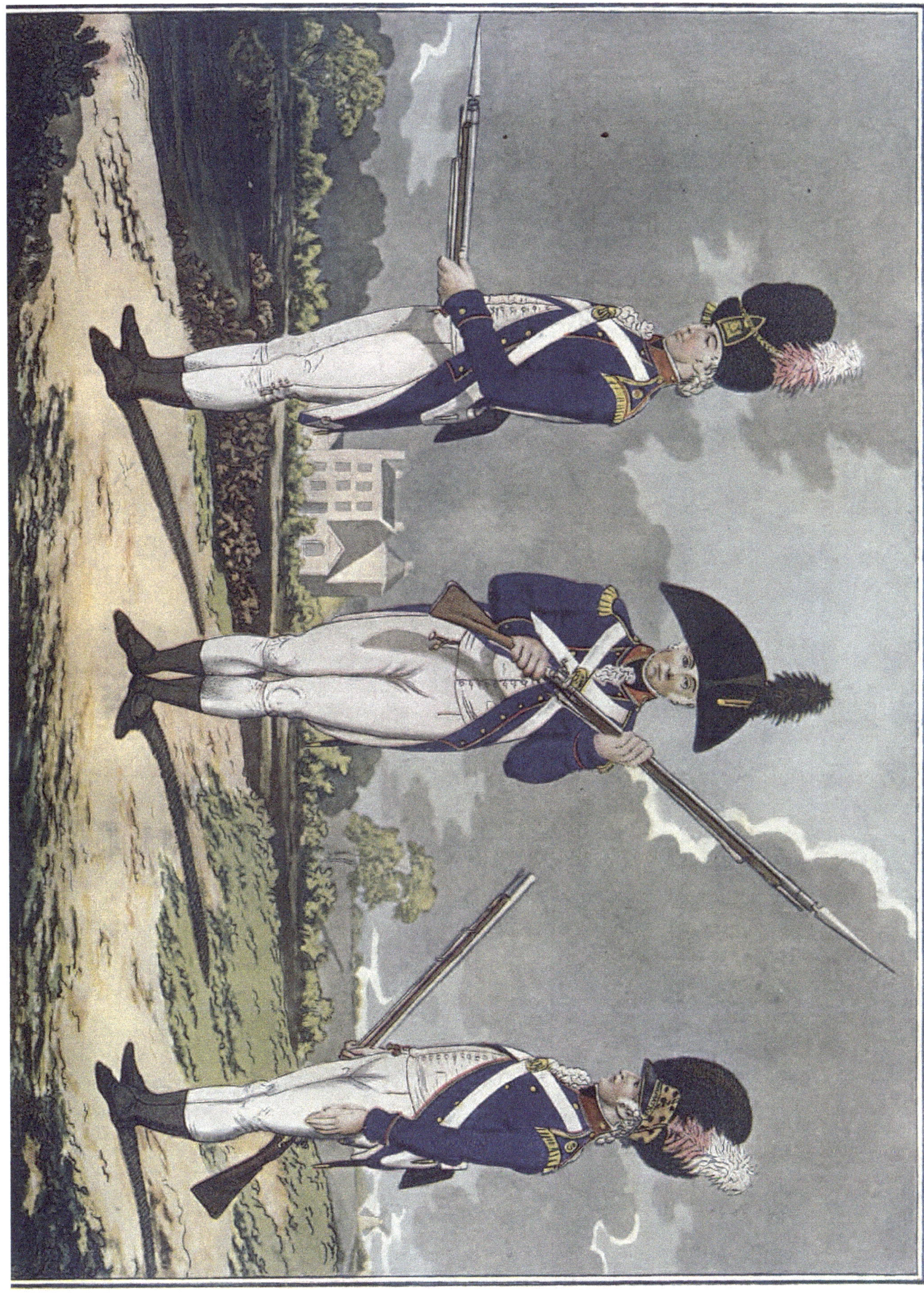

24 – SERGEANT OF THE LOYAL BIRMINGHAM VOLUNTEERS, 1803

Colour plate from *The History of the 1st Volunteer Battalion The Royal Warwickshire Regiment and its Predecessors* by Colonel Charles J Hart, VD and published by the Midland Counties Herald Ltd, Birmingham, 1906. Here we have a single standing figure in a red coat with yellow collar, shoulder straps and cuffs, white breeches and black gaiters buttoned to just below the knee. As a sergeant, he carries a tall pike which he holds at his right side.

Formed in 1803, the Loyal Birmingham Volunteers soon comprised three battalions, the colonel of all three being George, Earl of Dartmouth. Each battalion consisted of eight battalion companies, one grenadier and one light company. In this plate of a sergeant at time of formation, we see a detailed figure following closely the dress regulations laid down by the corps in 1803. Gone were the blue jackets with red facings of the old disbanded Birmingham Volunteers; scarlet and yellow were chosen for the new regiment. Here in the illustration we see a white-over-red plume in the shako indicating that the wearer is of a battalion company. He is a sergeant and therefore is permitted to be armed with a pike. Regarding breeches, the regulations stated that they should be white cloth made to button up high on the waist and with four buttons at the knee. Gaiters were to be black and to sit close full up to the knee in the front and with a small hollow behind. The sash was crimson and yellow worsted tied in a small knot on the right side. Although the plate is dated as 1803, the headdress being worn seems to be of the pattern introduced in 1812, the so called 'Waterloo Shako'.

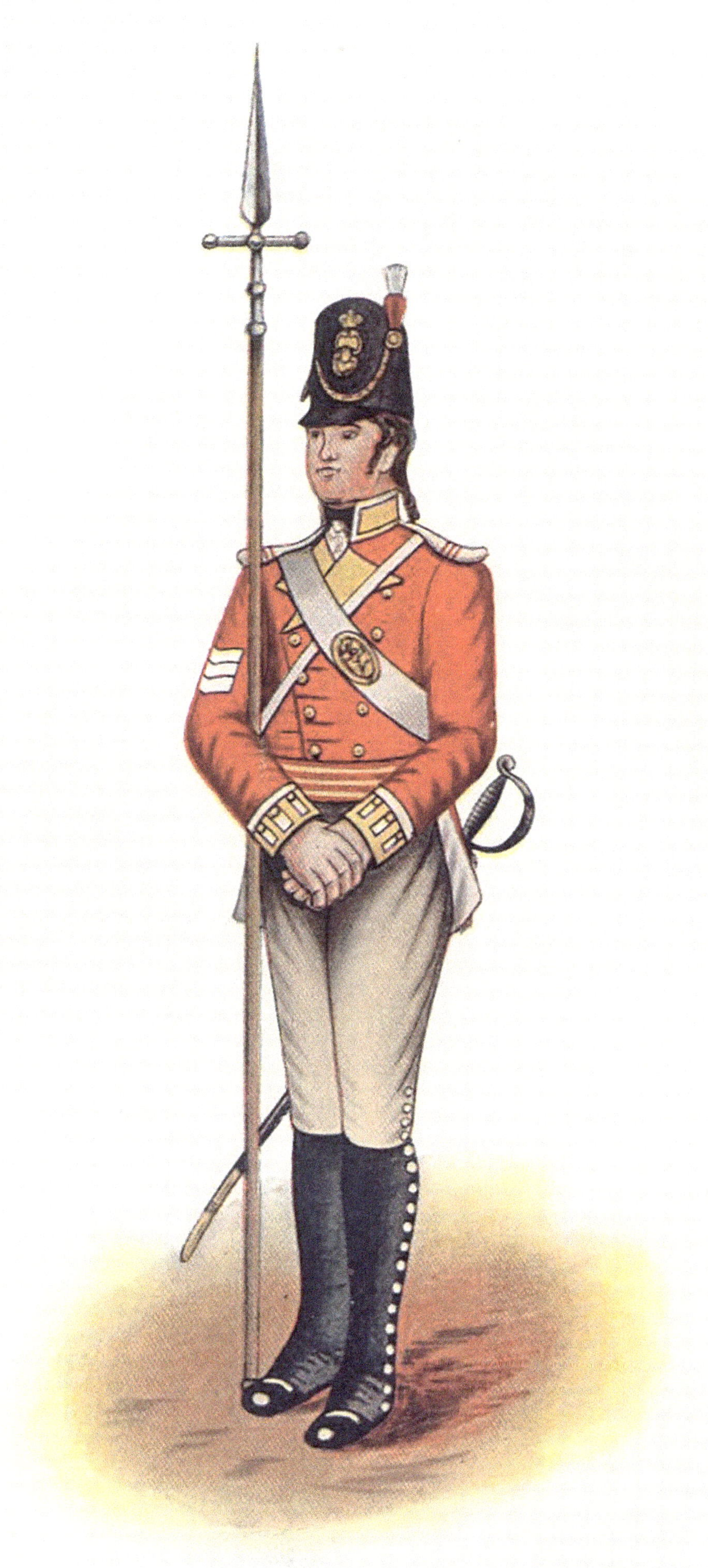

25 – SURREY YEOMANRY

Plate 2, designed and etched by Thomas Rowlandson from the Cavalry section of Rudolph Ackermann's *Loyal Volunteers of London and Environs Infantry and Cavalry in their Respective Uniforms*. Published 12 August 1799.

His horse in full gallop, a volunteer fires his musket. He wears a blue coat with red collar, cuffs and turnbacks, white breeches and a white pouch-belt. The helmet has a red plume, black fur crest and a turban of blue with dark stripes.

In the accompanying text to the plate, Ackermann notes the colonel of the regiment as the Rt Hon Lord Leslie. Other officers mentioned are a lieutenant-colonel Evelyn, Major Sir Thomas Turton, Captains John Rice, William Strode and Charles Dunking, a Lieutenant-Captain Jons, Lieutenants Barines and George Brown. Here are two cornets, Evans and Norris, and an Adjutant Wathen.

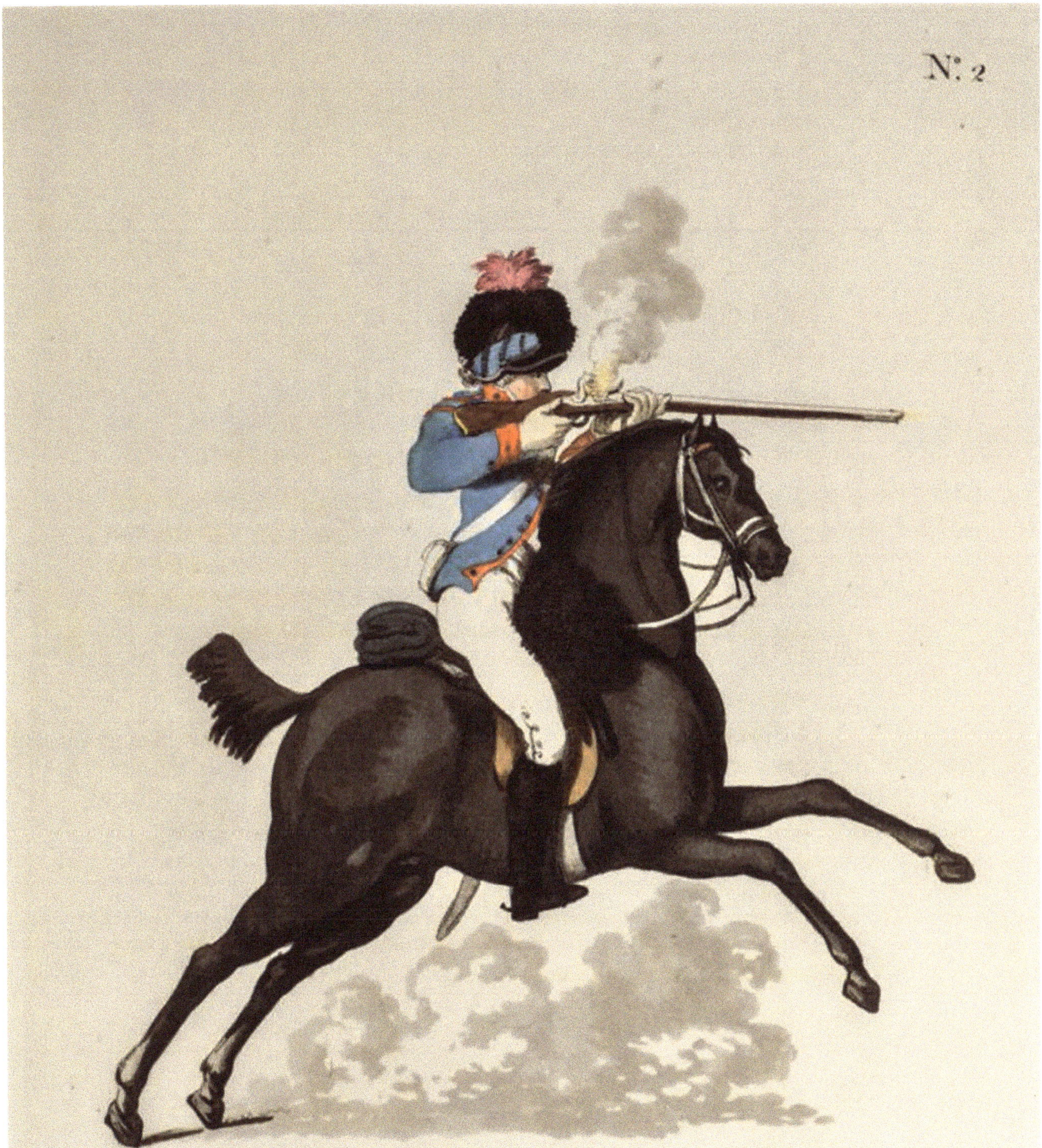

N° 2

26 – St GEORGE'S VOLUNTEERS

Hand-coloured caricature after James Gillray published by Hanna Humphrey of Bond Street, London on 1 March 1797 with the amended caption, 'St George's Volunteers Charging down Bond Street After clearing the Ring in Hyde Park, & Storming the Dunghill at Marybone'. The 'down Bond Street' part of the line was a later addition, possibly an afterthought. Three elderly and grotesque-looking volunteers dressed in red coats with blue facings and gold lace, white waistcoats and breeches charge rapidly and fiercely along a pavement. Their uniforms are ragged, the breeches and hose torn and holed, the headdress a mixture of varying types—a tall fur cap, a large cocked hat with damaged brim and a peaked helmet with red spiky plume. With bayonets fixed they scatter a terrified crowd of shoppers, only legs and petticoats are visible, off to the right as other soldiers wearing grenadier caps follow.

Close to Hanna Humphrey's premises in Bond Street was St George's Hannover Square, but the corps raised there wore blue uniforms. Wearing red though, was the St George's Volunteers at Southwark in South London. The Ring in Hyde Park was created by Charles I as an area where members of the royal court could drive their carriages, the so called 'Dunghill' at Marylebone (spelt wrongly in the caption) needs no explanation.

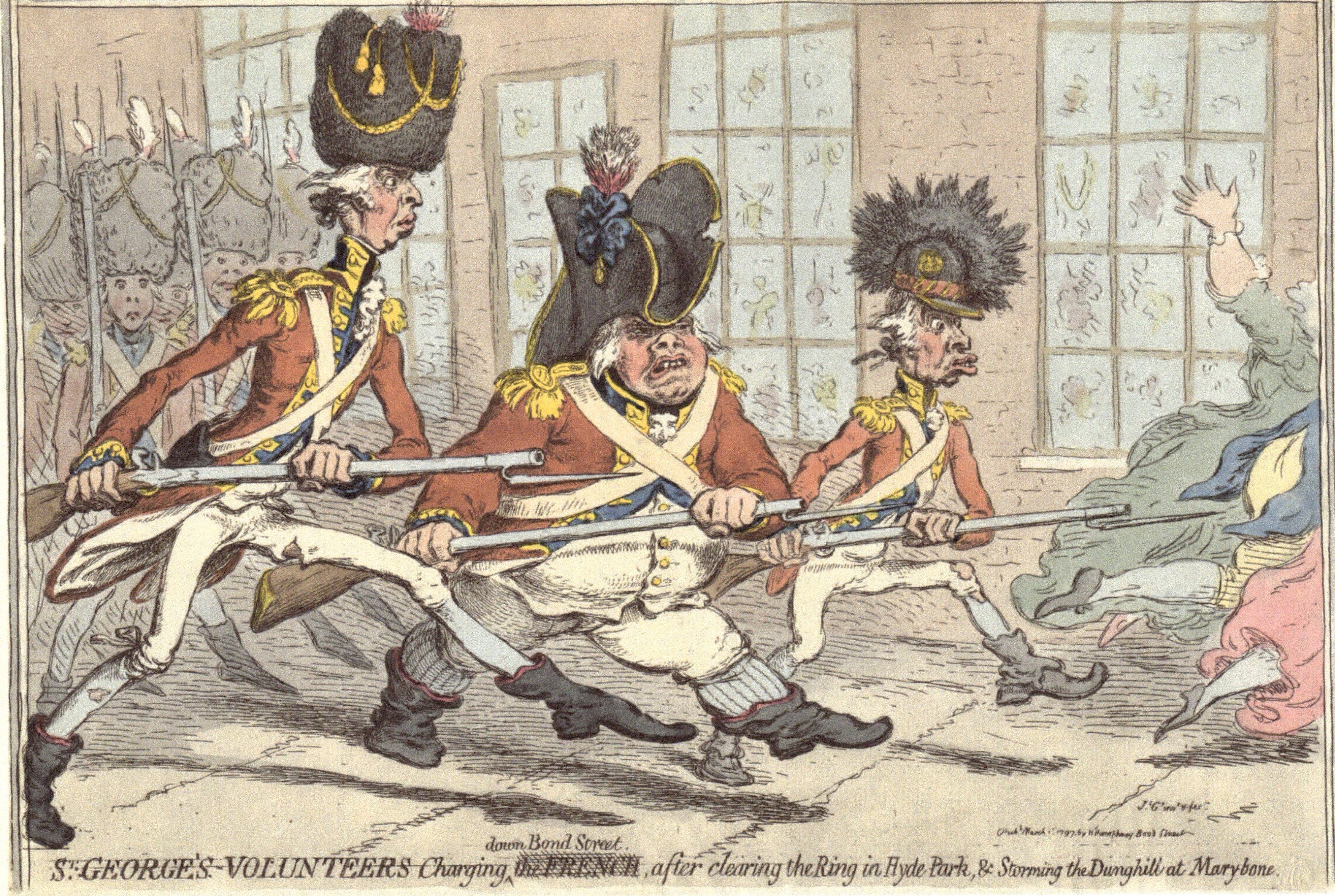
down Bond Street.
S^t. GEORGE'S-VOLUNTEERS Charging ~~the FRENCH~~, after clearing the Ring in Hyde Park, & Storming the Dunghill at Marybone.

27 – KING GEORGE III REVIEWING LONDON VOLUNTEERS IN HYDE PARK

Hand-coloured engraving by J & J Cundee published with the caption 'The Volunteers of London Reviewed In Hyde Park By His Majesty King George The Third, Accompanied By The Prince Of Wales, Duke Of York &c.' The King, and one other wearing a Tarleton helmet, return the salute of a volunteer officer standing on the ground. Three other members of the royal party look on as a Standard is flown bearing a GR cypher. Dismounted, another officer is bareheaded and stands with his hat held in his right hand, and a curved sword is held tucked under his left arm. A parade of red-coated volunteers stand to the left, their Colours flying high in the wind.

King George III reviewed the Volunteers of London and surrounding areas in Hyde Park on a number of occasions, notable those held on 4 June 1799, 4 June 1800 and twice in 1803 of which many prints were made.

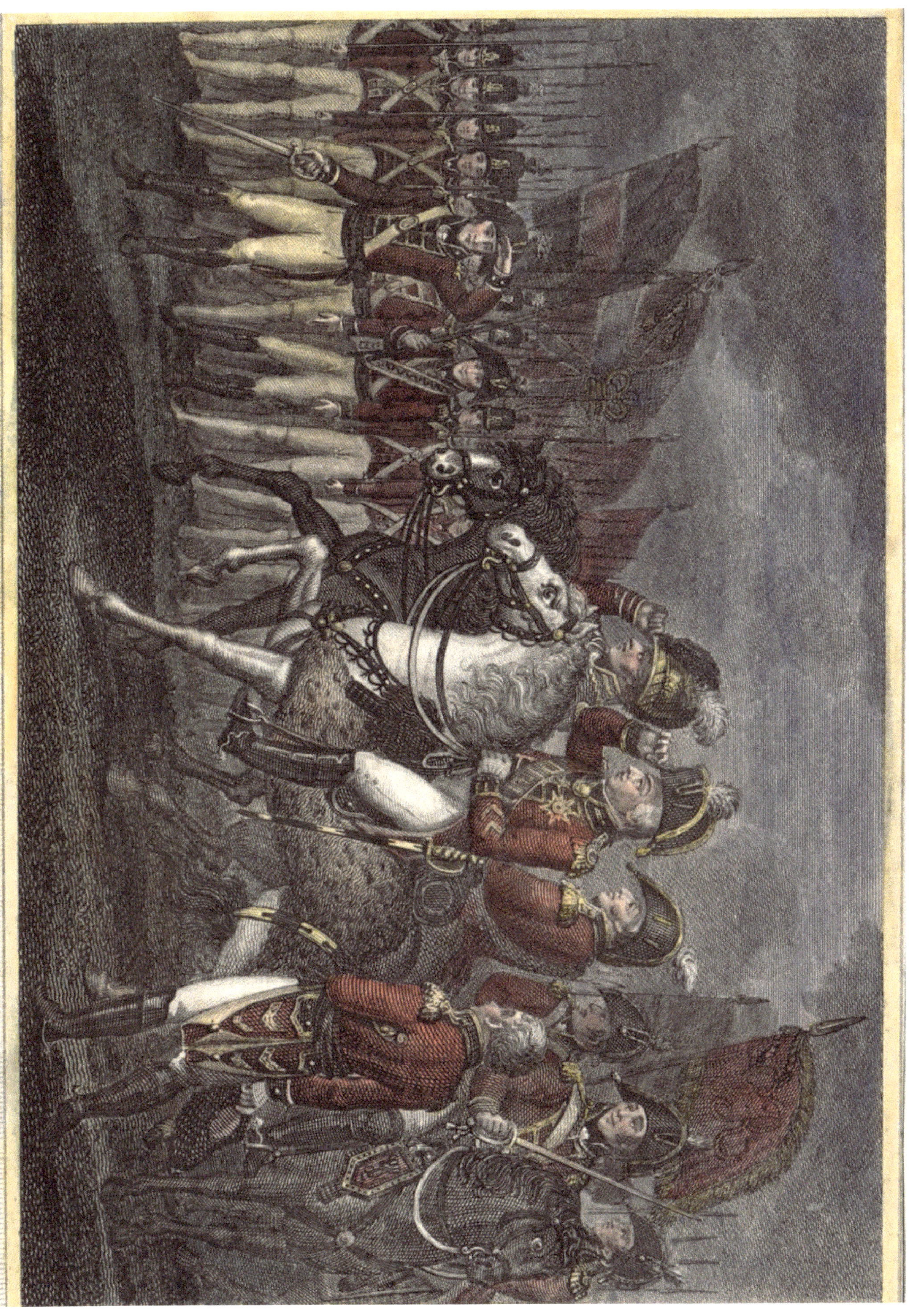

28 – 3RD LOYAL LONDON VOLUNTEERS

Colour aquatint published by John Walls Junior of 16 Ludgate Hill on 6 January 1804 with the following dedication, 'To John Pooley Kensington Esq Lieutenant Colonel Commandant The Officers and Privates of His Majesty's Third Regiment of Loyal London Volunteers This Print is respectfully dedicated by their obedient humble Servant John Wallis Junior.' The caption is printed on either side of the figure of a lion standing on a rock and surrounded by sea. Against a cloudy background, through which the dome of St Paul's can be seen poking through, a private of the regiment poses with one foot on a rock. He wears a red coat with yellow lace across the chest, a dark blue collar edged with yellow and dark blue cuffs with yellow buttonhole decoration. His Tarleton helmet has a tall white plume and a leopard skin turban. The white cross-belts display a yellow metal oval plate on which the cypher GR can just be made out. A rolled cloak is being worn on the back, a pouch on the right hip. The breeches are dark grey. In the background, one volunteer lies firing on the ground, behind him two ranks, one standing, the other kneeling, take aim.

The War Officer publication, *A List of the Officers of the Militia, The Gentlemen & Yeomanry Cavalry and Volunteer Infantry* for 1805 reveals that John Pooley Kensington's commission as lieutenant-colonel was dated 17 September 1803. Kensington was born in 1764 and with other members of his family carried on business as bankers in Lombard Street, City of London. He died in 1818. The corps comprised ten infantry companies and one of riflemen. John Wallis Junior was a private in No1 Company.

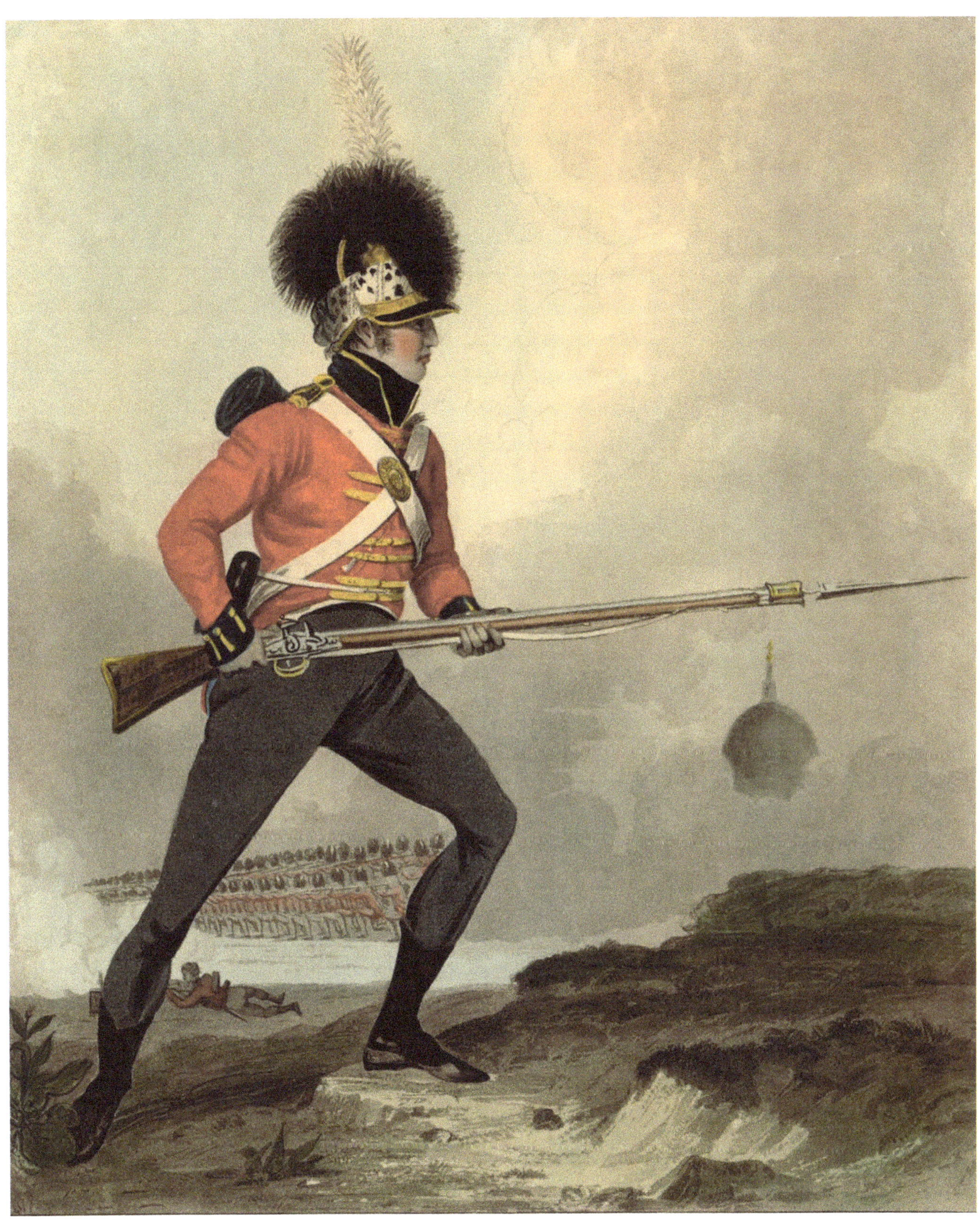

29 – PENDENNIS ARTILLERY VOLUNTEERS

Colour aquatint designed and engraved by Charles Tomkins, published by Egerton Thomas of on 1 February 1800. The image carries the dedication, 'To Lt. Coll. Burgess, the Officers and Gentlemen of the Pendennis Artillery Volunteers this Portrait and representation of their Uniform is inscribed by the Proprietors.' The wording appears on a tablet flanked by two Colours: left, a King's Colour comprising the Union flag charged with the letter PAV within a wreath of laurels, right, a blue Regimental Colour made up of a Union Flag in the top left-hand corner, a shield charged with three cannons and three cannon balls within a wreath. Above this, a crown and below, a three-part scroll inscribed 'Pendennis Artillery Volunteers'. A single figure holding a drawn sword wears a blue coat with red collar and cuffs, two gold epaulettes and edgings of gold down the front and around the pocket flaps. The coat turnbacks are white, as are the breeches, and the headdress sports a tall red-over-white plume. On the shoulder-belt, an oval plate engraved with the Ordnance arms as seen on the Regimental Colour. Artillery volunteers man guns facing out to sea, upon which a three-masted ship passes by. On the right side of the image more guns can be seen in front of a fortress and two smaller buildings at the top of a grassy hill. There are four more distant figures, three dressed in blue and one in red.

Colonel Isaac Burgess's commission was dated 26 May 1803 and he had commanded the former Pendennis Artillery Volunteers disbanded in 1802. The War Officer publication, *A List of the Officers of the Militia, The Gentlemen & Yeomanry Cavalry and Volunteer Infantry* for 1805 reveals Lieutenant-Colonel Henry Williams and Major John Hooton as his senior fellow officers. A Return made in 1803 gave the corps as comprising eight companies, each of seventy-one members, and a total strength of 568. (*Image courtesy of the Anne SK Brown Military Collection, Brown University Library*)

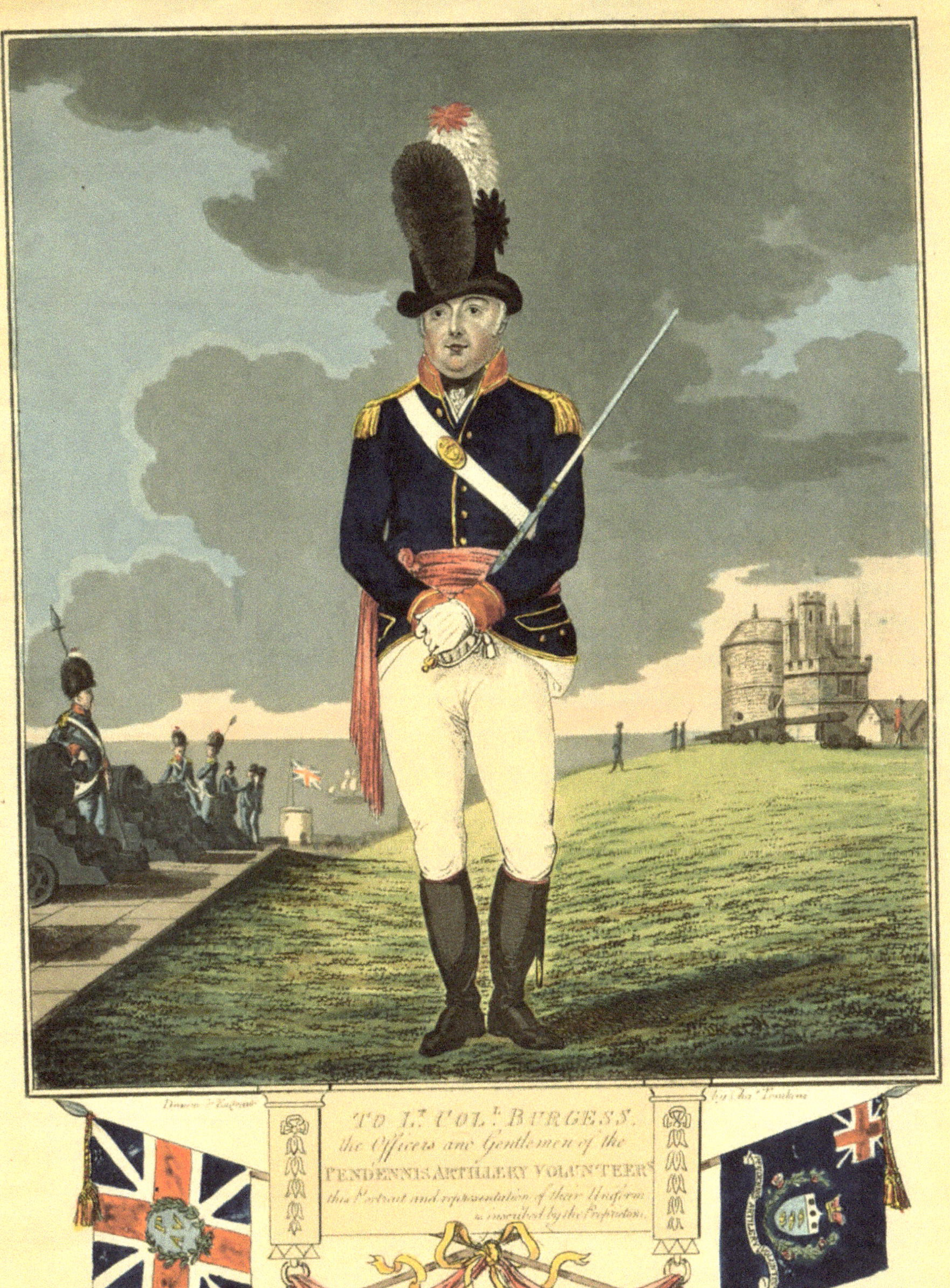

Pubd. as the Act directs Feby. 1, 1800 for the Proprietors by Egerton Whitehall

30 – LOYAL MACCLESFIELD FORRESTERS AND VOLUNTEER INFANTRY, 1805

One of four colour lithographs from *Historical Records of the 5th Administrative Battalion Cheshire Rifle Volunteers* by Captain Astley Terry and printed by Colour Sergeant Eachus of the 16th Cheshire Rifle Volunteer Corps, Sandbach, 1879. Against a backdrop of a tented camp, two officers stand in conversation. Both wear cocked hats with white over red plumes, black boots rising to just below the knee and scarlet coats. The collar, cuffs, lapels and breeches of the figure on the left are dark and he wears gold lace, gold epaulettes and a gorget. To the right, the second figure is dressed similarly, save that his epaulettes and breeches are white. Both men wear shoulder belts with oval gold plates and crimson waist sashes.

The services of the Loyal Macclesfield Foresters were accepted on 8 September 1803, its commanding officer being Lieutenant-Colonel Commandant Davis Davenport. The corps comprised four companies and wore red coats with blue facing and breeches. The officers' lace was gold.

Its services accepted on 20 August 1803, the Loyal Macclesfield Volunteer Infantry (sometimes referred to as the Old Macclesfield Volunteers), was commanded by Captain Jasper Hulley, the uniform of the corps being red coats with blue facings and white breeches. The officer's lace was silver. Captain Terry tells how for some years the Colours of the corps hung in the parish church, but were afterwards removed to the care of Captain Hulley's family. The Queen's Colour was of dark blue silk, with the royal arms in the centre, the Regimental Colour being of crimson silk with the Union flag in the upper canton, the arms of Macclesfield—a lion rampant holding a garb and the motto *Nec virtus nec desunt* (Neither virtue nor plenty are lacking)—being displayed in the centre within a wreath of oak leaves and acorns.

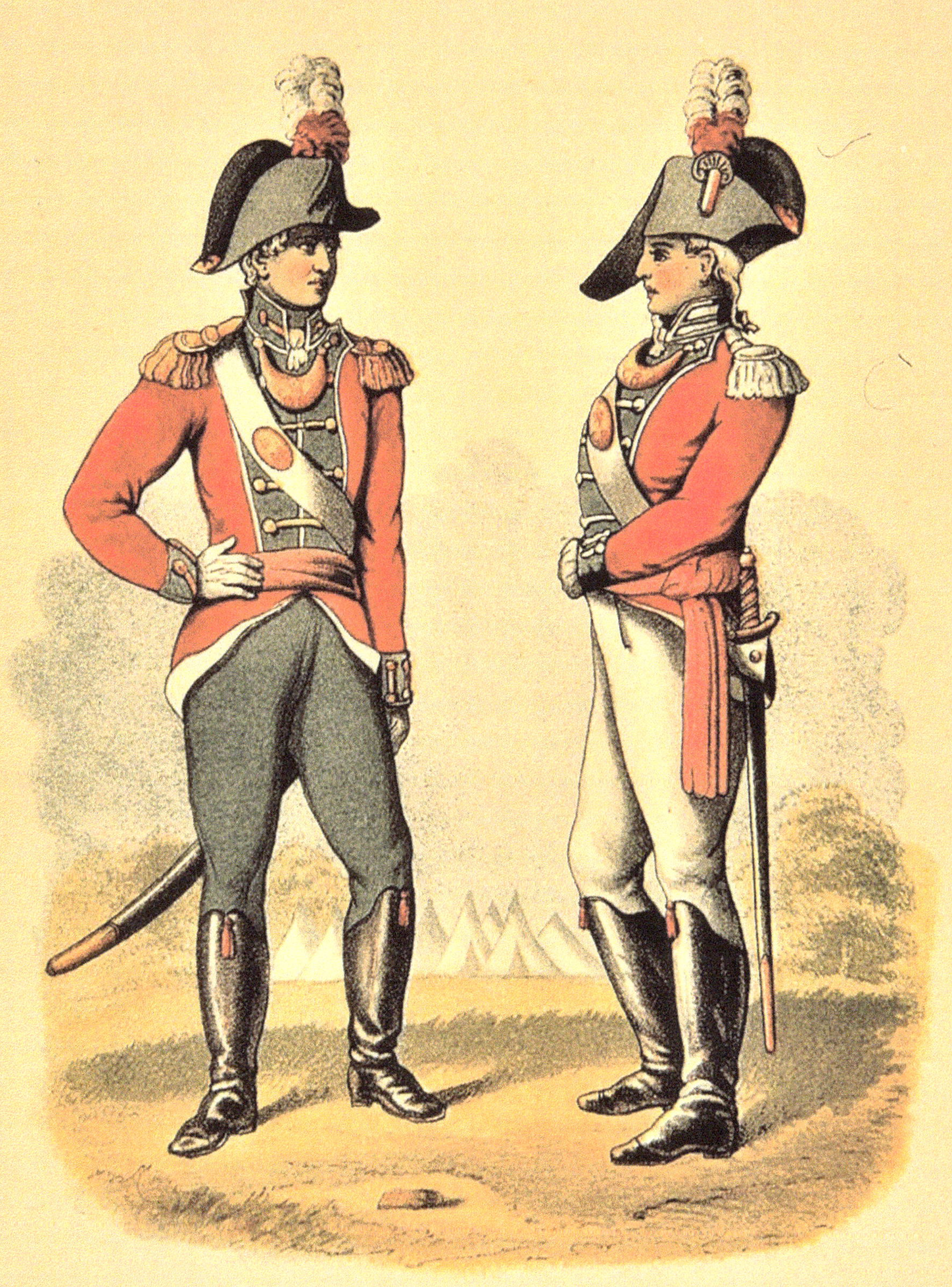

LOYAL MACCLESFIELD FORRESTERS AND VOLUNTEER INFANTRY, 1805.

31 – LEICESTERSHIRE LIGHT HORSE VOLUNTEERS

Hand-coloured caricature printed by Charles Williams and published in May 1806 by Samuel William Fores of No 50 Piccadilly. Wearing a red coat with blue cuffs, yellow breeches and a Tarleton helmet with tall white over red plume, an extremely fat cavalryman waves a drawn sword. His mount rears up and is also exceptionally large. At bottom left, a blue-coated, hatless figure holds up his arms as if pleading for mercy and cries out, 'Parbleu!! if dis be de specimen of de English light Horse, Vat vil de Heavy Horse be!! Oh by Gar I will put off de Invasion for an oder time.' Printed below the image is the following caption: 'Two Wonders of the World. Or a Specimen of a New Troop of Leicestershire Light Horse. – Mr Daniel Lambert who at the Age of 36 weighed above 50 Stone, 14 Pounds to the Stone—measured 3 yards 4 inches round the Body and 1 yard 1 inch round the Leg, 5 feet 11 Inches high. – The Famous Horse Monarch, the largest in the World, is upwards of 21 hands high (above 7 feet) & only 6 years Old .'

The blue-coated Napoleon would have been wise to postpone his invasion plans, should he believe that Britain's part-time light cavalry was made up of men like Daniel Lambert and horses like Monarch. The cartoon, typical of the many published between 1794 and 1808 portraying local volunteers as a strong threat to the French leader. Born 13 March 1770, Daniel Lambert was indeed a 'Wonder', the *Leicester Mercury* writing in 2009 that he was '...one of the city's most cherished icons.'

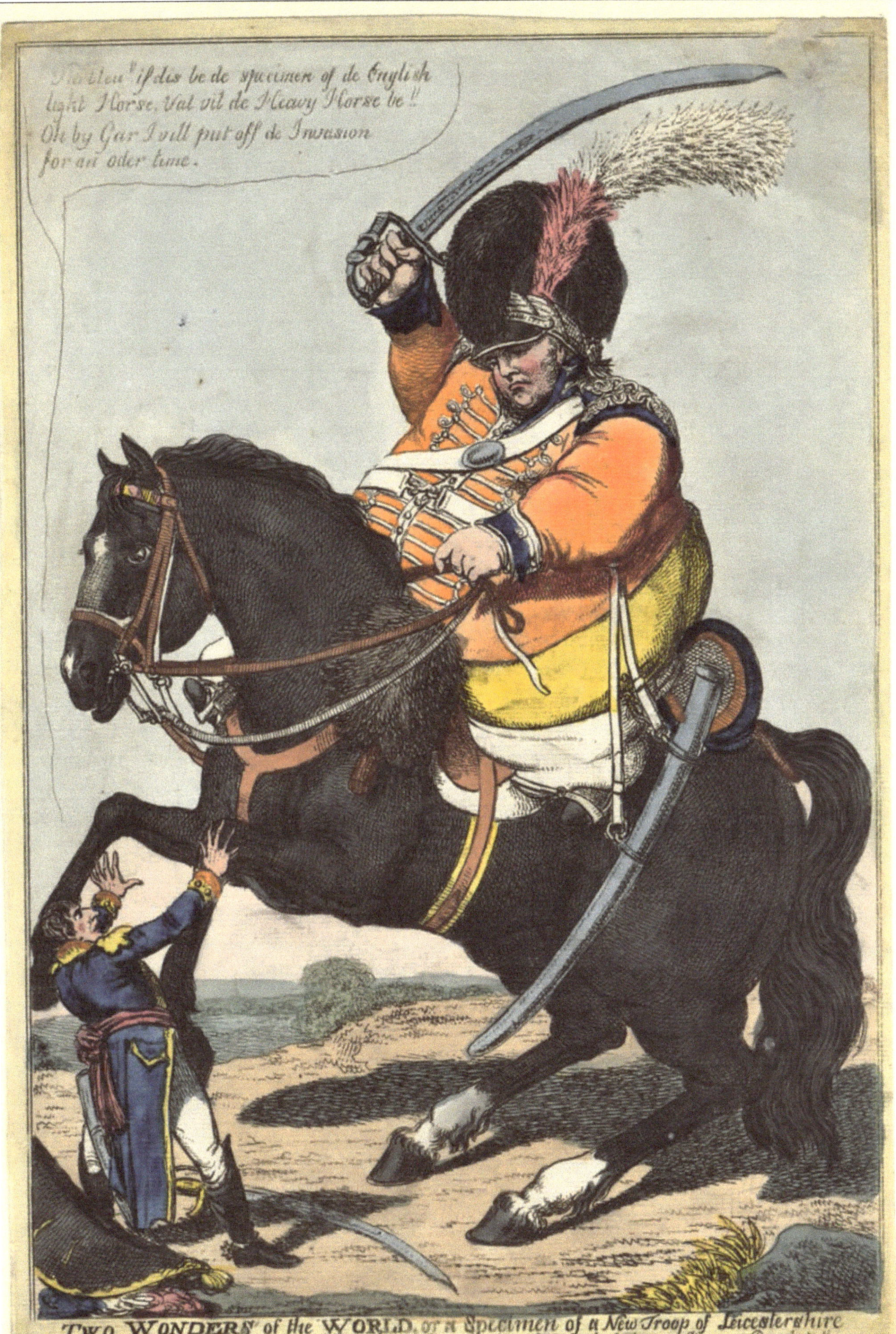
if dis be de specimen of de English
light Horse, Vat vil de Heavy Horse be!!
Oh by Gar I vill put off de Invasion
for an oder time.
TWO WONDERS of the WORLD, or a Specimen of a New Troop of Leicestershire LIGHT HORSE. — Mr Daniel Lambert who at the Age of 36 weighed above 50 Stone, 14 Pounds to the Stone — measured 3 Yards 4 Inches round the Body and 1 yard 1 Inch round the Leg, 5 feet 11 Inches high. —
The Famous Horse Monarch, the Largest in the World, is upwards of 21 hands high (above 7 fut) & only 6 Years Old

32 – LANGBOURN WARD VOLUNTEERS

Plate 52 from Rudolph Ackermann's *Loyal Volunteers of London and Environs Infantry and Cavalry in Their Respective Uniforms*. Illustrations by Thomas Rowlandson. A single figure is in the act of priming and loading as a centre rank. The caption below gives: 'The same as front rank Excepting the firelock which is held a little above the hip.' The volunteer wears a red coat with dark blue collar, cuffs and shoulder straps and gold braid. The headdress has a black fur crest, white over red plume and a turban of green and gold. The waistcoat, turnbacks and breeches are white. Two shoulder belts are being worn, one having an oblong yellow metal plate. Black half gaiters are worn.

The text accompanying the image is as follows: 'Langbourn Ward Volunteers. Major Commandant, Walter Powell, Jun. This Volunteer Corps was formed in May, 1798, Sir John Eamer, Knight and Alderman, in the Chair, when they resolved, with the approbation of His Majesty, to call themselves the Langbourn Ward Association; to furnish themselves with Arms and Clothing at their own expense; and that it be understood the persons forming the Association are not to be considered as enlisted Soldiers, but as Citizens, learning the use of Arms for the sole purpose of protecting their own property, and of supporting the Chief and other Magistrates, in case of Invasion, Rebellion, Insurrection, Riot, &c; nor were they to go out of the City without their own consent; and that care be taken to obtain Commissions from His Majesty, in which there be a clause expressive of these conditions; to which His Majesty was graciously pleased to signify his approbation.'

The corps consisted of two companies of some 120 rank and file and commanded by Major Commandant Walter Powell, Jun. Commanding the first company was Captain Augustus Robert Hankey. The second by Captain Alexander Innes. The helmets bore no title or ornament, the breast-plate having the letters LWA in cypher. The button bore a crown only.

The narrow Langbourn Ward runs in a west-east direction within the City of London, Lombard Street (west) and Fenchurch Street (east) traditionally forming boundaries.

LANGBOURN WARD.
VOLUNTEER.

No. 52

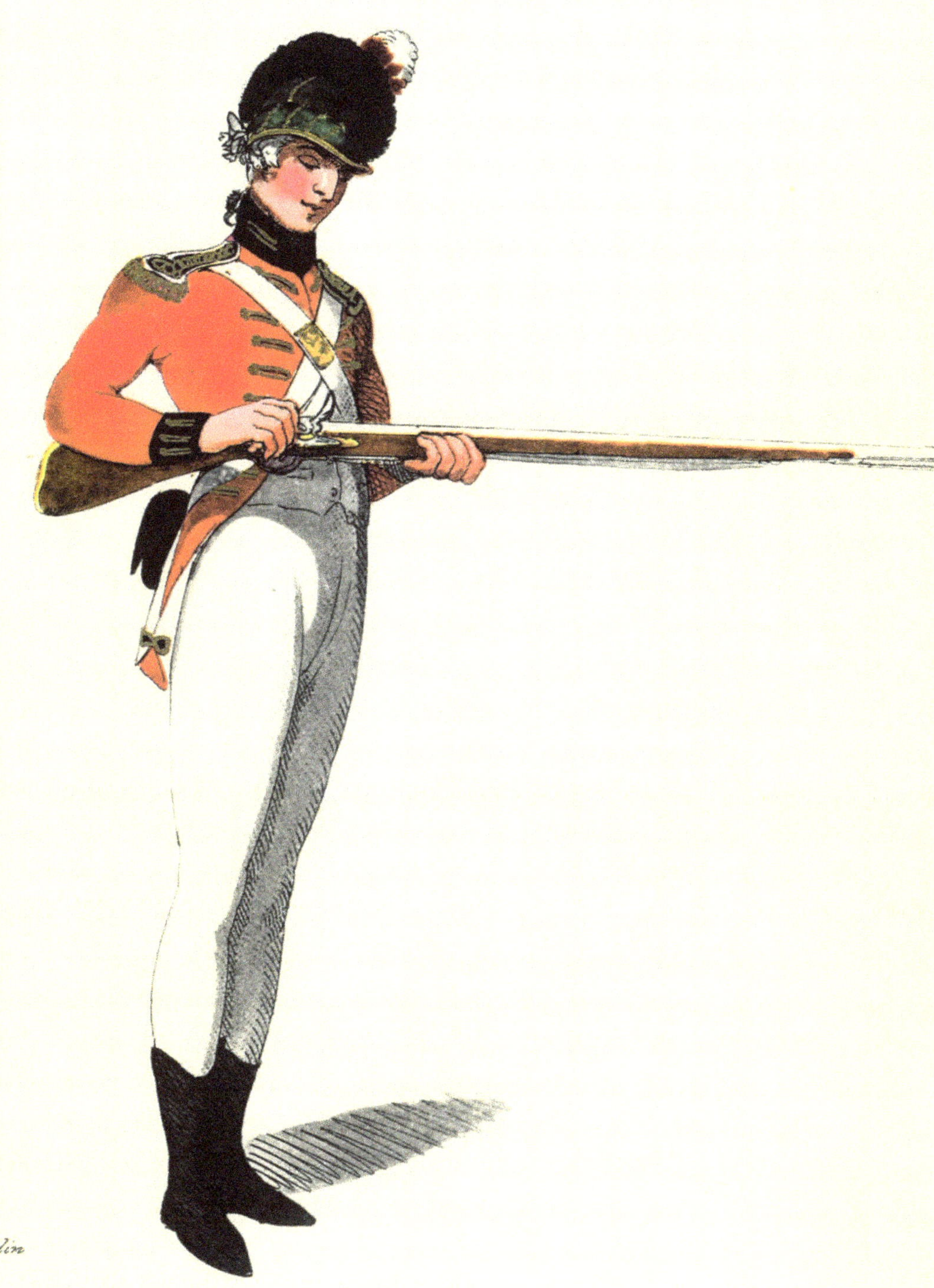

PRIME & LOAD *(as a Center Rank.)*

The same as front rank, Excepting the firelock which is held a little above the hip

London Pub Oct. 5 1798 at Ackermanns Gallery No. 101 Strand

33 – OFFICER, HUDDERSFIELD VOLUNTEERS, 1794

Colour lithograph from *A History of the Formation and Development of The Volunteer Infantry, From The Earliest Times, Illustrated By The Local Records Of Huddersfield And Its Vicinity, From 1794 To 1874* by Robert Potter Berry and published 1903 in London by Simkin, Marshall, Hamilton, Kent & Co of 4 Stationers' Hall Court, and in Huddersfield by J Broadbent & Co, High Street and Albion Street. After PW Reynolds, the image shows a single figure holding a drawn sword. He wears a black hat with gold tassels and white over red plume. The long, tailed coat is red with dark blue collar, lapels and cuffs, the right shoulder having a gold, fringed epaulette. A white waistcoat with gold buttons is worn with a crimson sash tied around the waist. The breeches are white, the gaiters black. A gold gorget hangs from the neck and an oval plate is fixed to a white shoulder-belt.

A proposal to raise a corps of volunteers in Huddersfield was put forward at meeting presided over by Sir George Armytage, Bt held at the George Inn on 28 June 1794. The response by the town's citizens was enthusiastic and as a result it was quickly agreed to raise a force consisting of not more than 200 men. For a title, 'The Huddersfield Corps of Fusilier Volunteers' was settled upon and on 6 December the names of the following appointed officers appeared in the London Gazette for 6 December 1794: Major Commandant Sir George Armytage, Captains Richard H Beaumont, Northend Nichols and Joseph Haigh, First Lieutenants Joseph Scott and William Horsfall and Second Lieutenants Walter Stables, Bramwell Dyson and John Hudson. Their commissions bore the date 18 November 1794.

From Robert Potter Berry's book, details of the officers' uniform decided upon are given as follows: 'The uniform of the corps was the cocked hat of the period, worn across the head, coats of red cut away at the hips and faced with blue, white breeches buttoned down the length of the leg and presenting a gaiter-like appearance.' As we can see from PW Reynolds's painting, the hat included a white over red plume and has two gold tassels. A gilt gorget is being worn, the buttons also gilt and appearing down each of the lapels, on the cuffs and collar. A crimson sash is worn around the waist and over the waistcoat, and a white leather shoulder-belt displays an oval gilt plate.

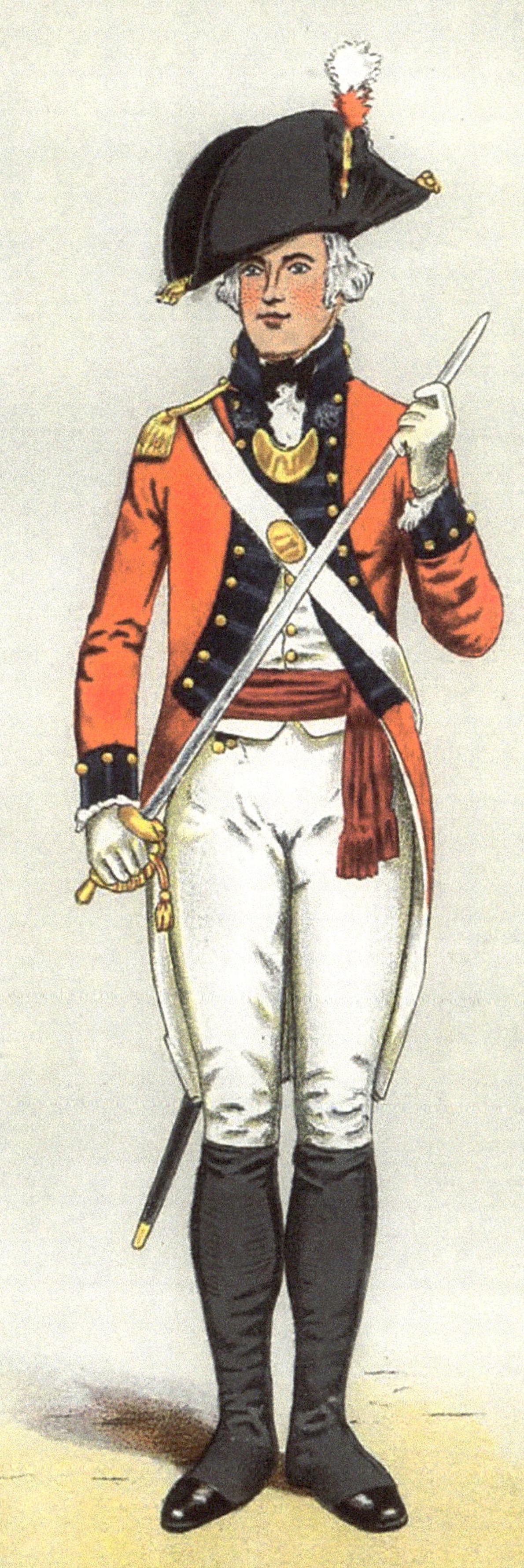

34 – SERGEANT OF THE LOYAL BIRMINGHAM VOLUNTEERS, 1803

Colour plate from *The History Of The 1st Volunteer Battalion The Royal Warwickshire Regiment And Its Predecessors* by Colonel Charles J Hart, VD and published by the Midland Counties Herald Ltd, Birmingham, 1906. A single figure posed holding a tall pike cradled in his right arm. He wears a red short-tailed coat with yellow collar, lapels and cuffs, a yellow and crimson girdle, buff breeches and long, black gaiters buttoned at the sides. The black headdress has a gold plate, chin-strap and white-over-red plume.

Formed in 1803, the Loyal Birmingham Volunteers soon comprised three battalions, the colonel of all three being George, Earl of Dartmouth. Each battalion consisted of eight battalion companies, one grenadier and one light company. In this plate of a Sergeant at time of formation, we see a detailed figure following closely the dress regulations laid down by the corps in 1803. Gone were the blue jackets with red facings of the old disbanded Birmingham Volunteers, scarlet and yellow being chosen for the new regiment. Here in the illustration we see a white-over-red plume in the shako indicating that the wearer is of a battalion company. He is a sergeant and therefore is permitted to be armed with a pike. Regarding breeches, the regulations stated that they should be white cloth made to button up high on the waist and with four buttons at the knee. Gaiters were to be black and to sit close full up to the knee in the front and with a small hollow behind. The sash was crimson and yellow worsted tied in a small knot on the right side. Although the plate is dated as 1803, the headdress being worn seems to be of the pattern introduced in 1812, the so called 'Waterloo Shako'.

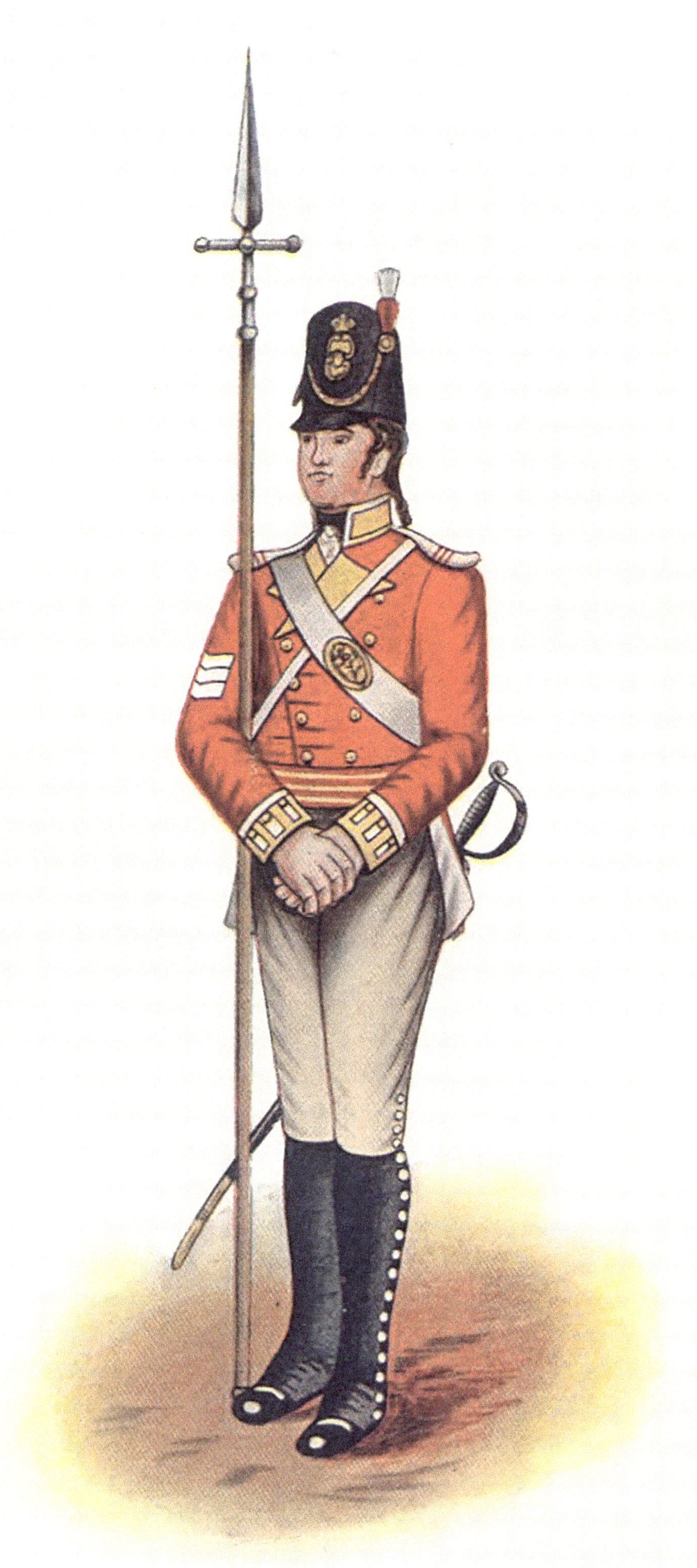

35 – SIR MARTIN BROWNE FOLKES, NORFOLK RANGERS YEOMANRY CAVALRY

Colour reproduction of an original painting from *Record Of The Norfolk Yeomanry Cavalry To Which Is Added The Fencible and Provisional Cavalry Of The Same County From 1780 To 1908* compiled by Lieutenant-Colonel JR Harvey and published in 1908 by Jarrold & Sons of 10 and 11 Warwick Lane in the City of London and London and Exchange Streets, Norwich. Tipped into the book, the image appears with the following caption printed separately below: 'Sir Martin Brown Folkes, Bart., Hillington Hall, Norfolk, Norfolk Rangers Yeomanry Cavalry, 1783, From the picture in possession of Sir Willian ffoulkes, Bart.' The portrait shows Sir Martin, bareheaded and wearing a green coat with gold buttons and epaulettes which unbuttoned reveals a white waistcoat. A white shoulder-belt is worn which has an oval plate bearing a shield engraved with the letters NR below a crown.

The Norfolk Rangers dates from 1782 and we read in the Norwich Mercury for 14 September of that year the following: "On Saturday se' night, the Right Hon. Lord Viscount Townshend and his Lady arrived at their family seat at Raynham; and on the Sunday morning a very respectable body of gentlemen, farmers, and tradesmen, waited on his Lordship as volunteers to serve in a corps (styled the Norfolk Rangers) in order to protect the county of Norfolk from any insults from the enemy. The foot being upwards of fifty, were clothed in a genteel green uniform, with black caps and green feathers, at his Lordship's expense." As a follow up, the Norwich Mercury a week later commented: 'Lord Townshend's corps of volunteers have already increased in number to 150...Lord Townshend's uniform is green, faced with black....'

About the time of formation a song was composed with the following words: 'Gird on your swords, / And pass your words, / To combat toils and dangers; / When foes assail ' We'll turn not tail, / But join the Norfolk Rangers'.

Come the formation of volunteer corps throughout the country in 1794, the Norfolk Rangers were already trained and equipped to a high standard. A government 'List of the Officers of the Corps and Troops of Gentlemen and Yeomanry' published in that year gives George, Marquis Townshend as major commandant and Sir Martin B Folkes, Bt as one of three captains. Sir Martin, the subject of the illustration, was created a baronet on 26 May 1774. He served as High Sheriff of Norfolk and was thirty-one years member of parliament for Lynn. He died on 11 December 1821.

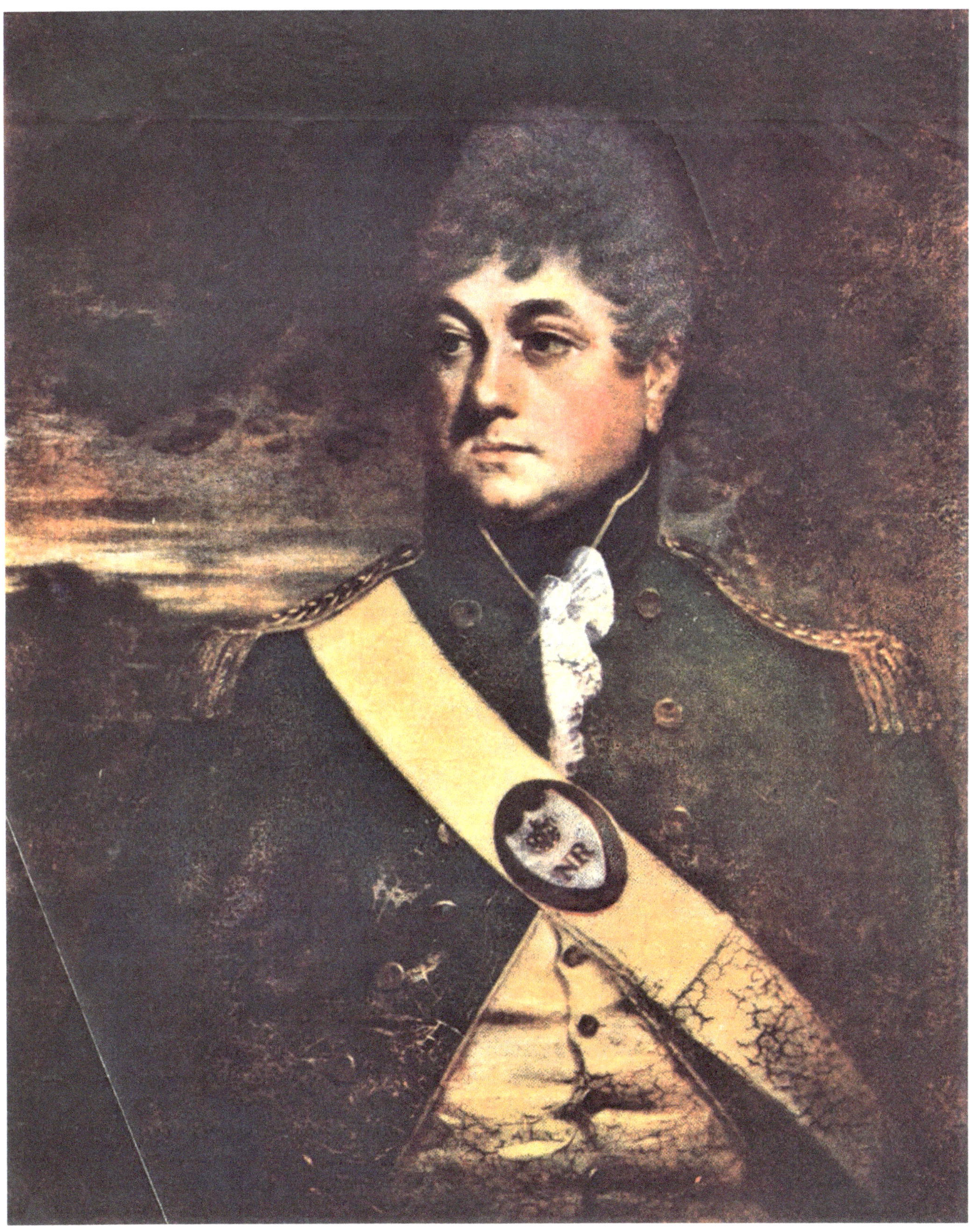

36 – LIEUTENANT WILLIAM PALGRAVE, YARMOUTH VOLUNTEER CAVALRY, 1799

Reproduction of an original painting from *Record Of The Norfolk Yeomanry Cavalry To Which Is Added The Fencible and Provisional Cavalry Of The Same County From 1780 To 1908* compiled by Lieutenant-Colonel JR Harvey and published in 1908 by Jarrold & Sons of 10 and 11 Warwick Lane in the City of London and London and Exchange Streets, Norwich. The image is tipped in opposite page 100 and is shown with the following caption printed below: 'Lieut. William Palgrave, Yarmouth Volunteer Cavalry, 1799.' The officer is shown wearing a headdress adorned with a fur crest and feather plume, his coat having fringed shoulder epaulettes. His left hand grips the scabbard of a sword. The coat was scarlet with black facings and gold lace.

Colonel Harvey records in his book how, 'At Yarmouth, there was formed in April, 1798, a troop of Yeomanry Cavalry, supplying themselves with an outfit at their own cost, and each man contributing sixpence a week to a fund which in two or three years amounted to nearly £200.' Mention is also made in the history of a presentation of Colours by Lady Bacon on 30 August 1798, '...from the Angel balcony to the Yarmouth Yeomanry Cavalry, with which they proceeded to the Parish Church, where the colours were consecrated at the altar and a sermon preached by the Rev. Lovick-Cooper.' The Angel is possibly the Angel Hotel which dates from around 1652.

William Palgrave was commissioned by the Duke of Portland on 20 June 1798, his short biography being included in Colonel Harvey's book telling how '...his portrait in the gay uniform of his corps was in 1879 in the possession of his eldest surviving son, Thomas Palgrave, Esq', of Bryn-y-gynog, Llansaintffraid, near Conway, North Wales. Palgrave was collector of customs at the Port of Great Yarmouth and in 1814 had been elected as Mayor of the Borough. He died in Dublin on 11 January 1838, aged sixty-eight.

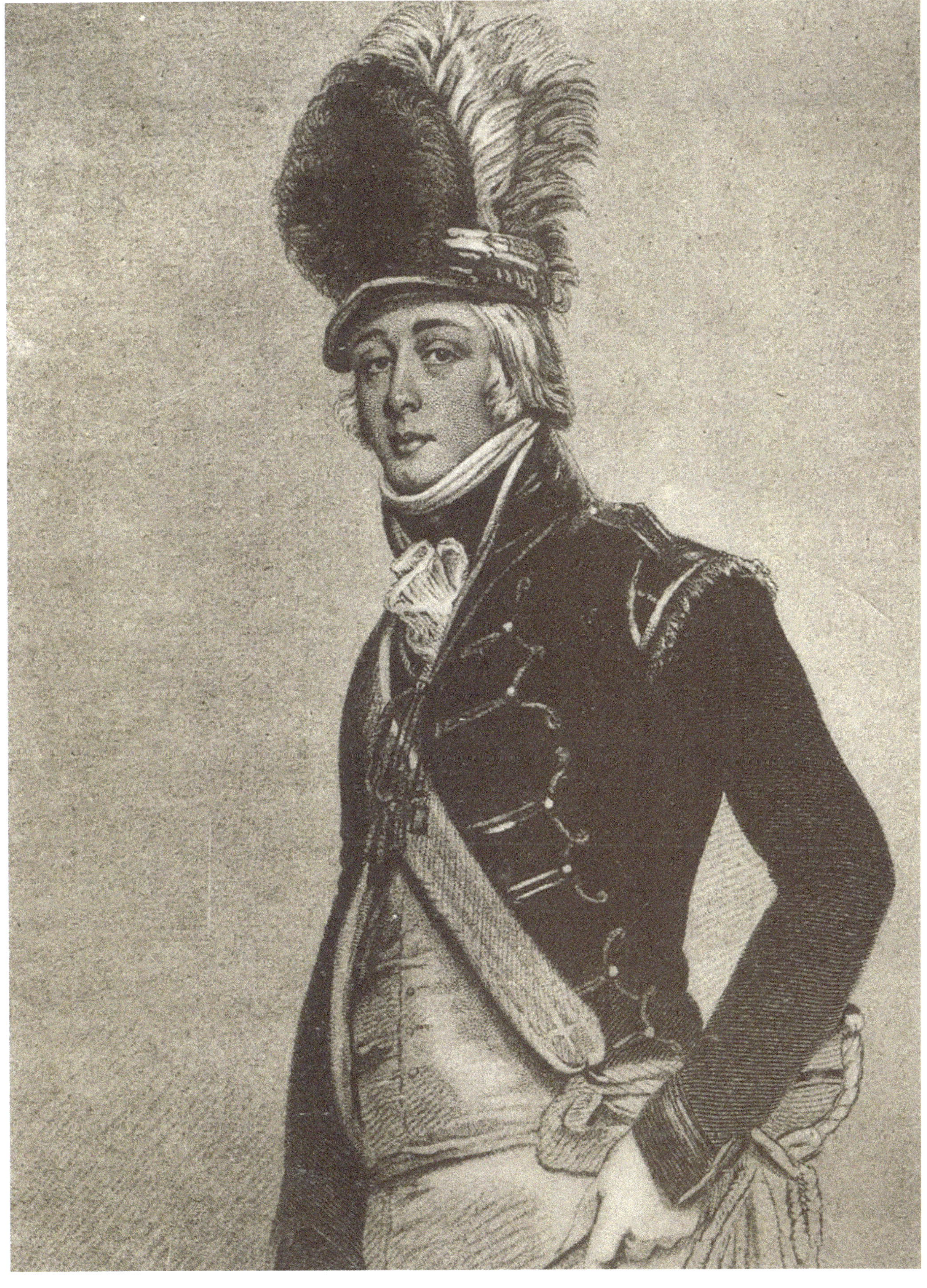

37 – SHARP-SHOOTERS ATTACKED BY CAVALRY

One of a pair of coloured aquatints by Thomas Rowlandson published by Laurie & Whittle of 53 Fleet Street, London on 12 May 1804. To the left of a fast running stream, a party of men defend their position against an oncoming cavalry charge. The infantrymen wear light brown uniforms with red collars, cuffs and piping and tall black shakos sporting red plumes. Several men are in the action of firing, one from high up in the boughs of a tree, another, from a ground position, is lying flat. Others, kneeling, await the enemy with fixed bayonets and one to the far left of the image reloads his firelock. To his right, a bugler sounds a call.

The charging cavalry are in blue coats with red collars and cuffs and wear black bicorn hats with tall red feather plumes. One of their number has just been hit, another lies wounded on the ground.

The second image in the set can be seen in 38 below. (*Image courtesy of the Anne SK Brown Military Collection, Brown University Library*)

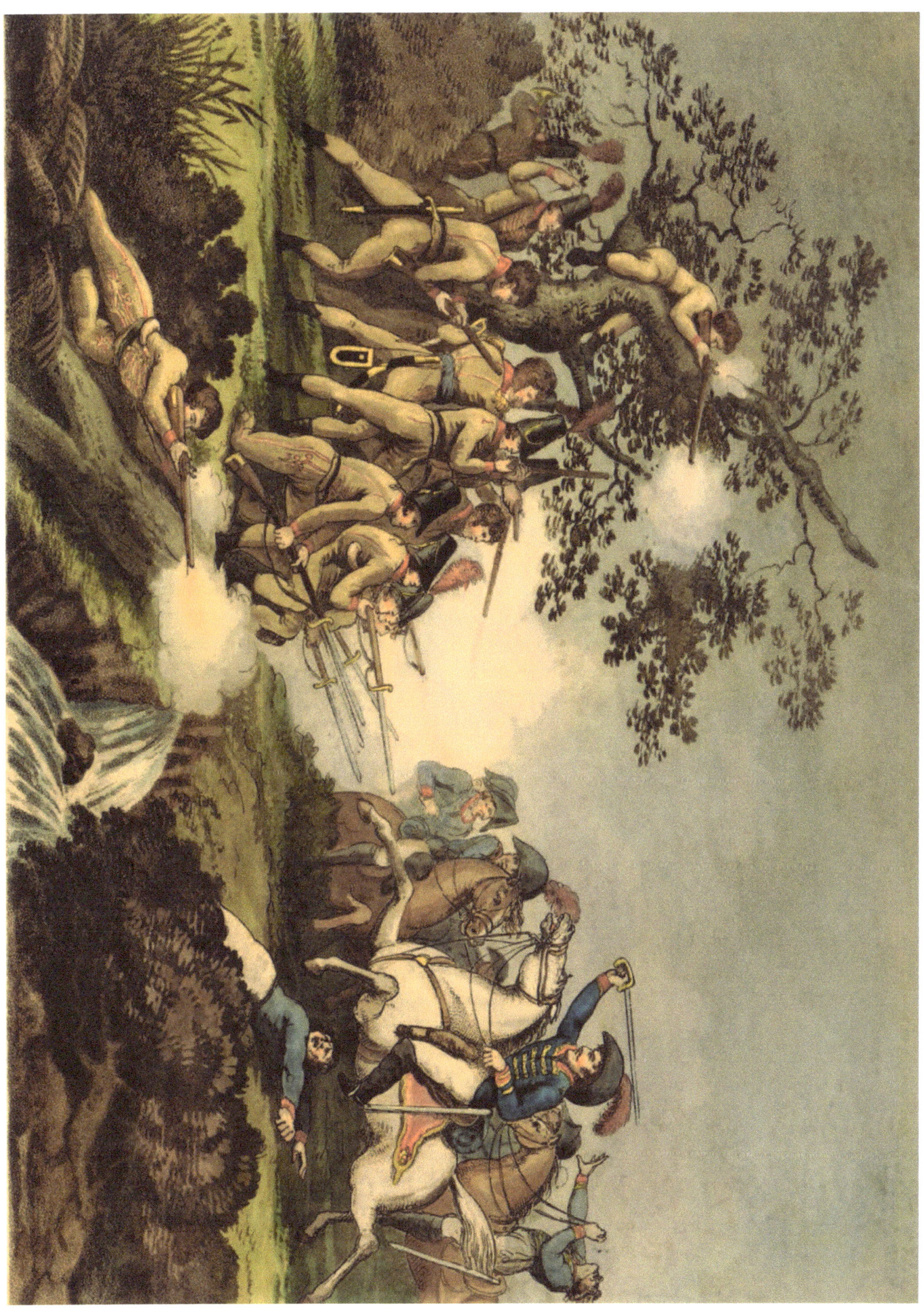

38 – SHARP-SHOOTERS FIRING IN AMBUSH

One of a pair of coloured aquatints by Thomas Rowlandson published by Laurie & Whittle of 53 Fleet Street, London on 12 May 1804. From high ground a party of sharpshooters dressed in light brown uniforms with red collars, cuffs and piping fire towards an unseen enemy. High up, an officer with sword drawn directs the action while another hatless and with a pistol tucked into his sash, instructs a bugler who wears wide red shoulder decoration to his coat. Lying on his back with feet and head raised, one man fires from a classic rifleman position.

The other image in the set can be seen in 37 above. (*Image courtesy of the Anne SK Brown Military Collection, Brown University Library*)

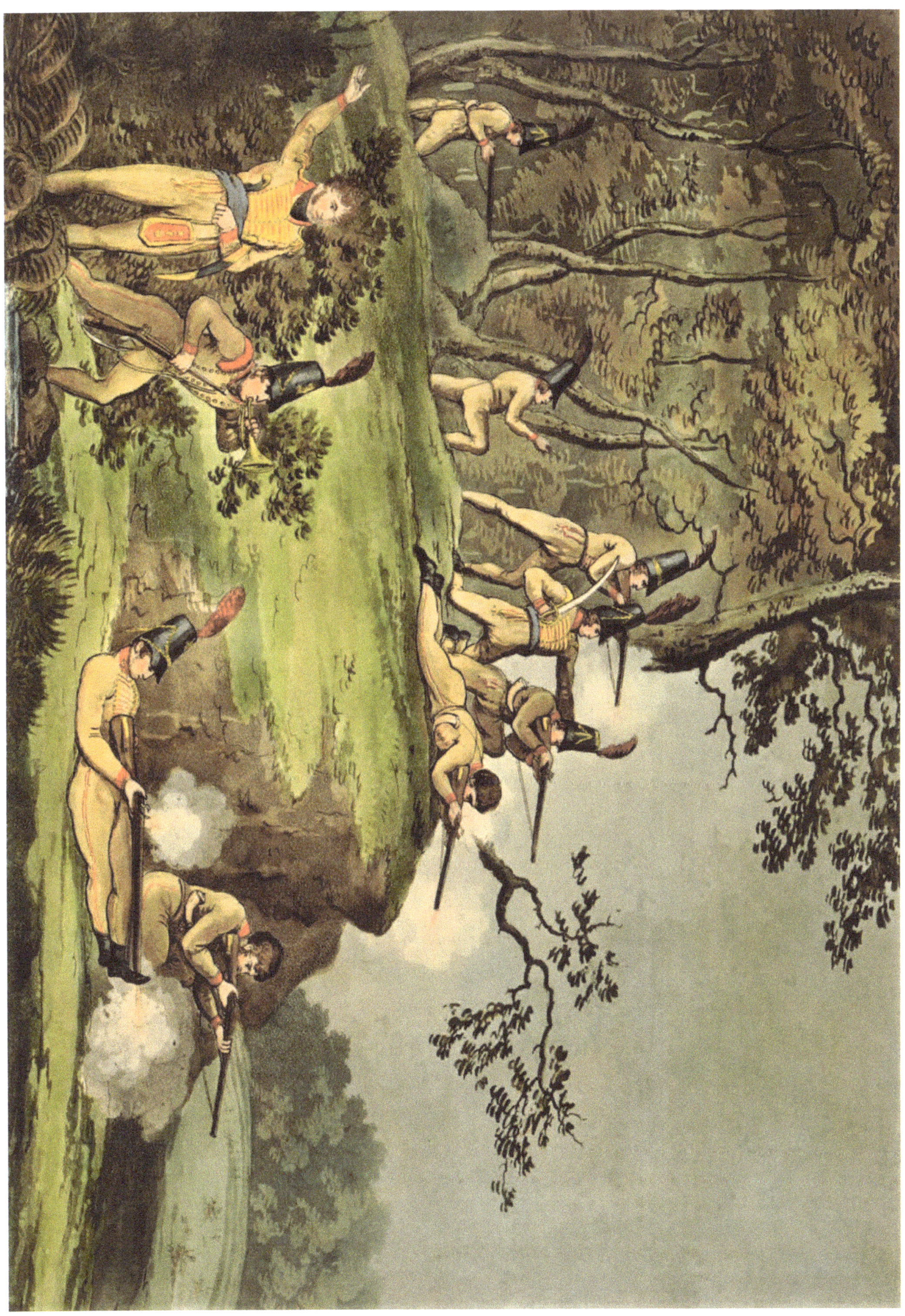

39 – THE VOLUNTEER SUNG BY MR INCLEDON AT VAUXHALL

Coloured etching song sheet published on 4 April 1804 by Laurie & Whittle of 53 Fleet Street, London bearing the title 'The Volunteer Sung by Mr Incledon at Vauxhall.' The image carries the printed number '342' and the following lyric:

1 A Scarlet coat and a smart cockade,
Are passports to the fair;
For Venus self was kind 'tis said
To Mars the God of War.
Then since my country calls to arms,
Love's livery I'll wear,
Nor seek rewards, save Nanny's charms,
But go a Volunteer.

2 Should fortune smile, and grant me fame,
The laurel shall be thine;
The flowers of love I only claim,
Ah let their sweets entwine—Then since, &c

3 All hardships seem as light as air,
While British maids we guard;
Each soldier has one darling care,
Her smiles his best reward—The since, &c

On a cliff top commanded by an embattled-walled encampment, a group of volunteers dressed in red coats and grey breeches have set up a marquee which flies the Union flag. Inside, a long table, around which eight men raise glasses in a toast, is laden with bottles. Featured, and standing by three groups of piled firelocks, a volunteer holds the hand of a young woman dressed in a black coat worn over a long pink dress. Two cannon look out to sea where three ships can be seen in the distance just below the horizon.

Mr Incledon, Mr Charles Benjamin Incledon (1763-1826), was a Cornish tenor whose career led him to be reckoned as one of the country's leading performers of theatre music and ballads. Vauxhall, Vauxhall Gardens in fact, was from 1785 to 1859 a London pleasure area on the south bank of the River Thames and one of the capital's important venues for public entertainment. In 1817 a re-enactment of the Battle of Waterloo took place involving more than 1,000 troops.

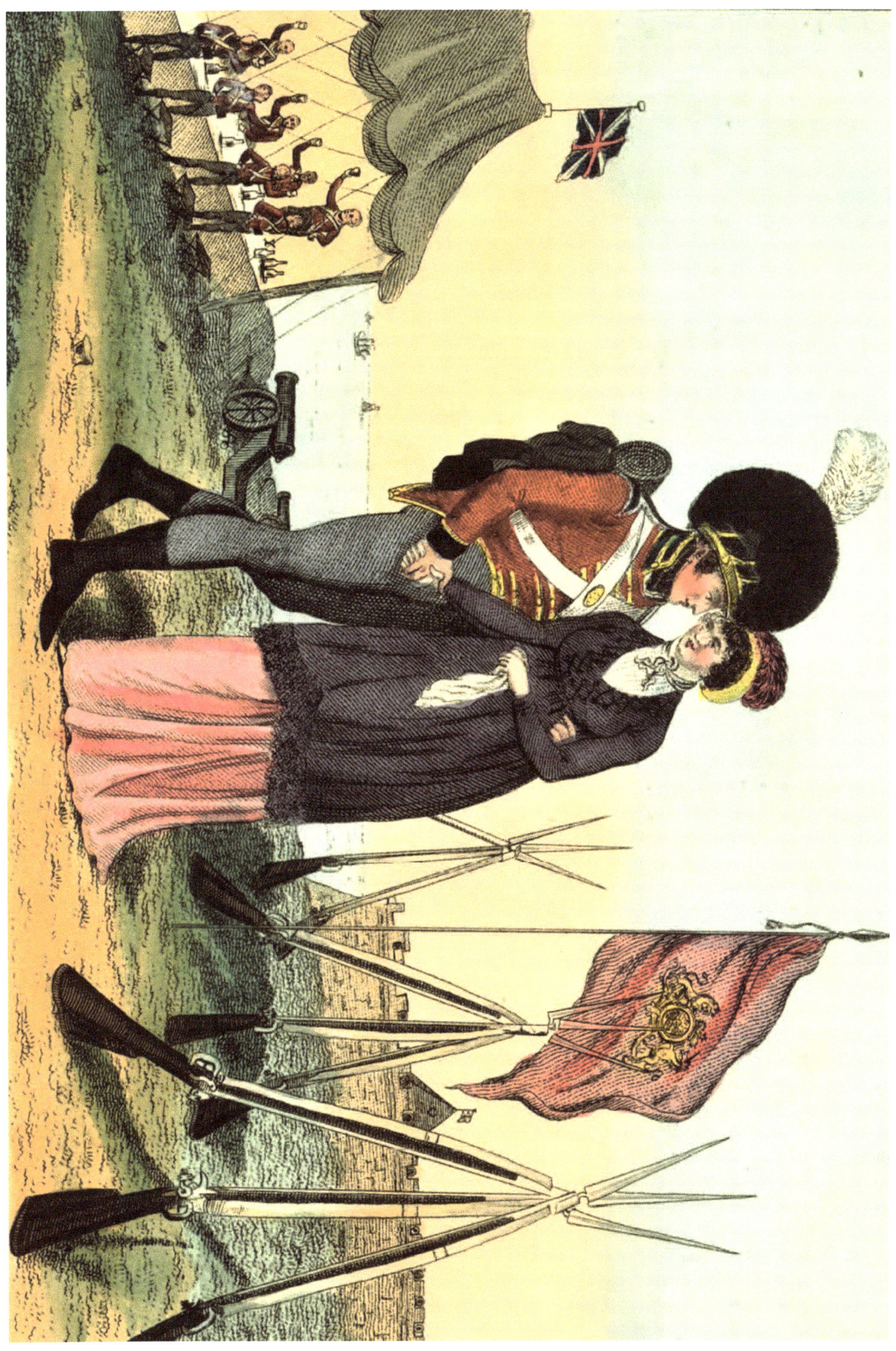

40 – 10th REGIMENT OF LOYAL LONDON VOLUNTEERS

From a series of ten 'dedicated' prints to Loyal London Volunteers drawn and engraved by Peltro William Tomkins and published by Elizabeth Walker of 7 Cornhill in the City of London on 1 June 1804. The dedication reads: 'To Lieutenant Colonel Combe, The Officers & Privates of the Tenth Regiment of Loyal London Volunteers, This Print Representing their Uniform, is Respectfully Dedicated by their Obligd Sert E. Walker.' Dividing the dedication is the shield from the City of London's arms supported by two volunteers in uniform. Carrying his firelock at the trail in his right hand, a volunteer raises his left arm, his index finger pointing to his front. He wears a short white coat with dark facings, dark breeches and a Tarleton helmet. To his left, two men stand close to a target. Beyond that is a group of houses and the tower and steeple of a church.

The services of the 10th Loyal London Volunteers were accepted on 4 August 1803, Colonel Harvey Christopher Combe's commission being dated 17 September of that year. Regarding uniform, Willson's chart of 1806 gives the coats as red, the facings and breeches as blue. Gold lace was worn by officers. (*Image courtesy of the Anne SK Brown Military Collection, Brown University Library*)

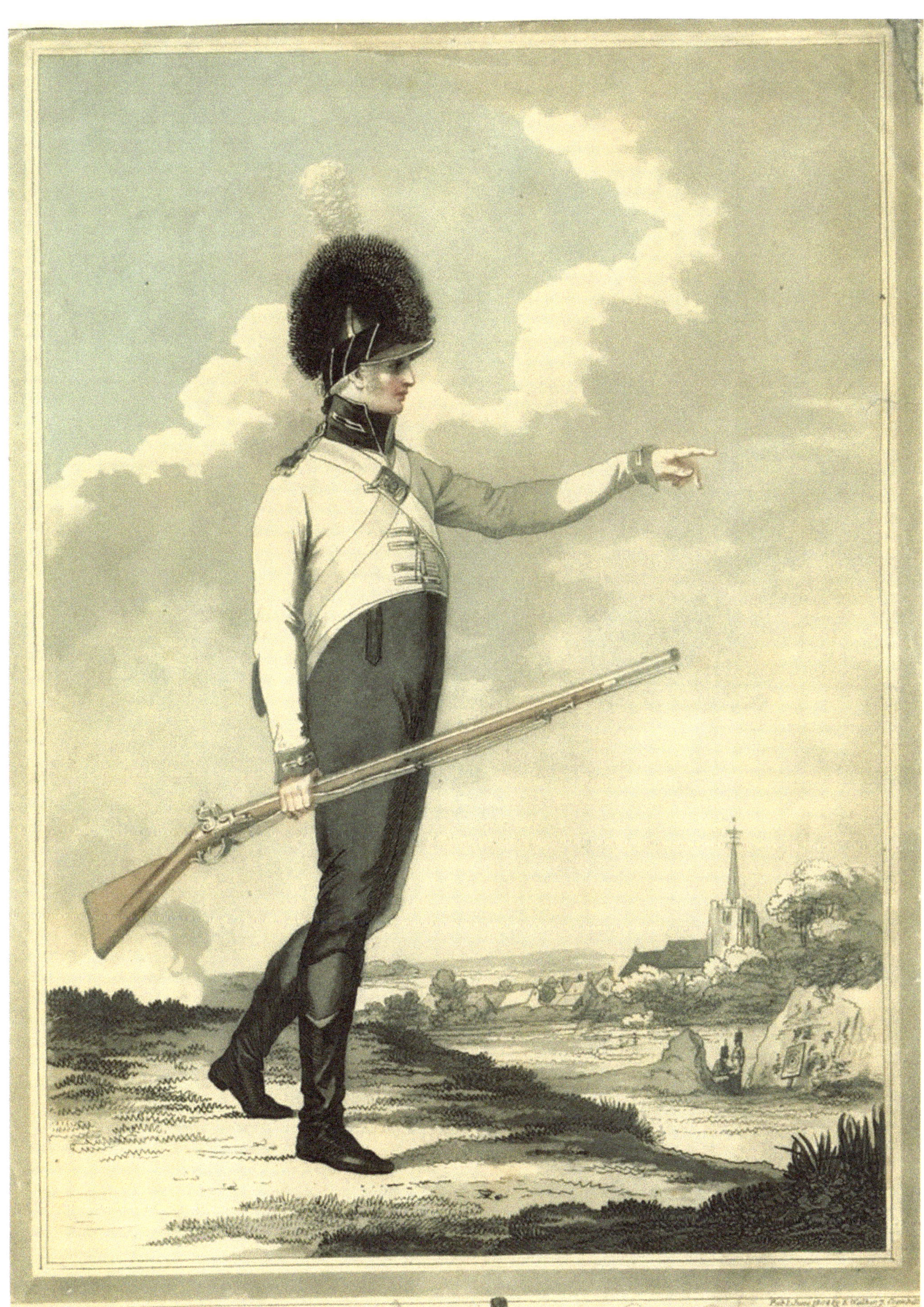

To Lieutenant Colonel Combe, The Officers & Privates of the Tenth Regiment of Loyal London Volunteers, This Print Representing their Uniform is Respectfully Dedicated by their Oblig.^d Servt E. Walker

41 – BLOOMSBURY AND INNS OF COURT ASSOCIATION

Hand coloured stipple engraving after George Hounsom, engraved by F Bartolozzi and published on 1 January 1799 by George Hounsom of 167 Fleet Street and G Shepheard of 13 Church Row, St Pancras. The image carries the following dedication: 'To the Gentlemen of the Bloomsbury and Inns of Court Association this print of Lieut Colonel Cox is inscribed, by their obedient humble Servant George Hounsom.' Colonel Cox is seen in a scarlet coat which has a yellow collar, lapels and cuffs and gold epaulets. He wears a white waistcoat with gold buttons, white breeches, a shoulder-belt with an oval gold plate, and a Tarleton helmet with white plume. A yellow flag can be seen in the background which bears the title of the corps and the figure of Britannia looking out to sea.

This corps was formed in June 1797 and comprised six companies under the command of Lieutenant-Colonel Samuel Compton Cox, Master in Chancery of the High Court. Colours were presented by Lady Loughborough on 2 June of the following year. The Bloomsbury and Inns of Court Volunteers were made up of lawyers, a profession much disliked by King George who referred to them as 'The Devil's Own', a name that remained with the regiment throughout its history. See also illustration 42 below. (*Image courtesy of the Anne SK Brown Military Collection, Brown University Library*)

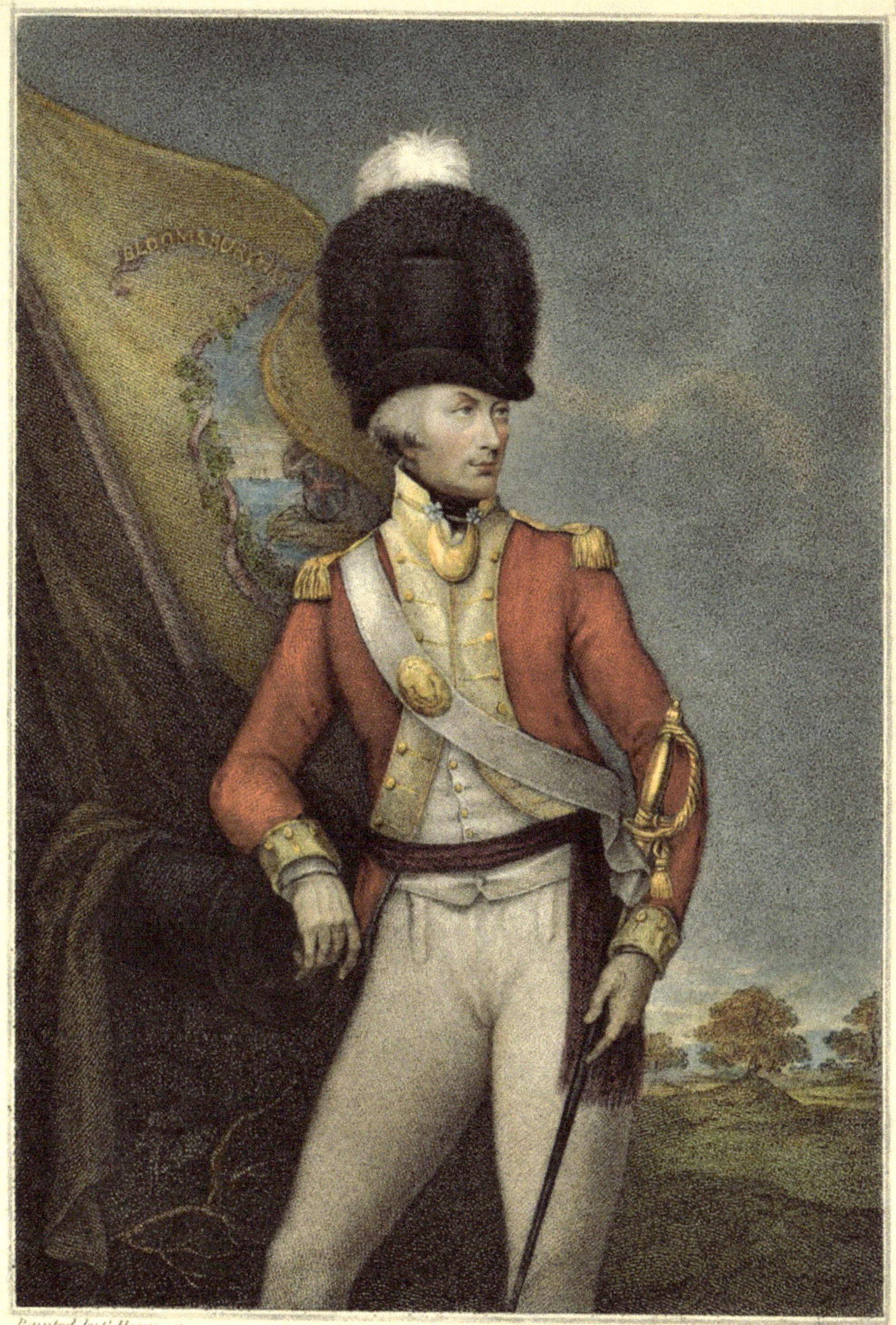

Painted by G. Hounsom — Engraved by F. Bartolozzi R.A.

To the Gentlemen of the
BLOOMSBURY and INNS of COURT ASSOCIATION
this Print of Lieu.t Colonel Cox, is inscribed,
by their obedient humble Servant.
George Hounsom.

London Publish'd Jan.y 1.st 1799 by G. Hounsom No. 167 Fleet Street,
& G. Shepheard No. 14 Church Row St. Pancras.

42 – BLOOMSBURY AND INNS OF COURT ASSOCIATION

Drawn and engraved by PW Tomkins and published on 1 November 1803 by Elizabeth Walker of Cornhill in the City of London. From a series of ten images featuring London volunteers, the print shows a private of the regiment holding his firelock in the 'Charge Bayonet' position. He wears a red coat with yellow collar, lapels, shoulder straps and cuffs. His waistcoat and breeches are white. The tall headdress has a white feather plume. The private is shown against a background of the Foundling Hospital, in the grounds of which can be seen a party of volunteers drilling, a mounted officer and numerous civilian men, women and children. The image was published with the following dedication below: 'To the Gentlemen of the Bloomsbury & Inns of Court Association, this Print representing the Uniform is respectfully dedicated by their Obt. Servt. E Walker.' Between the wording a representation of Britannia within a wreath.

The regiment's commander, Lieutenant-Colonel Samuel Compton Cox was Governor of the Foundling Hospital. Now demolished, the hospital was located on Lamb's Conduit Field in Bloomsbury.

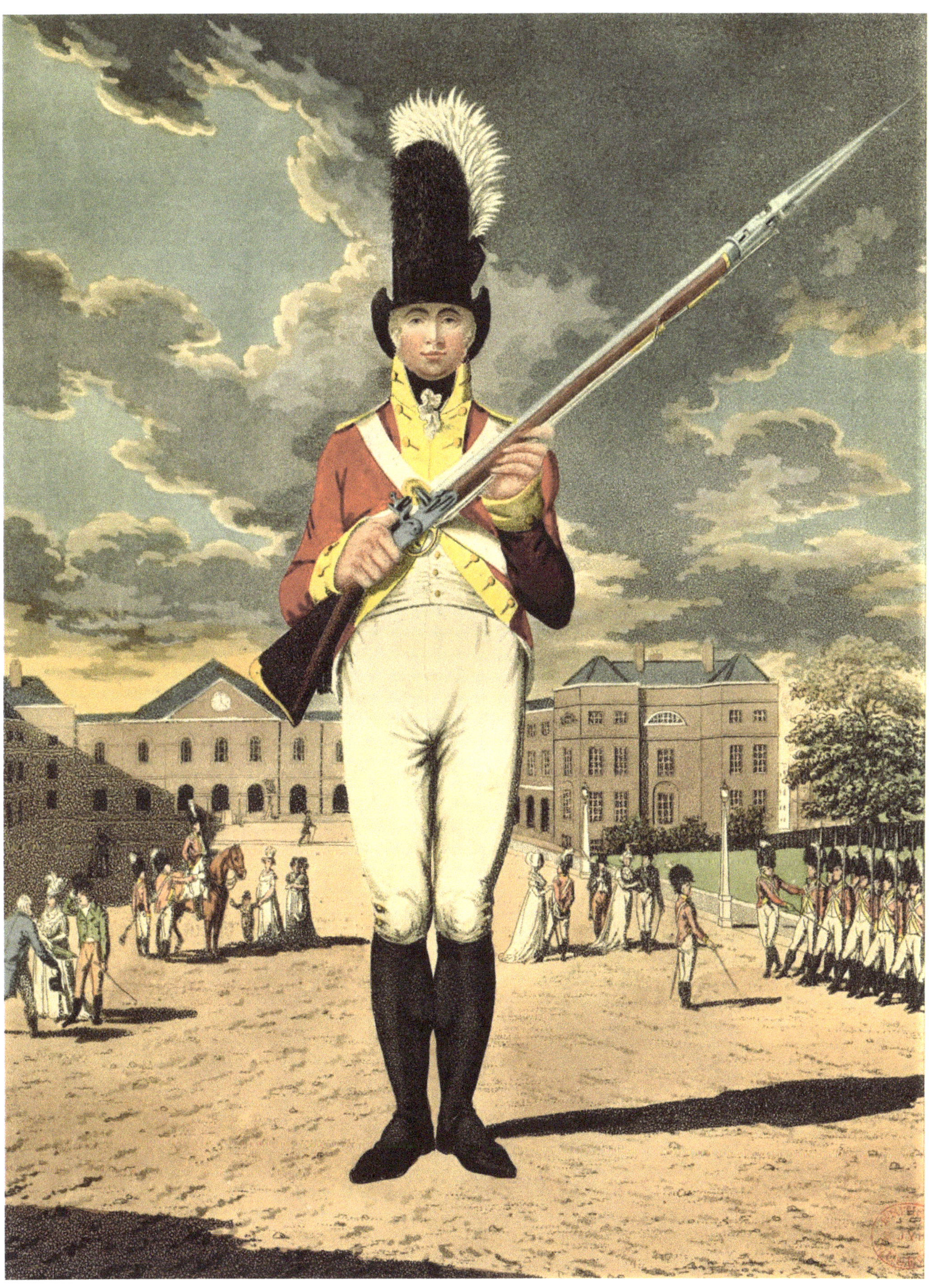

43 – JOHN BULL GUARDING A TOYSHOP

Caricature credited to John Cawse and published by Samuel W Fores of Piccadilly, London on 20 October 1803 as part of a set entitled 'Folios of Caricatures Lent Out For The Evening'. Wearing the uniform of a volunteer corps, John Bull stands in front of a toy shop in absolute defiance of Napoleon. Looking like a spoilt child, the French leader wipes his eyes and cries, 'Pray Mr Bull let me have some of the toys if 'tis only that little one in the corner.' Wearing a large hat and a sword almost as big as himself, Napoleon points to a model of none other than the Bank of England. But the symbol of all that is British stands firm with hand on hip and replies, 'I tell you – you shant touch one of them – so blubber away and be d——d.'

Playing an important role during the threat of invasion from France were the many thousands of volunteers who formed regiments, large and small, to defend Britain should the need arise. In this satirical cartoon by John Cawse we see good old John Bull dressed as one of them and guarding a toyshop full of model London buildings. And here is poor old Napoleon, so sad and pleading with this national personification of Britishness for just one. (*Courtesy of the Anne SK Brown Military Collection, Brown University Library*)

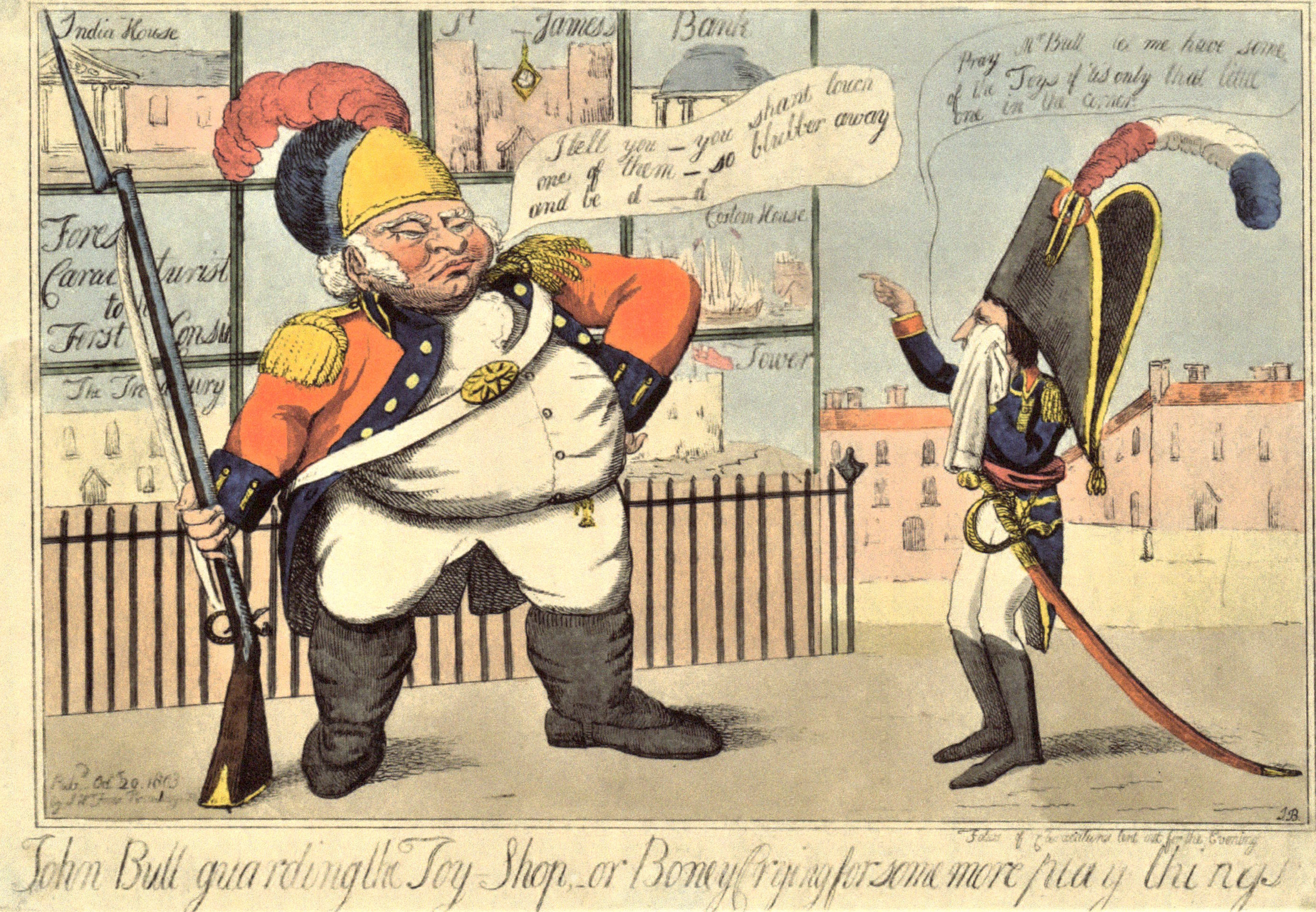

John Bull guarding the Toy-Shop, or Boney Crying for some more play things

44 – THE RIGHT HON WILLIAM PITT, CINQUE PORTS VOLUNTEERS

Colour aquatint engraved by Joseph Constantine Stadler after P Hubert and published by P Hubert & S White of 23 Villiers Street, London on 28 March 1804. Against a background of a large stone fortress and several civilian and uniformed figures, a mounted officer wearing a red coat with yellow collar, lapels and cuffs and dark blue breeches rides past with his sword held high. Below the image the following printed dedication: 'The Right Honbl William Pitt Colonel / Commandant of the Cinque Port Volunteers / To the Gentlemen Volunteers, the Corporations and other Inhabitants of / the Cinque Ports, This Plate is respectfully inscribed by their / Most obedient humble servant Saml White.' Between the lettering, the arms of the Cinque Ports.

The 1805 War Office List reveals that the Colonel Commandant of the Cinque Ports Volunteers was the Right Honourable William Pitt, the former Prime Minister and after 1792, Lord Warden of the Cinque Ports. Much useful information regarding the Cinque Ports Volunteers can be found on the 'Romney March The Fifth Continent' website. It tells how the corps was reformed in 1803 under the command of William Pitt who was then living at the Lord Warden's official residence, Walmer Castle. He had written to Secretary of State for War, Lord Hobart on 27 July 1803 as follows: 'I have the honour of transmitting enclosed Memorandum of the proposal which I laid before your Lordship this morning for raising a Regiment of Volunteers within the Cinque Ports, to serve in case of invasion in any part of England, and to consist of three Battalions: and I have to request that your Lordship will submit the same to His Majesty's consideration.' Pitt's proposal was subsequently accepted, and 3,000 men would be enrolled between July and November 1803. The officers, note the records, were all local gentry and aristocracy, the rank and file being in the main skilled labourers and artisans that could be relied upon to leave their businesses for long periods. After Pitt's death on 23 January 1806, both the 1st and 2nd Battalions formed a guard of honour at his Westminster Abbey burial on the following 22 February. The 3rd Battalion was disbanded in the same year.

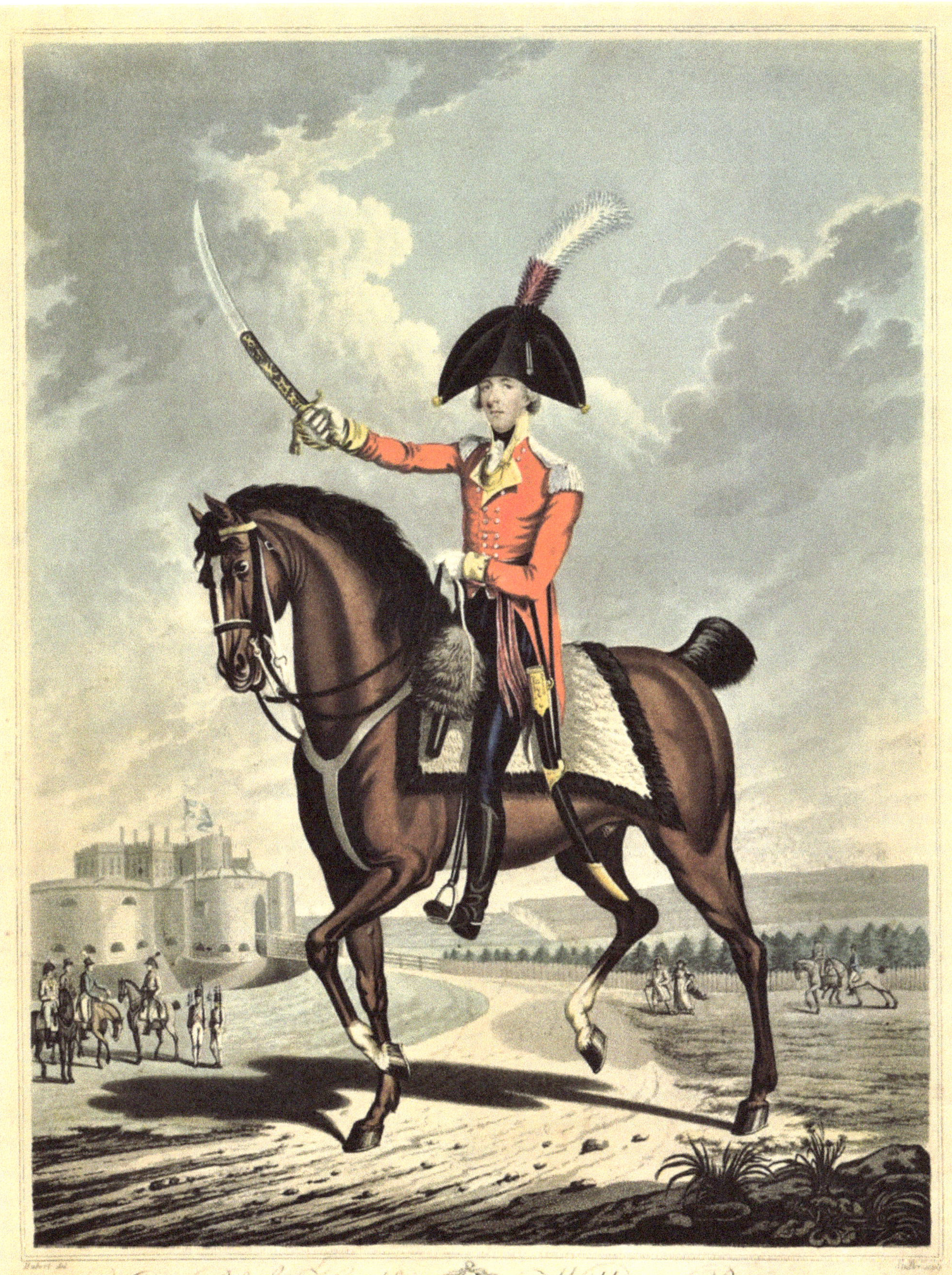

The Right Honble William Pitt
COLONEL Commandant of the Cinque Port VOLUNTEERS
To the Gentlemen Volunteers, the Corporations and other Inhabitants of the Cinque Ports, This Plate is respectfully inscribed by their
Most obedient humble Servant Saml White

45 – St CLEMENT DANES VOLUNTEERS

Plate 7 from Rudolph Ackermann's *Loyal Volunteers of London & Environs* and published in 1799 from artwork supplied by Thomas Rowlandson. A single figure posed with his firelock in the 2nd motion 'shoulder arms' position. He wears a red coat with dark blue collar, lapels, shoulder straps and cuffs, a white waistcoat and white breeches. The headdress sports a red over white plume. The 2nd motion shoulder arms position is described at the bottom of the image: 'At the word Arms, the Piece is at once flung to the left shoulder & caught in the left hand. Keeping the Body square & perfectly upright.'

The following text accompanies the image: 'This corps was formed May 1st 1798, to keep the peace within their own limits. They consist of two Companies of Light Infantry; and received their Colours on the 3rd June, 1799, from the hand of Miss Edwards, daughter of Captain Edwards; and these are decorated with the Anchor, and the words "St Clement Danes Association." Their Committee is composed of all the officers and seven Privates.'

A list of officers is also given: Samuel Edwards (Captain Commandant), William Sandby, Jun (Second Captain), Richard Twining (First Lieutenant), John Paternoster (Second Lieutenant), John Prince and Benjamin Marshall (Ensigns).

The helmets are noted as having black-purple ribands and red over white feathers, the oval breast plates having the title St Clement Danes Association around an anchor.

No. 7

St. CLEMENT DANES
VOLUNTEER

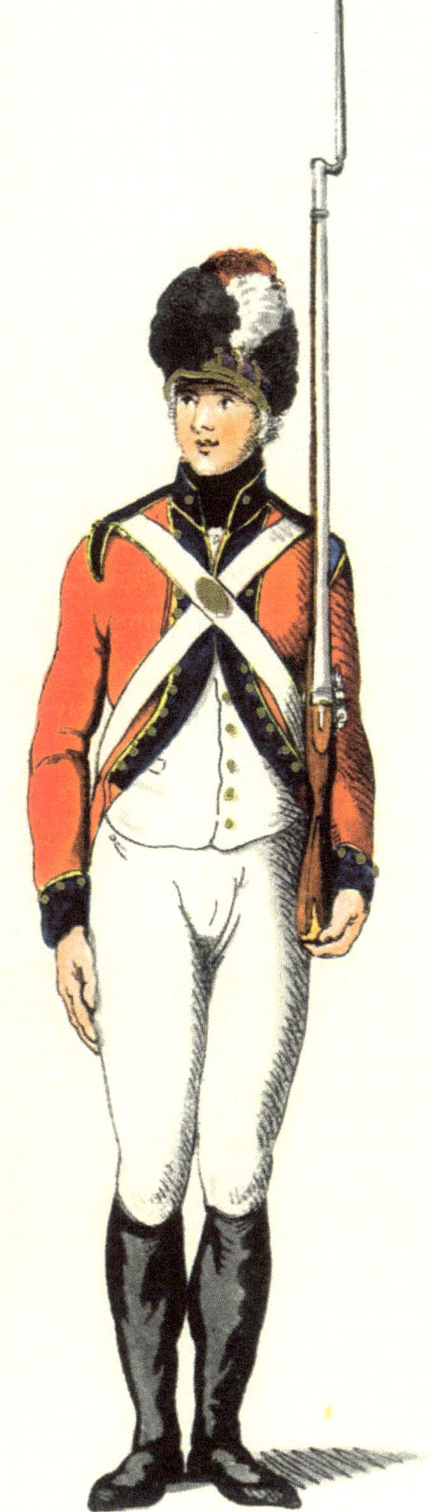

Rowlandson Delin

SHOULDER ARMS 2d. Motion

At the word Arms, the Piece is at once flung to the left Shoulder, & caught in the left han[d] Keeping the Body square & perfectly upright.

London Pub June 1 1798 at Ackermann's Gallery No. 101 Strand

46 – THE GRAND TRIUMPHAL ENTRY OF THE CHIEF CONSUL INTO LONDON

Cartoon after Charles Ansell Williams published by SW Fores of 50 Piccadilly on 1 October 1803 with the caption, 'The Grand Triumphal Entry of the Chief Consul into London. A representation of a defeated Napoleon is seen riding in procession through a London street. A gathered crown jeer and poke fun as the French leader passes hatless sitting in disgrace, backwards on his horse, the missing headgear now hoisted high on a flagstaff from which flies a Union flag and that of France. From a crowded high window someone shouts 'For St Pauls'; another from down in the street replies, 'We may thank our Volunteers for this glorious sight.'

Two volunteers, one carrying the flagstaff, the other with a piece of cloth marked 'For St Pauls' dangling from his cuff, lead the chief consul's horse through the crowd. Behind them, mounted volunteers similarly dressed in red coats and yellow facings, follow on as others march at their sides with bayonets fixed. Someone close to them shout, 'I say Boney you have got past the Bank I thought you was to call on the Old Lady in Threadneedle Street.'

In this imaginary spectacle it would seem that the St Pauls Volunteers are being credited with the defeat of Napoleon and with it the subsequent invasion of Britain. One of his many recorded ambitions, had he reached London, was to take control of the Bank of England—the so called 'Old Lady of Threadneedle Street'. (*Image courtesy of the Anne SK Brown Military Collection, Brown University Library*)

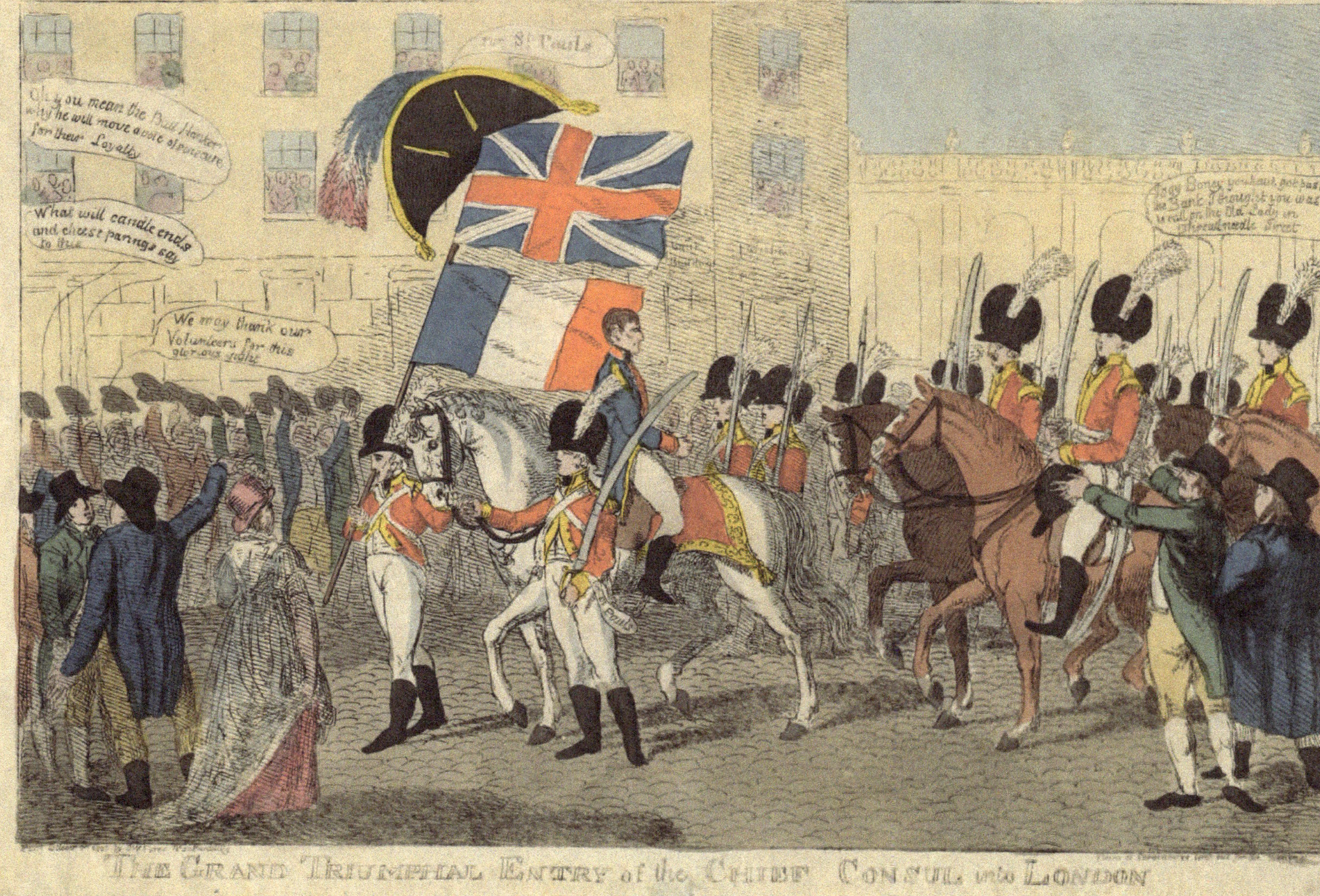

THE GRAND TRIUMPHAL ENTRY of the CHIEF CONSUL into LONDON

47 – CAPTAIN ALEXANDER ADAIR

Mezzotint after Martin Archer Shee, RA of Captain Alexander Adair, 9th Suffolk (Loyal Southelmham) Yeomanry Cavalry. Publisher, Charles Turner of 50 Warren Street, Fitzroy Square, London on 18 September 1813. The following dedication appears below the image, 'To Mrs Adair, This Print of Alexr. Adair Esqr, / Captain Commandant of the 9th Suffolk, or Loyal Southelmham Yeomanry Cavalry / Is, at the particular request of that Corps, inscribed by their obedient & Humble Servt C Turner'. The text is divided in the middle by a shield charge with three open right hands, above which is a severed bearded head, and below on a scroll the motto '*Loyal au mort*' (Loyal to the dead)—the arms of Adair. With his shako placed on a ledge to his right and a small party of mounted cavalry to the left, the captain stands with his sword drawn. He wears a sash around the waist and a narrow sword-belt with snake-hook fastening. The jacket has three rows of buttons and many lines of horizontal lace.

A glance at the War Officer List of Officers of the Militia, Gentlemen & Yeomanry Cavalry and Volunteer Infantry for 1805 reveals that there were nine (1st to 9th) yeomanry cavalry corps then in existence. Captain Adair is shown with two other officers, Lieutenant Robert Aggar and Cornet Thomas Drake, all three having commissions dated 5 September 1803. Published in 1806, James Willson's, 'Volunteer Chart', records the uniform of the 9th Troop as red coats faced yellow, gold lace and white breeches. (*Image courtesy of the Anne SK Brown Military Collection, Brown University Library*)

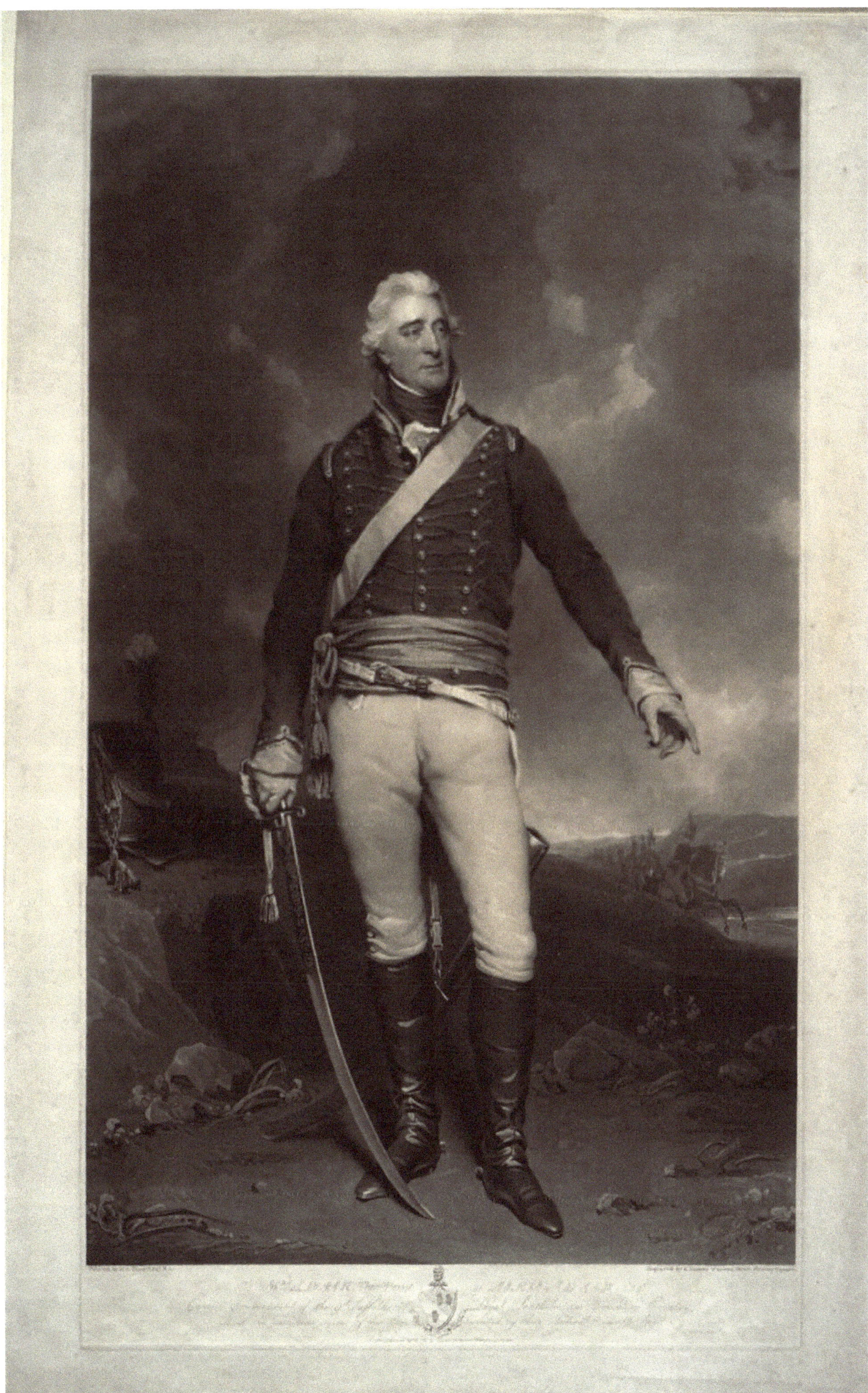

48 – SIXTH REGIMENT OF LOYAL LONDON VOLUNTEERS

Aquatint drawn and engraved by PW Tomkins and published by Elizabeth Walker of 7 Cornhill, London on 1 October 1804. A rifleman dress in green and with a tall black shako sporting a large green feather plume is featured with several others in the background wearing similar uniforms. The scene is set at a water's edge from which the men are firing and loading their firelocks. Long cord lines hang from the headdress which reach down to the waist where a black sash is tied. A caption below the image reads, 'To Robert Wigram Esqr. M.P. Lieutenant Colonel Commandant, The Officers & / Privates of the Rifle Corps Attached to the Sixth Regiment of Loyal London / Volunteers, This Print is Respectfully Dedicated by their Obt Sert. E Walker.' The text is divided in the middle by a sketch of a seated, bearded, man holding a wreath of laurel and a staff headed with a fleur de lis. By his side, a lion.

One of a set of ten from Elizabeth Walker and featuring London Volunteers, the print is dedicated to Lieutenant-Colonel Robert Wigram whose commission as commandant of the 6th Loyal London Volunteers was dated 17 September 1803. Born at Wexford on 30 January 1744, Wigram was the only son of a Bristol merchant. Having moved to London, he would become a fully qualified surgeon later serving on board the East Indiaman Admiral Watson in that capacity. He developed a successful family mercantile business and in 1802 became Member of Parliament for Fowey, Cornwall. He was created a baronet on 20 October 1805, acted as High Sheriff of Essex between 1812-13, and died at his home in Walthamstow in November 1830.

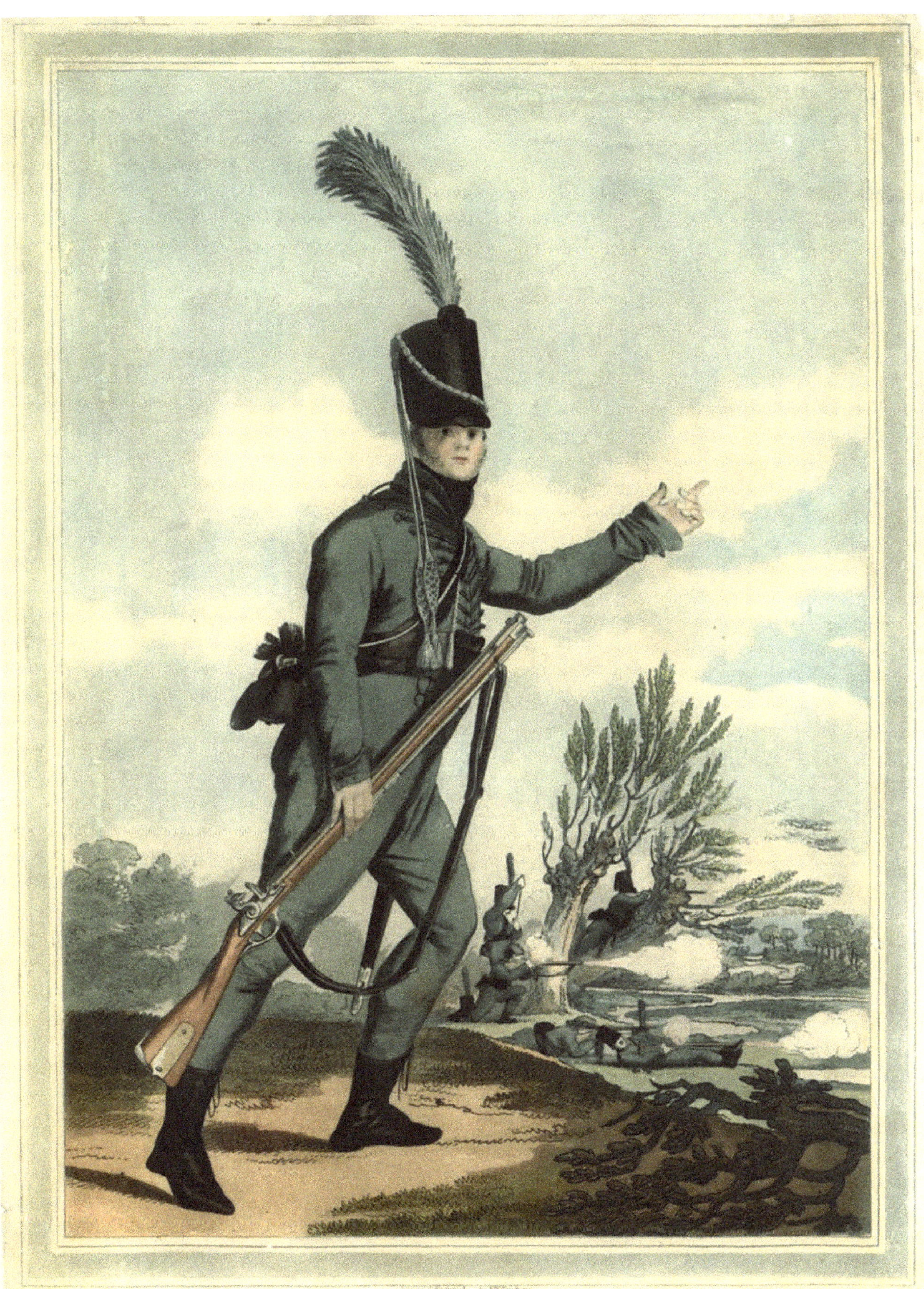

To Robert Wigram Esqr. M.P. Lieutenant Colonel Commandant, The Officers & Privates of the Rifle Corps Attached to the Sixth Regiment of Loyal London [illegible] This Print is Respectfully Dedicated by their Obt. Servt. G. Walker

49 – FIRST SURREY REGIMENT OF VOLUNTEER INFANTRY

Colour aquatint after S Creed published by S Creed of 2 Surrey Side Westminster Bridge and sold by principle booksellers in the borough. A single figure wearing a red coat with blue collar, shoulder wings and cuffs, white lace and white breeches. A white belt is worn under the left shoulder, another around the waist fastened by a circular white metal clasp bearing a lion mask. The headdress has a wide peek, fur crest rising from front to back, and a tall white over red feather plume. In the background, a windmill and three uniformed figured standing before a low single-storied building. Below the image, the following dedication: 'To Thomas Gaitskell Esq Lieutenant Coll Commandant, the Officers and Privates / of the First Surry Regiment of Volunteer Infantry , this Print / us respectfully dedicated by their obedient Servt. S. Creed'. ['Surry', an earlier spelling of Surrey].

Thomas Gaitskell was a partner in the Bermondsey wine merchant and distiller firm of Thomas and Henry Gaitskell. He had joined the Bermondsey Volunteer Infantry as a captain on 23 July 1794, rising later to major-commandant in April 1798. The Bermondsey corps was disbanded as a result of the Peace of Amiens in 1802, but re-raised a year later as the 1st Surrey Regiment at which time Thomas became its commander. His business partner Henry, also served in the Bermondsey and later 1st Surrey, Volunteers. (*Image courtesy of the Anne SK Brown Military Collection, Brown University Library*)

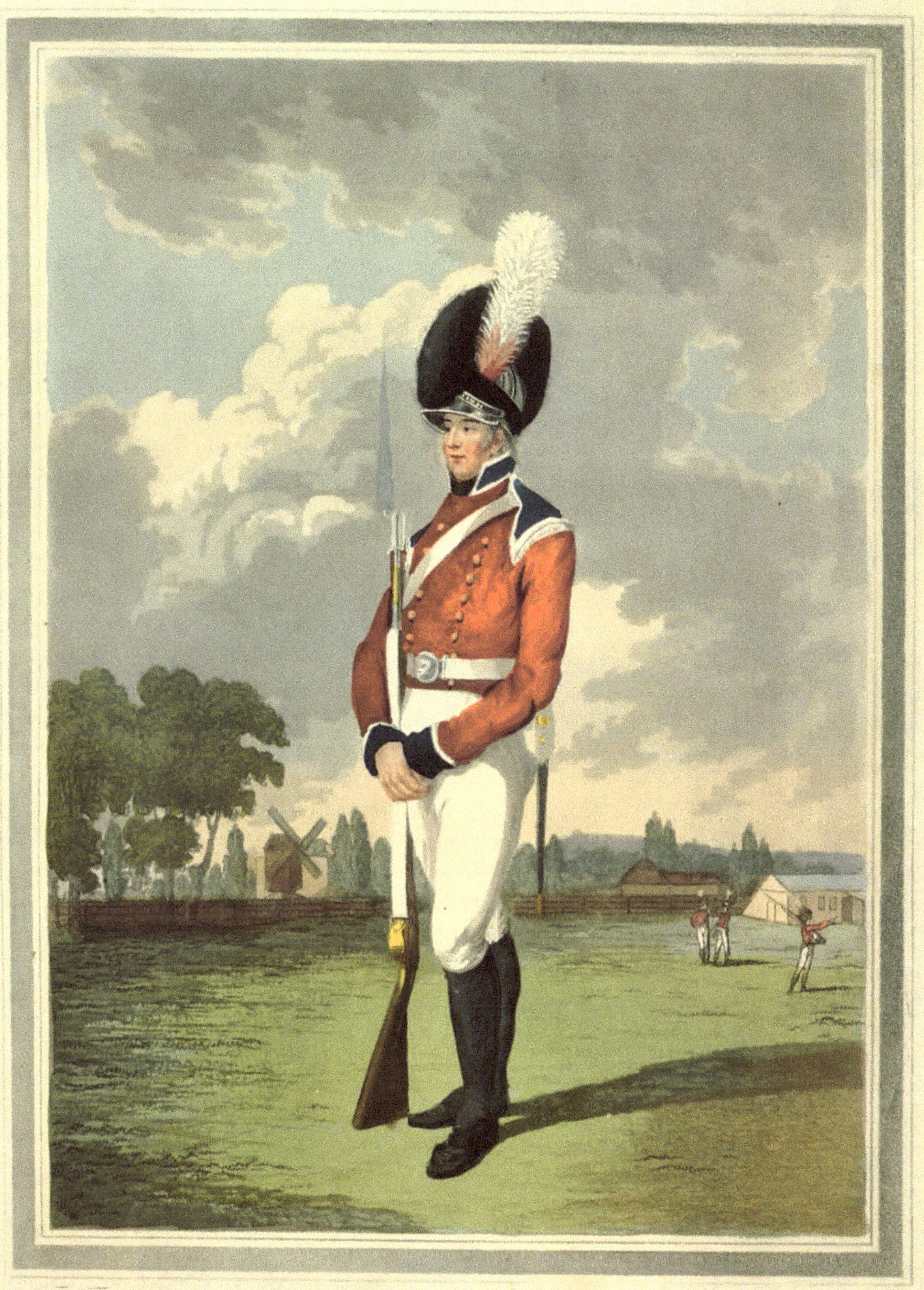

To Thomas Gaitskell Esqr Lieutenant Col.^l Commendant the Officers, and Privates of the **FIRST SURRY REGIMENT** of **VOLUNTEER INFANTRY**, this Print is respectfully dedicated by their obliged Servt S. Creed.

Pub. by S. Creed N.º 2, Surry Side Westminster Bridge. and Sold by the Principle Booksellers in the Borough.

50 – LOYAL SOMERSET PLACE VOLUNTEERS

From a series of four colour aquatints drawn, engraved and published by R Page c1804-05. Against a country background of trees and a body of water, a single figure wearing a red coat with dark blue collar, shoulder straps and cuffs, white breeches and a tall black shako sporting a white over red plume and yellow plate, stands pointing to his left. He carries his firelock in the 'advance arms' position. The image carries the following printed caption below: 'To Sir Andrew Hamond Colonel Commander / Officers & Privates of the Loyal Somerset Place Volunteers / This print Representing The Uniform Of The Corps / is with permission humbly inscribed / by their most obedient & humble Servant R. Page'.

Sir Andrew Snape Hamond's commission as Lieutenant-Colonel Commandant of the Somerset Place Volunteers was dated 18 September 1804. Born at Blackheath, Kent on 17 December 1738 he was a British naval officer who went on to act as Lieutenant Governor of Nova Scotia and back home, Controller of the Navy between 1794 until his death in 1828. Famously, possibly, he was one of the several naval officer involved with the court martial of capture crewmembers involved in the Mutiny on the Bounty. Somerset Place is the location of London's Somerset House. It was rooms at this location that the Navy Board moved into in 1789. (*Image courtesy of the Anne SK Brown Military Collection, Brown University Library*)

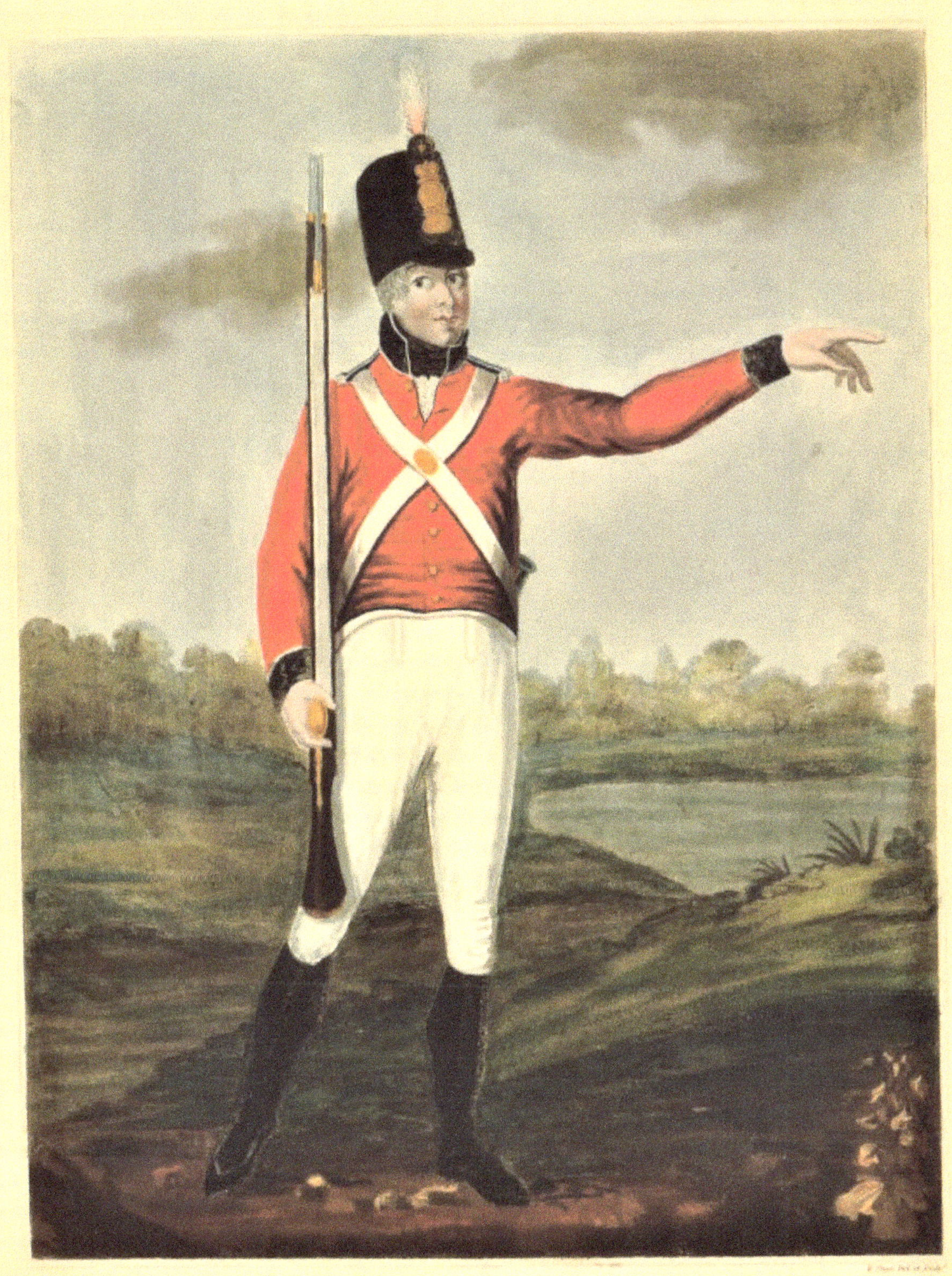

To Sir Andrew Hamond Colonel Commander
OFFICERS & PRIVATES of the LOYAL SOMERSET PLACE VOLUNTEERS
THIS Print REPRESENTING THE Uniform OF THE Corps
is with permission humbly inscribed
by their most obedient & humble Servant R. PAGE

1805

51 – TEMPLE ASSOCIATION

Plate 14 from *Loyal Volunteers of London and Environs* published by Rudolph Ackermann with illustrations by Thomas Rowlandson. A single figure is in the present arms position and wearing a red coat with black collar edged with white piping, black lapels with gold buttons, black cuffs edged white and with three buttons, black epaulettes edged and fringed with gold. The waistcoat and breeches are white, the gaiters black. The helmet is fur crested with red over white plume and leopard's skin, the cross-belts bearing an oval plate.

The following caption appears below the image: 'Present Arms 3rd Motion / The firelock is by a quick motion brough down from the Poize to the extent of the right Arm with the cock turned to / the left groin, the right hand holding the piece by the small of the butt, keeping the little finger out of sight, while the firelock is bring- / ing down the right foot steps close behind the left. The left hand quits the piece & firmly meets it when at the rest keeping / the thumb between the barrel & stock, the little finger to touch the feather spring & the left chiefly supporting the firelock.'

The plate is accompanied by the following text: This Corps was first formed in April, 1798, under Robert Graham, Esq. (a King's Council, and Attorney General to his Royal Highness the Prince of Wales) for the protection of the Temple, &c. It consists of three Companies; it has a Committee of thirteen persons, chosen by ballot from their own Association. Their Colours were presented in the Temple Gardens, June 20th, 1799, by Her Royal Highness the Princess Charlotte of Wales, the Right Hon. The Countess Dowager of Elgin being proxy for the Princess Charlotte.' The Colours displayed the red cross of the Knights Templars with the Motto, *In hoc signo vinces* (Under this this sign thou shall conquer) and the armorial bearings of the two Temples. The officers of the corps at time of publication included Captain Commandant Robert Grantham, who as mentioned above was a King's Council, and the Rev Thomas Rennell, Master of the Temple, appointed Dean of Winchester Cathedral in 1805, who served as chaplain.

Unseen in the image are the arms of the two Temples below a crown borne as a badge on the helmet and the letters TA in cypher inscription on the breast plate.

TEMPLE ASSOCIATION

N°. 14

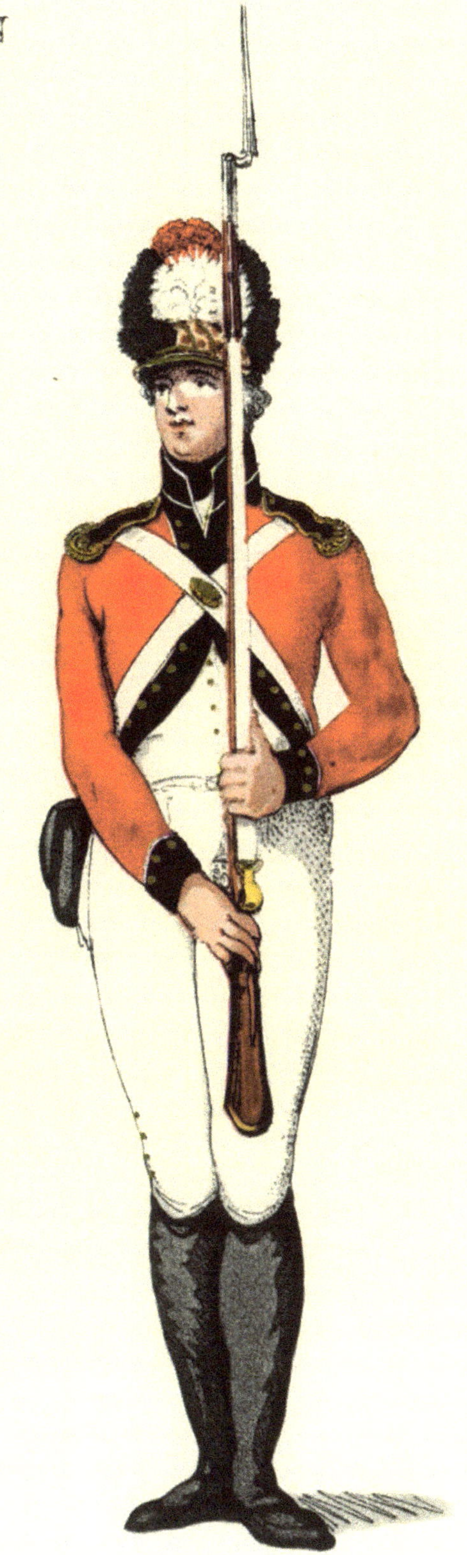

Rowlandson Delin

PRESENT ARMS 3.^d Motion

or Bringing the Piece to the Rest.

The Firelock is by a quick motion brought down from the Poize to the extent of the right Arm with the cock tu the left groin, the right hand holding the piece by the small of the butt: keeping the little finger out of sight: while the firelock -ing down the right foot steps close behind the left: The left hand quits the piece & firmly meets it when at the rest k the thumb between the barrel & stock, the little finger to touch the feather spring & the left chiefly supporting the firelo

52 – AFTER THE INVASION – THE LEVÉE ON MASSE – OR BRITONS STRIKE HOME

Caricature credited to Charles Ansell Williams and published by Samuel William Fores of Piccadilly, London on 6 August 1803 as part of a set entitled 'Folios of Caricatures Lent Out For The Evening'. Three men stand, two wearing military uniform of red coats with blue facings, gold lace and epaulettes, a third in country clothing, but with military-style cross-belts. To the right, the soldier holds a pitchfork upon which is impaled a severed head. Close by is this caption: 'Here he is Exalted my Lads, 24 Hours after Invasion.' In answer to this, the man on the left exclaims in dialect, 'Dang my Buttons if that beant the Head of that Rogue Boney I told our Squire this morning, what do you think say's I the lads of out Village can't cut up a Regiment of them French Mounsheers, and as soon as the Lasses had given us a Kiss for good luck I could have sworn we should do it and so we have'.

Holding a bicorn hat decorated with sprigs of oak and a ribbon bearing the words, 'Britain's never will be slaves', the central figure answers, 'Why Harkee, d'ye zee, I never liked Soldiering afore, but some how or other when I thought of our Sal the bearns, the poor pigs, the cows and the Geese, why I could have killed the whole Army my own self.'

In the distance, blue-coated troops are being forced back off a cliff by British soldiers while two women in brown dresses pick the pockets of French dead, one remarking, 'Why this is poor finding I have emptied the pockets of a score and only found one head of garlic 2 onions & a parcel of pill boxes'.

Published at the height of the invasion scare of 1803, it will be safe to assume that the image is one of many produced to promote the existence of volunteers for home defence. There they are, ready and waiting within moments of the enemy landing. In possession of a hat identical to the uniformed pair, the central figure seems to suggest that, save for his cross-belts, he had not had time after leaving his farmyard duties to put on his full uniform. And a poke at the French cannot be resisted, of course, their pockets carrying nothing but garlic, onions and pills. (*Image courtesy of the Anne SK Brown Military Collection, Brown University Library*)

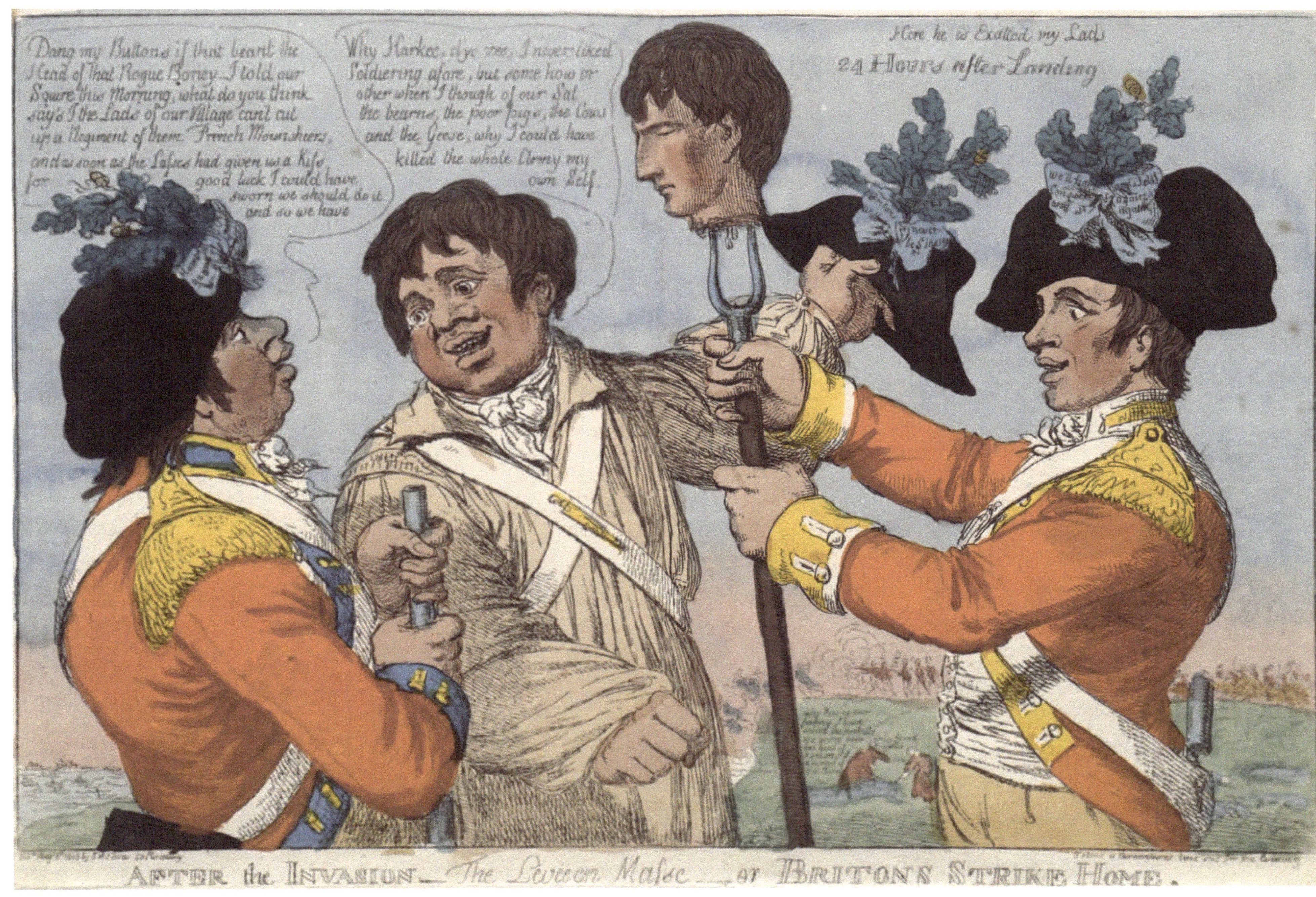

AFTER the INVASION — The Levee en Masse — or BRITONS STRIKE HOME.

53 – INSPECTING A VOLUNTEER CORPS IN HYDE PARK

Hand-coloured etched caricature by James Gillray published by Hannah Humphrey of 27 St James's Street, London on 4 December 1803. A mounted, blue-coated figure (the Earl of Harrington) wearing a large cocked hat with gold tassels and a tall white-over-red plume. He sits astride his horse as red-coated volunteers discharge their firelocks in the distance.

Charles Stanhope, 3rd Earl of Harrington, was commissioned into the Coldstream Guards in 1769 and later served as colonel of the 85th, 65th and 29th Regiments, then finally until his death in September 1829, the 1st Life Guards. London's Hyde Park was the scene of many reviews throughout the volunteer period, notably those held on 1799, 1800 and 1803. The image was one of a collection of forty-three mixed military subjects after James Gillray published by Hannah Humphrey. One of London's leading print sellers, Hannah Humphrey's first shop in St Martin's Lane, and her latter premises in St James Street were much frequented by the capital's leading gentry. As well as Gillray, who for a time lived above the James Street shop, Humphrey published work by Thomas Rowlandson and James Sayers.

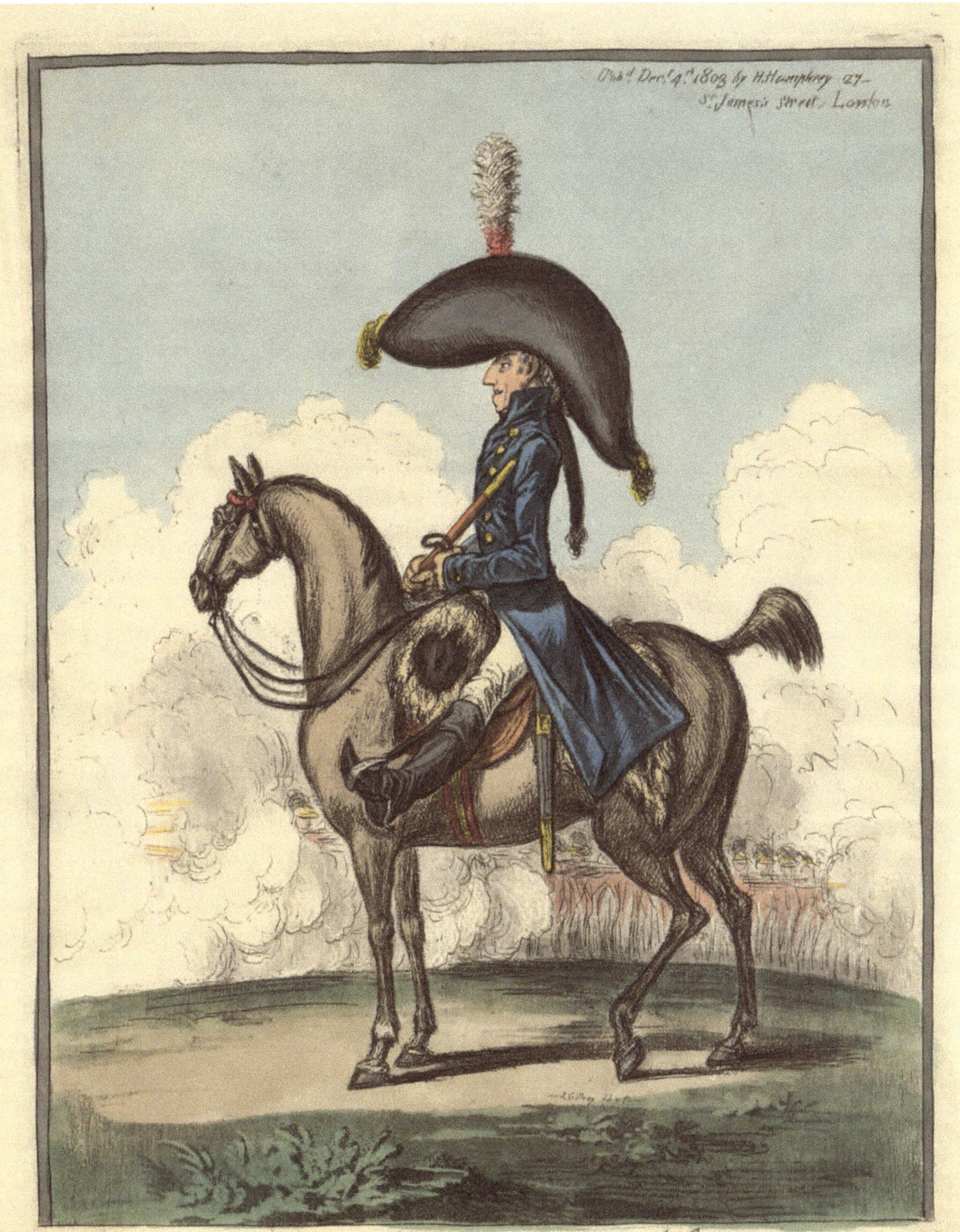

Inspecting a Volunteer Corps, in Hyde Park.

54 – CLERKENWELL VOLUNTEERS

Original watercolour signed in the bottom right hand corner by O [Orlando] Norie and including a hand-written date of 1809 below the image. Two figures dressed in red coats with white collars, cuffs and turnbacks, white breeches and black gaiters rising to just below the knee. One man, a private possibly, holds his firelock by his left side, his coat being double breasted and buttoned. He wears a white shoulder-belt, white waist-belt fastened with a circular clasp and a fur-crested black helmet. He is in conversation with an officer whose coat is open to reveal a white waistcoat and crimson sash tied at the left side. He carries a sword which is hung from a white belt to which is fixed an oval silver plate. His headdress is also fur crested and has a white over red plume. Both men are posed against a background of bushes and a dull sky.

The services of the Loyal Clerkenwell Volunteers were accepted on 3 August 1803, its establishment being ten companies under the command of Lieutenant-Colonel Commandant Francis Magniac whose commission was dated 10 November 1803. His second in command, Major Thomas Maynard. James Willson's Volunteer Chart of 1806 gives the uniform as red with blue facings and white breeches, the officers having gold lace. (*Image courtesy of the Anne SK Brown Military Collection, Brown University Library*)

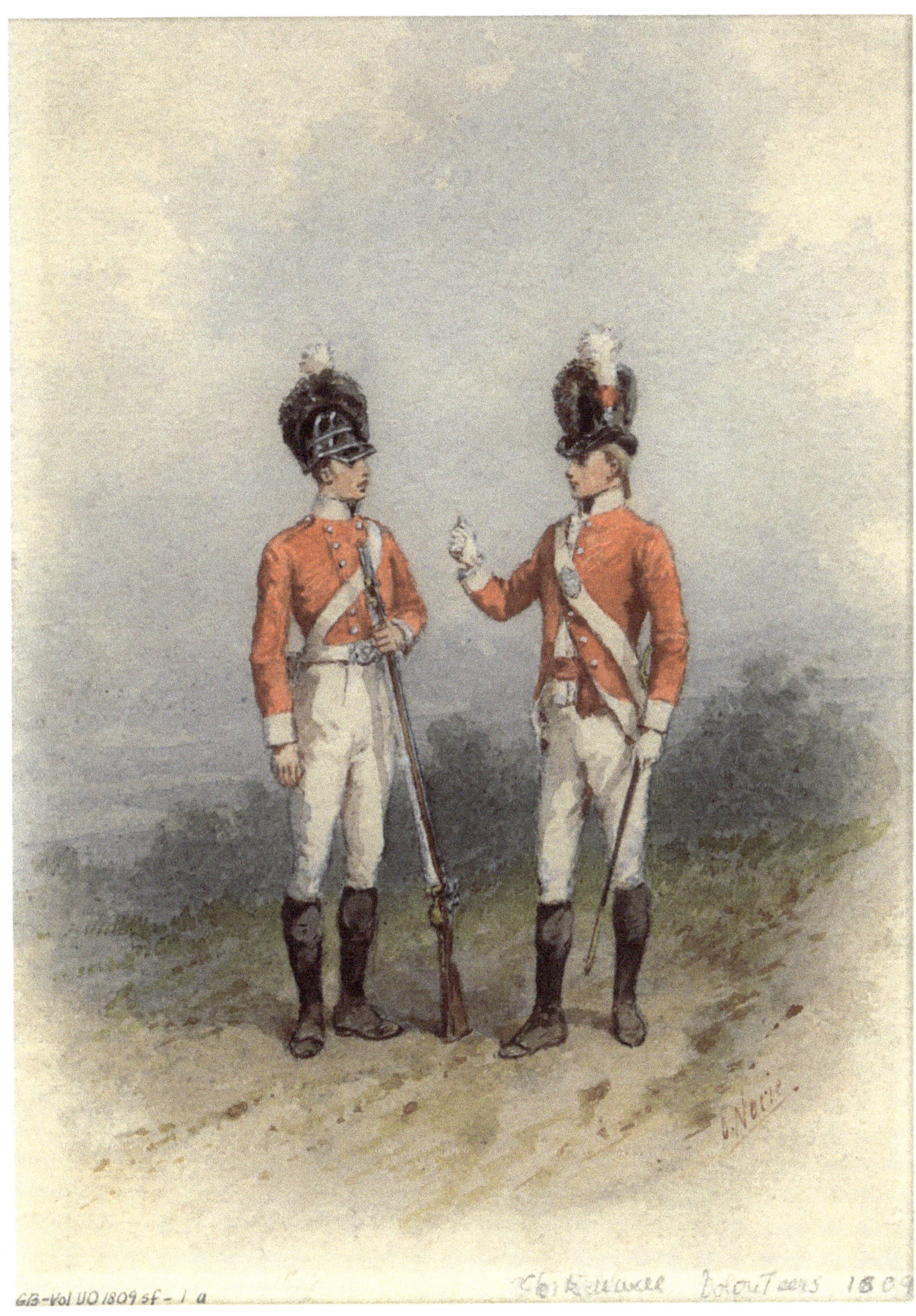
GB-Vol UO 1809 sf - 1 a

55 – CLERKENWELL VOLUNTEERS

Plate 58 from *Loyal Volunteers of London and Environs* published by Rudolph Ackermann of 101 The Strand, London on 16 November 1798 after Thomas Rowlandson. A single figure against a plain background holds a firelock in the 'Advance Arms' position. Below the image, the following text: 'Advance Arms. The 1st and 2nd Motions of advance are the same as the 1st & 2nd of present, see No 12 & 13, at the motion the forelock is from the poize flung to the right side, & caught by the swell in the left hand, and at the Lock in the right hand taking care to place the guard between the forefinger & thumb, the cock resting on the other fingers.'

The uniform consists of a scarlet coat, the blue collar having a gold button on either side with plain buttonhole. The lapels are blue edged with white piping and ornamented with gold buttons and plain buttonholes. Cuffs are also blue, edged around the top with white piping and with gold buttons, the shoulder straps blue with gold decoration. The coat is open to reveal a white waistcoat, the breeches, white, the half gaiters black and shoulder-belts are worn, one with an oval plate. The helmet is crested with gold fittings and a purple turban, the top of the feather white.

The accompanying text to the plate tells how the corps was formed in May 1797 under the direction of Marmaduke Sellon, Esq '...not to go out of their own District, and to assist the Magistrates in the preservation of Tranquillity.' The strength of the corps is given as one company consisting of eighty-six privates, the helmets having the title Loyal Clerkenwell Association at the front. Breast-belt plates omitted the word Loyal, the cartouch carried a star with the letters CA in cypher, the buttons were plain. In addition to Captain Commandant Marmaduke Sellon, three other officers are named: Captain Magniac and Lieutenants William Cook and J Robins.

CLERKENWELL
ASSOCIATION.

No. 58.

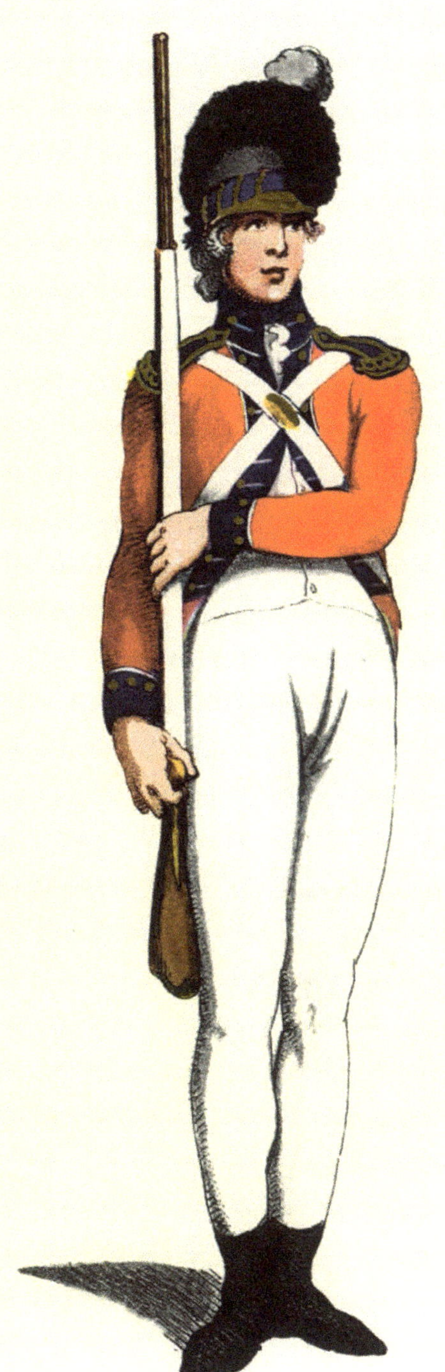

Rowlandson Delin.

ADVANCE ARMS.

The 1st & 2d Motions of advance are the same as the 1st & 2d of present, see No. 12 & 13. at the motion the firelock is from the poize flung to the right side, & caught by the swell in the left hand, & at the Cock in y right hand, taking care to place the guard between the forefinger & thumb, the cock resting on the other fingers.

London Pub. Nov. 16 1798. at Ackermann's Gallery. 101 Strand.

56 – CLERKENWELL CAVALRY

Plate 7 from *Loyal Volunteers of London and Environs* published by Rudolph Ackermann of 101 The Strand, London on 1 November 1798 after Thomas Rowlandson. A single mounted figure against a plain background turns to his right with sword drawn. He wears a short scarlet jacket with dark blue collar and cuffs and decorated with gold lace. The fur-crested helmet has a purple turban and white plume, the breeches are white.

This troop was formed shortly after the Clerkenwell Infantry (see 55 above) under the same commanding officer, Captain Marmaduke Sellon. There were two other officers, Lieutenant Sturges and Cornet Seward. The helmets had the name Clerkenwell Cavalry at the front, the right side having the device of a garter and crown. The breast-plates were plain, the buttons, according to the text accompanying the plate, engraved with the letters CWLC in cypher.

No. 7

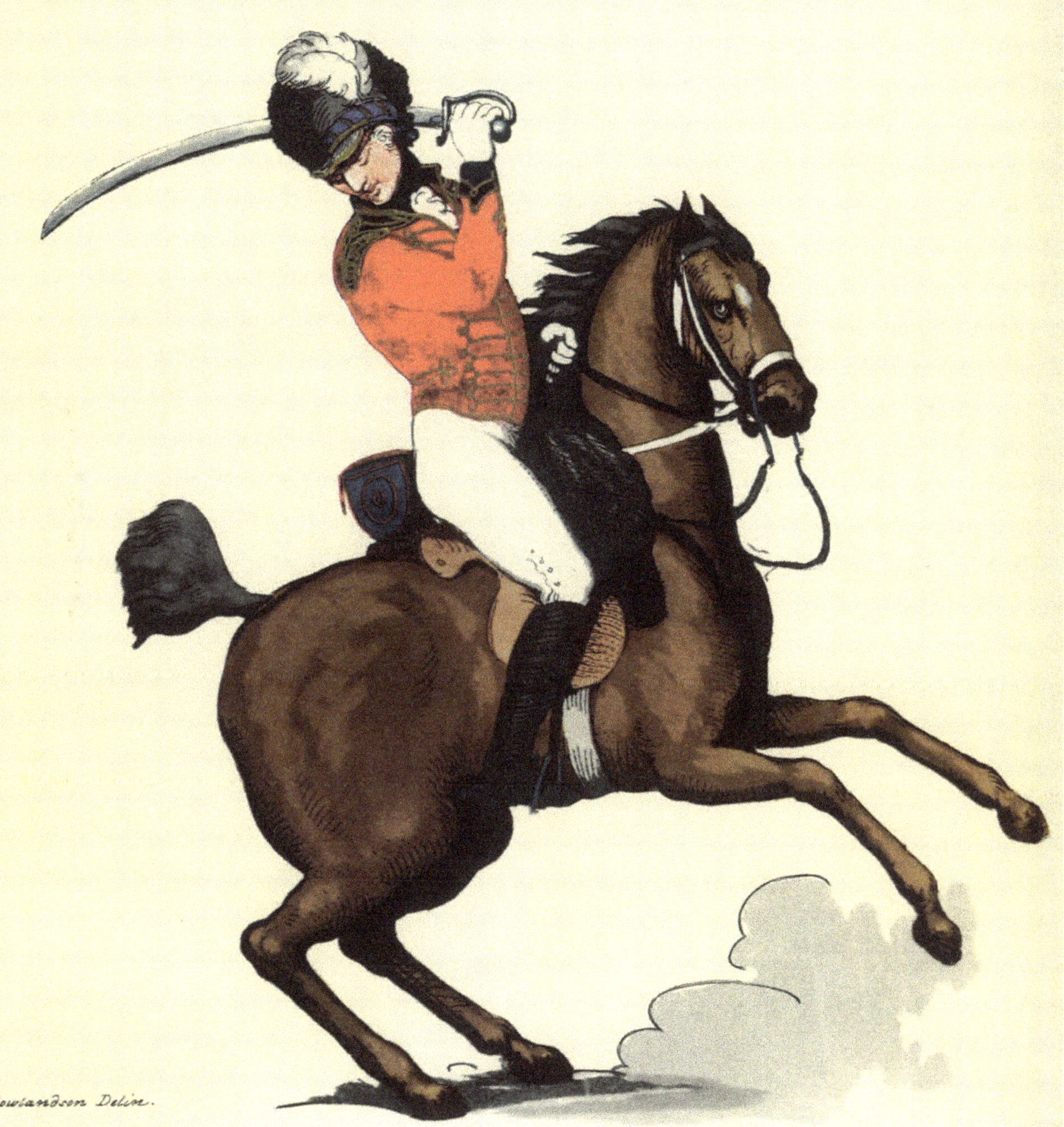

CLERKENWELL CAVALRY.

London Pub: Nov: 1. 1798. at Ackermann's Gallery 101 Strand.

57 – A SIDE DISH FOR JOHN BULL!!

Published by William Holland of 11 Cockspur Street, Pall Mall, London in November 1803 with the caption 'A Side Dish for John Bull!!' A representation of Napoleon, trussed and skewered and wearing a black hat trimmed with gold lace and sporting a large crimson feather, is depicted laying on a platter. By his side, a sword blade inscribed, 'Volunteer Carving Knife'. To the right of the image a large tankard, overflowing with froth, has a representation of the Royal Arms and the inscription, 'Destruction to the Enemies of Great Britain'.

Once again, and via the medium of the image, the print publisher makes it clear to all the Volunteer's intentions should France be foolish enough to invade. (*Image courtesy of the Anne SK Brown Military Collection, Brown University Library*)

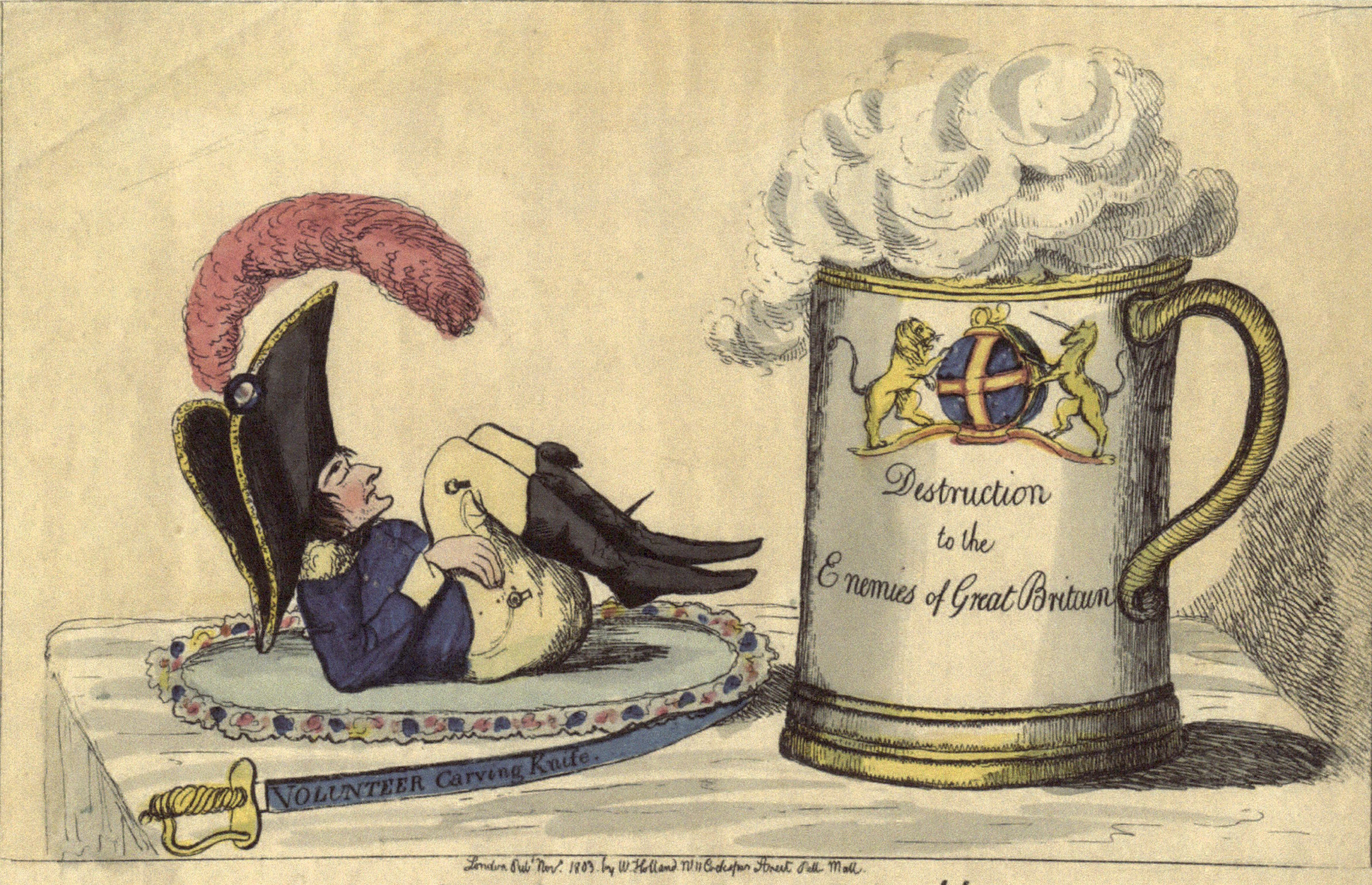

Destruction
to the
Enemies of Great Britain
VOLUNTEER Carving Knife.
London Pub.d Nov.r 1803 by W. Holland No 11 Cockspur Street Pall Mall
A SIDE DISH for JOHN BULL!!

58 – THE ASSOCIATION OFFICERS OR CITY DEFENDERS

Hand-coloured caricature published by Matthew Darley of 39 The Strand, London on 1 September 1780 with the caption, 'The Association Officers Or City Defenders'. Riding horses along a track, two volunteer officers belonging to undisclosed associations are seen in a race. In the lead, one wears a red coat with blue facings and gold lace and is shown with a large wig which has two braided queues flowing in the wind. He holds a tricorn hat in his left hand. In the other, a sword is held almost at the tip.

Coming up behind, a much slimmer volunteer has managed to keep his hat on. The queue of his wig, just one this time, is tied with a black bow and is possibly five to six feet in length. Almost as long is the cane held under his right arm. (*Image courtesy of the Anne SK Brown Military Collection, Brown University Library*)

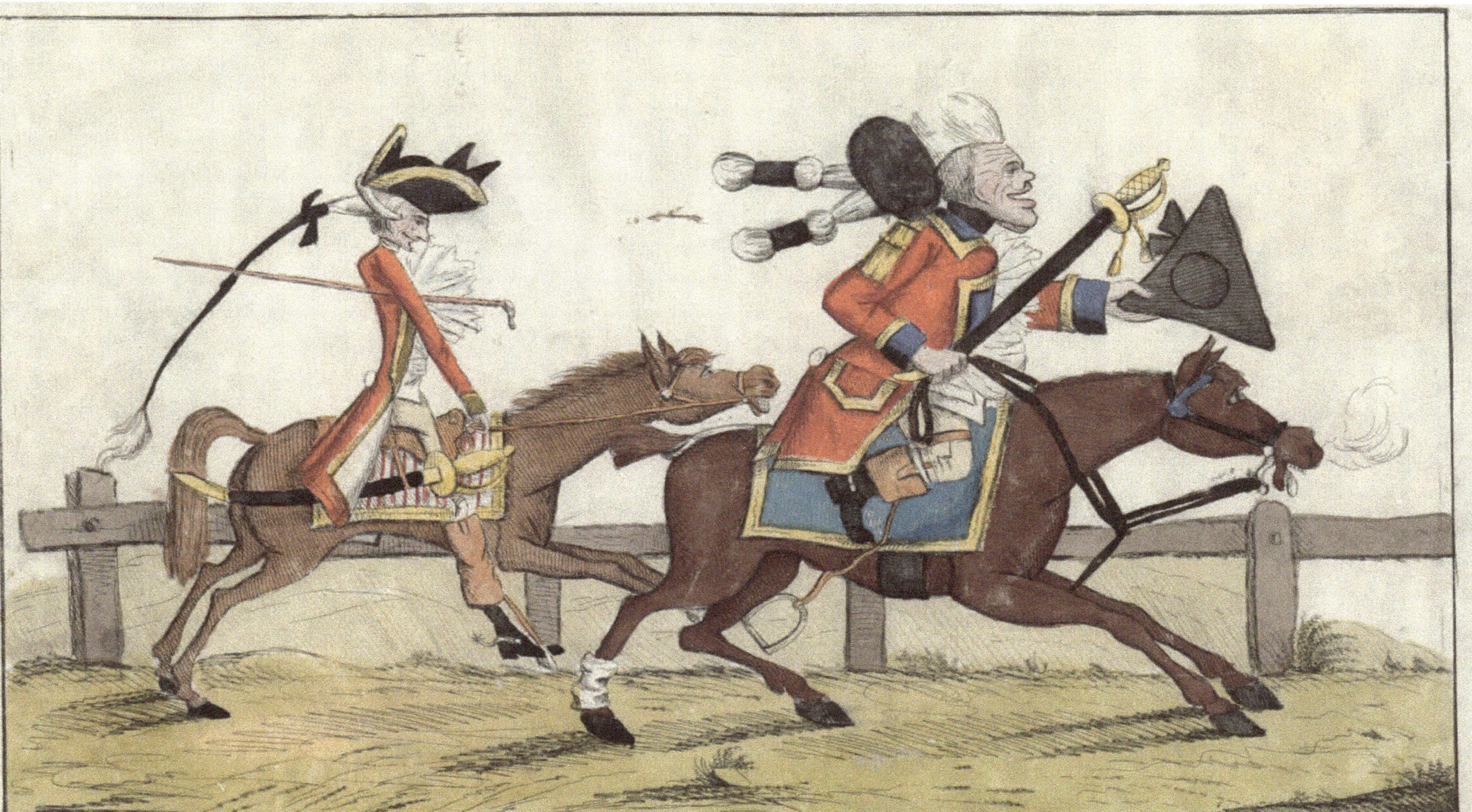

THE ASSOCIATION OFFICERS OR CITY DEFENDERS,

59 – LONDON VOLUNTEER CAVALRY AND FLYING ARTILLERY, HYDE PARK MAY 1804

Colour aquatint after Charles Cranmer, engraved by Mitan & Stadler and published by John Wallis, Jun of 16 Ludgate Street, City of London on 20 June 1805 with the following caption: 'To the Right Honble Lord Mayor, Court of Aldermen & Common Council of the City of London / This print, representing the London Volunteer Cavalry & Flying Artillery, under the Command of / Lieut. Coll John Proctor Anderdon, as Reviewed by the Honble Col. Blaquiere, in Hyde Park, on the 1st of May 1804. / Is most respectfully Dedicated by their obedient humble Servant / John Wallis Junr'. The foreground to the right shows a number of mounted officers, the uniform coats being both blue and red. All wear tall plumes, some plain white, some white over red. Mounted on a grey horse third from the left of the party, a bugler in a red coat is in the act of sounding a call. A rifleman dressed in green stands talking to a man in civilian clothing, while a cavalryman stands with his sword held under his left arm. The party on the left of the image is made up of civilian men, women and children, save for a soldier dressed in a red coat and fur-crested helmet who stands by his horse. In the far distance an audience is gathered to watch the sceptical of cavalry and guns. The Flying Artillery with a single gun and wagon carrying sixteen seated gunners can be seen moving forward from the right edge of the image. (*Image courtesy of the Anne SK Brown Military Collection, Brown University Library*)

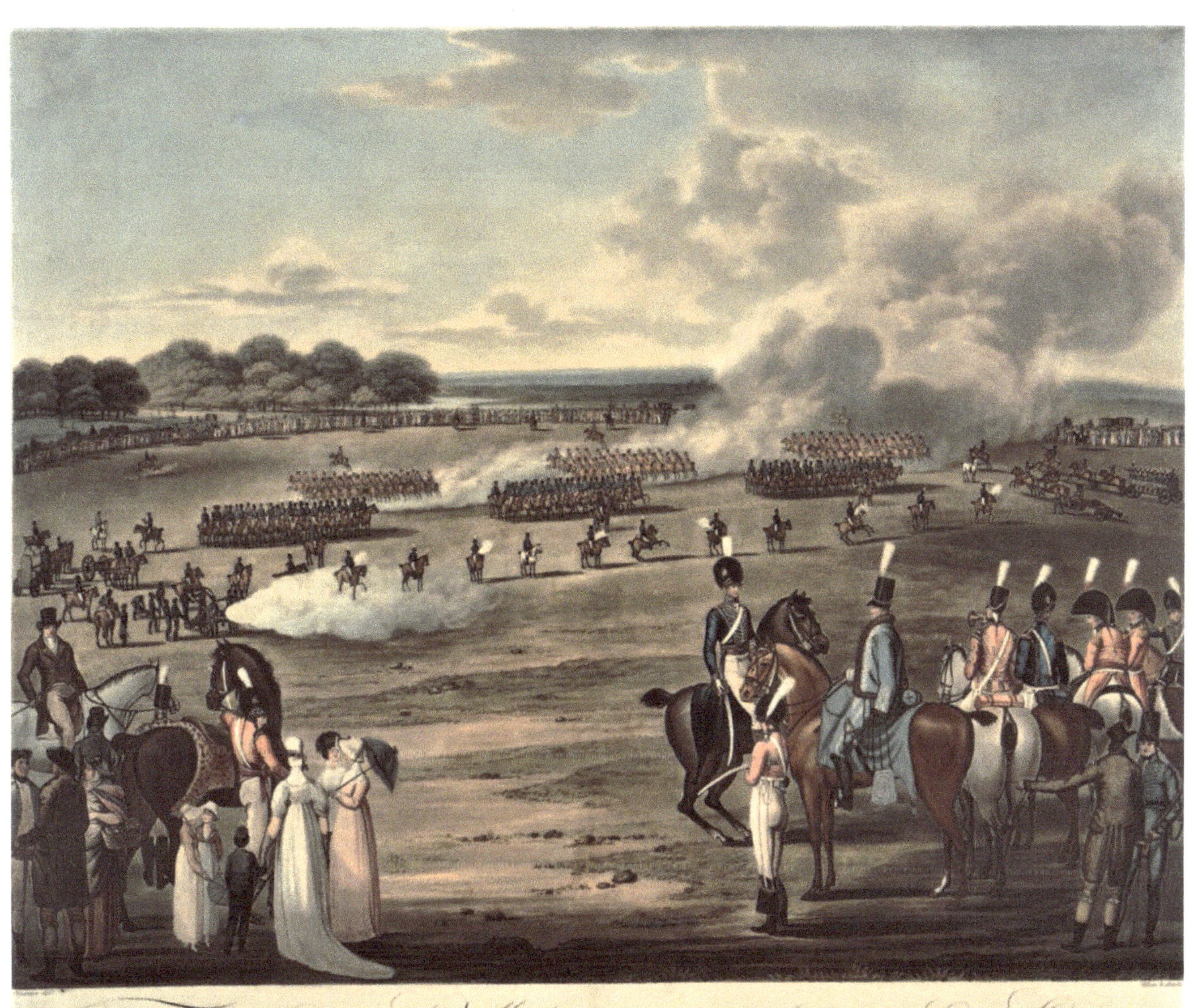

To the Right Honble the Lord Mayor, Court of Aldermen & Common Council of the City of London,
This Print, representing the LONDON VOLUNTEER CAVALRY & FLYING ARTILLERY, under the Command of
Lieut. Col. John Proctor Anderdon, as Reviewed by the Honble Col. Blaquiere, in Hyde Park, on the 1st of May 1804
Is most respectfully Dedicated by their obedient humble Servant
John Wallis Junr

60 – A FIELD DAY IN HYDE PARK

Colour aquatint drawn and etched by Thomas Rowlandson, aquatinting by T Maldon first published by SW Fores on 15 May 1789 with the caption 'A Field Day in Hyde Park'. A second impression was produced 12 August 1791. As a party of volunteers dressed in red coats, white breeches and black hats fire a volley, some of the crowd and horses gathered on the left of the image are startled. In the centre a man, a dog barking at his side, runs off in fear with his wife clinging onto his coat tails. Two men seem unable to control their mounts as they rear up in fright, one of them doing all he can to prevent a man and a woman who have fallen startled to the ground from being trampled. But three officers, two in red coats, one in blue, have seen this all before and they, and their horses, stay calm.

A FIELD DAY in HYDE PARK.

61 – WILLIAM GRINLY, LEITH VOLUNTEERS

By John Kay in 1795 and later published by Hugh Patron of Edinburgh between 1784 and 1816 in Volume II of *Original Portraits & Caricature Etchings*. The image shows a stout figure wearing a long red coat with green collar and cuffs, red shoulder straps and gold buttons, a white waistcoat, white breeches and white hose. A large black hat has gold decoration and a black cockade, and a white sword-belt with an oval gold plate is worn over the right shoulder. The subject of the image is Mr William Grinly, Quartermaster to the Royal Leith Volunteers, who is shown standing on an eagle which flies above a line of bushes or trees.

The Royal Leith Volunteers was embodied in 1795 as two companies under the command of Captain Commandant James Bruce. A list of officers for 1795 show in addition to Captain Bruce and Quartermaster Grinly, Captain William Oliphant, Lieutenants Alexander Waddell and John Scott, Ensigns John Jameson and Robert Strong, Chaplain Thomas Macknight and Surgeon John Cheyne. Colours were presented to Captain James Bruce on 26 September 1795.

Mr Grinly was from a family of shipowners based at Borrowstounness. He has been noted as no stranger to seafaring life, his adventures including being captured by pirates and many times shipwrecked. His biographer, John Kay, recalled how Grinly had a strange habit '...of throwing out his legs and arms in walking', a display that earnt him the nickname of 'Spread Eagle', (*Image courtesy of the Anne SK Brown Military Collection, Brown University Library*)

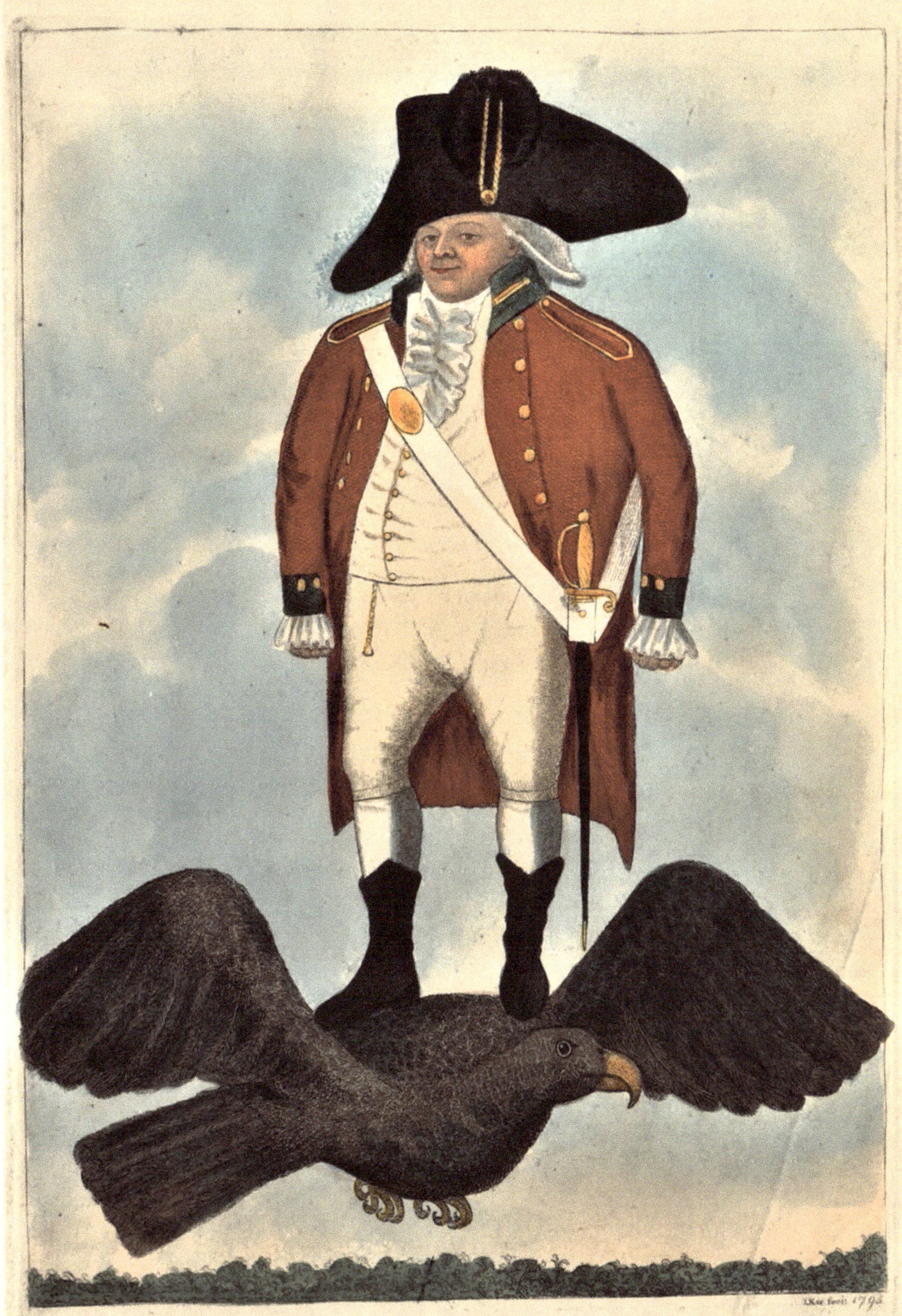

LEITH VOLUNTEER.

62 – ARCHIBALD GILCHRIST, EDINBURGH VOLUNTEERS

Un-coloured etching by and after John Kay, 1794 and later published by Hugh Patron of Edinburgh between 1784 and 1816 in Volume I of *Original Portraits & Caricature Etchings*. A single figure wearing a long coat which has epaulettes on both shoulders ending in tassels stands with a firelock at his side. He wears black cross-belts, one of whom has an oval plate engraved with the arms of Edinburgh. The waistcoat, breeches and hose are white. Three plumes issuing from a crown have been placed between the caption 'Edinburgh Volunteer'.

The Edinburgh (later Royal Edinburgh) Volunteers were embodied in 1794, John Kay recording that, 'The Volunteers were to bear all their own expenses of clothing and other necessaries; and half-a-guinea of entry-money was extracted from each member, towards defraying contingencies.' This, and other rules, had been decided upon at a meeting held in the Sheriff Court Rooms, Edinburgh, on 3 July 1794. The uniform chosen was to '...consist of a blue coat, with red cape and cuff, white lining turned up in the skirts, two gold epaulettes, and a button bearing the name of the corps and arms of the city; white cassimere vest and breeches, and white cotton stockings; short gaiters of black cloth; a round hat, with two black feathers and ne white; and black cross-belts.' Of the latter, Kay notes that 'The belts of the Edinburgh Volunteers were afterwards painted white, which soon gave the corps an awkward appearance, on account of the paint scaling off, and leaving portions of white and black alternately.' There were two grenadier companies which had bear skin and a grenade on the hat.

Archibald Gilchrist was a haberdasher by trade and, having opened new premises on the South Bridge, became haberdasher to the Prince of Wales. With this in mind, John Kay had included plumes and a crown with his image. Gilchrist has been noted as a well-respected citizen of Edinburgh, being elected as a member of the town council in 1796. He also held the office of treasurer, 1797-8, and was selected as a magistrate in 1801.

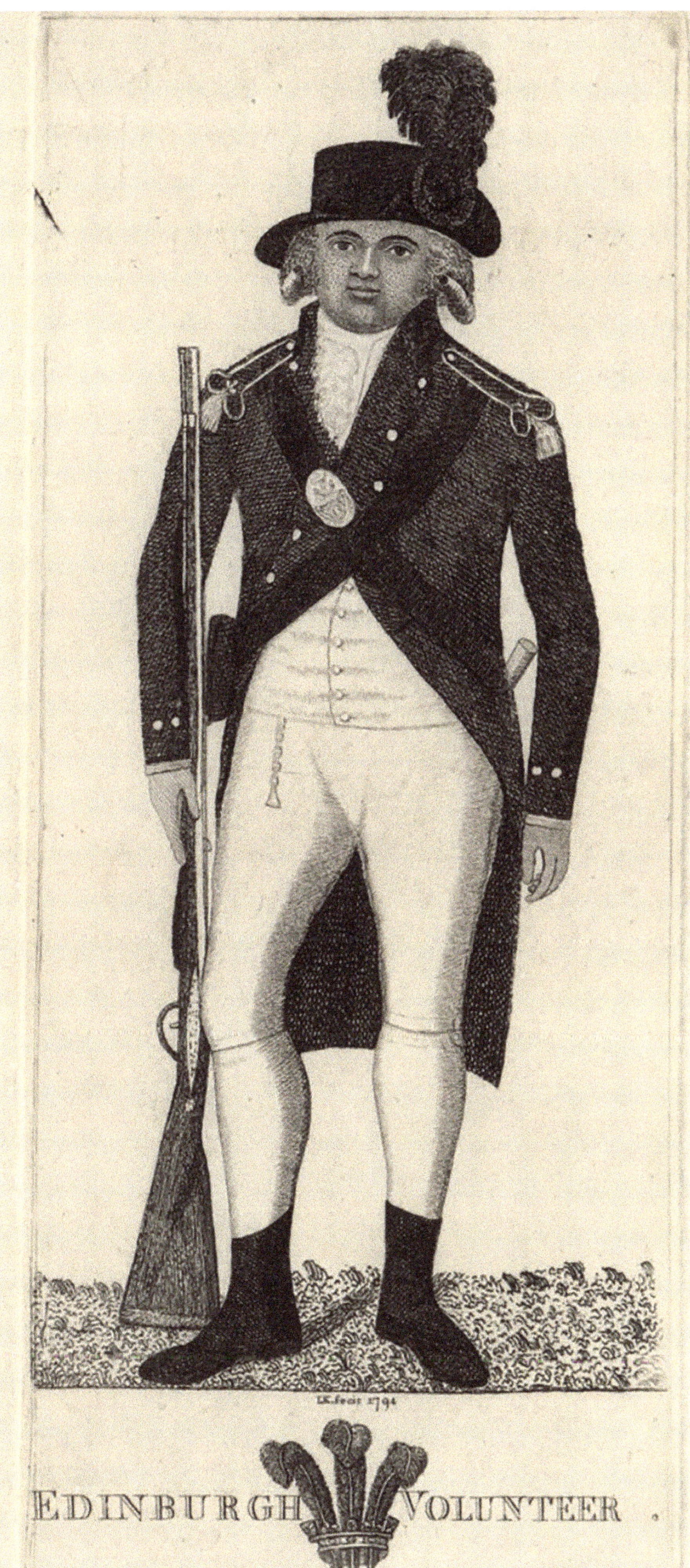
I.K. fecit 1794
EDINBURGH VOLUNTEER

63 – LORD VISCOUNT MILTON

Mezzotint engraving by John Jones after Thomas Beach published by Thomas Beach of Strand Green, Kew Bridge on 20 July 1795 with the following caption: 'The Right Honourable / Lord Viscount Milton. / Colonel of the Dorsetshire Volunteer Rangers.' The engraver, John Jones is described just below the image as being, 'Engraver Extraordinary to HRH the Prince of Wales, & Principle Engraver to His R.H the Duke of York.' A three quarter length portrait of an officer against a studio background of a country scene. Clearly seen on the open jacket are flat buttons with the letter D over VR.

The original painting by Thomas Beach was featured in the *Journal of the Society for Army Historical Research* (Volume 90, No 364, Winter 2012) and revealed that both the jacket and waistcoat were dark green and the breeches buff. The accompanying article tells how the general day of enrolment had taken place in Dorchester on 3 May 1794, the volunteers then having undertaken to provide their own horses and uniforms.

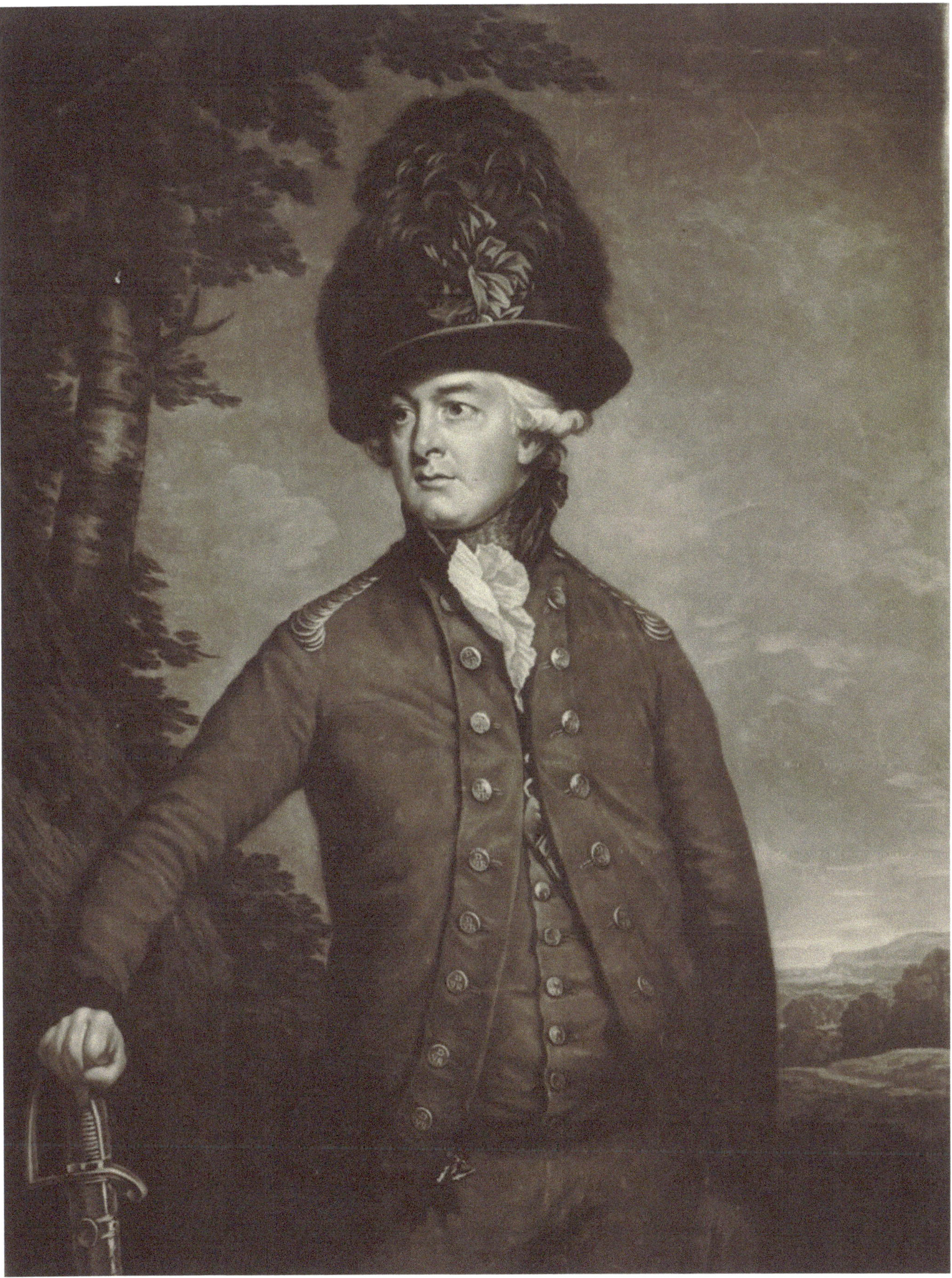

64 – REVIEW NEAR FRESHWATER BAY, ISLE OF WIGHT, 1798

Colour aquatint engraved by J Wells after Richard Livesay, Drawing Master to the Royal Academy, Portsmouth, and published by Livesay on 1 April 1799 with the following dedication printed below the image: 'To Major General Don Commander in Chief of the Forces in the Isle of Wight / This Plate of the Grand Review near Freshwater Bay on the 17th of June 1798; / Is inscribed with respectful acknowledgments, by his obliged humble Servant / Richard Livesay.' Between the lettering a representation of the arms and motto of Major-General George Don who had been placed in command of the Isle of Wight defences after returning to England in 1798 from service at the Prussian Court. The volunteers are just visible formed up on a distant hillside. Both red and blue uniforms are visible and smoke from guns can be seen. Several coaches make their way to the parade while parties of spectators stand in conversation in the foreground.

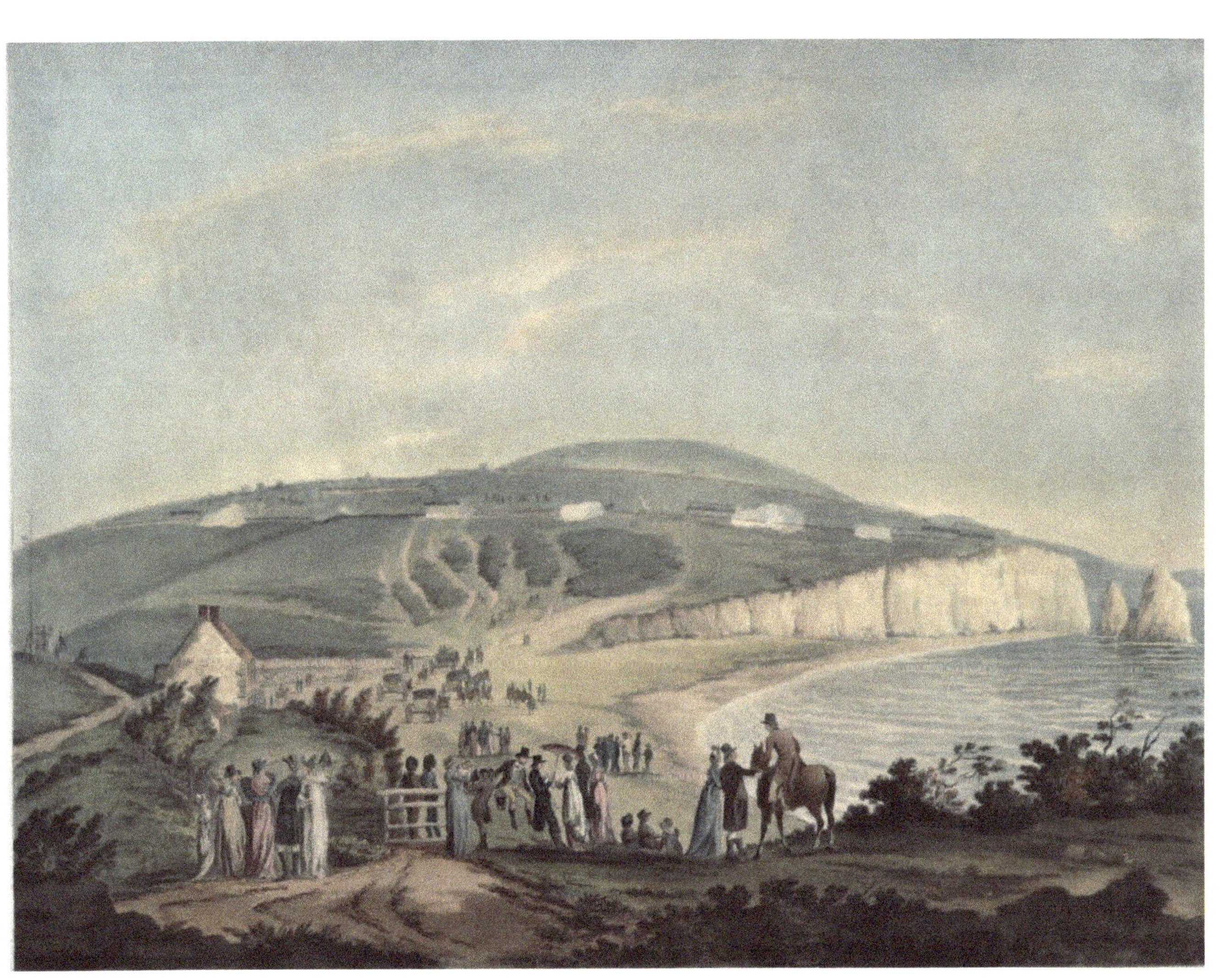

65 – GRAND REVIEW AT SANDHAM BAY, ISLE OF WIGHT, 1798

Colour aquatint engraved by J Wells after Richard Livesay, Drawing Master to the Royal Academy, Portsmouth, and published by Livesay on 11 January 1800 with the following dedication printed below the image: 'To the Rt Honble General Sir Willm. Pitt, K.B. Commander In Chief of the South Western District / This Plate of the Grand Review at Sandham Bay in the Isle of Wight on the 4th of June 1798; / Is most respectfully inscribed by his much obliged and most obedt. hble. Servant / Richd. Livesay.' Between the lettering a representation of the arms of General Pitt. Parties of troops can be seen parading far into the distance along the beach. Other line the walls of a long embattled wall. There are several rows of tents and a number of volunteers can be seen making their way up, or down a hillside via a narrow track. In the middle distance gunners attend their guns while others to the right of the image occupy the top of a Martello tower. Reaching up into the air are a collection of artillery ramrods and infantry pikes. Just below a musician stands holding a French Horn while riflemen dressed in green take aim under the direction of an officer. (*Image courtesy of the Anne SK Brown Military Collection, Brown University Library*)

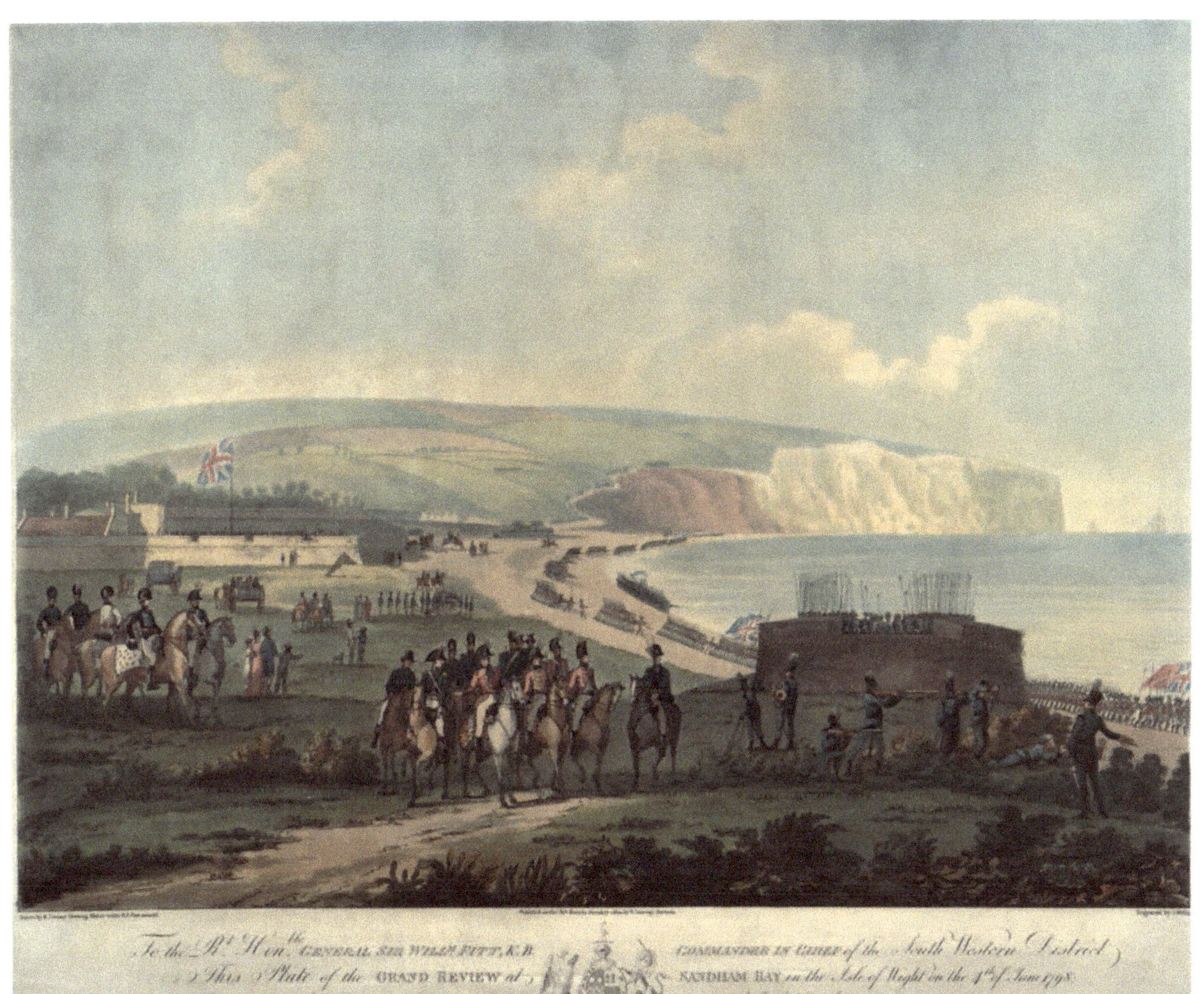
To the Rt. Honble GENERAL SIR WILLm PITT, K.B. COMMANDER IN CHIEF of the South Western District
This Plate of the GRAND REVIEW at SANDHAM BAY in the Isle of Wight on the 4th of June 1798
Is most respectfully inscribed by his much Obliged and most obedt. hble Servant Richd. Livesay

66 – PRESENTATION OF ISLAND BANNER AT CARISBROOKE CASTLE, 24 JUNE 1798

Colour aquatint engraved by J Wells after Richard Livesay, Drawing Master to the Royal Academy, Portsmouth, and published by Livesay on 1 June 1799 with the following dedication printed below the image: 'To the Right Hon Lord Bolton, Governor of the Isle of Wight / this Representation of the Volunteers receiving the Island Banner, presented to them by his Lordship / at Carisbrooke Castle on the 24th of June 1793 / by his lordship's much obliged and most obedt hble Servant / Richard Livesay.' The lettering is divided by an engraving of Lord Bolton's coat of arms against a background of the gateway to Carisbrooke Castle and a representation of 'The Needles' on the western side of the Isle of Wight. On a field before Carisbrooke Castle ranks of infantry volunteers wearing coats of red, blue and green are drawn up, their firelocks held at the present. Behind them stand the cavalry. To the left, an officer kneels before Lord Bolton to receive the Banner and all around crowds have gathered to witness the event. In the centre, a lone rifleman in green stands behind a band.

Harry Powlett, 6th Duke of Bolton had been appointed Governor of the Isle of Wight in 1782. (*Image courtesy of the Anne SK Brown Military Collection, Brown University Library*)

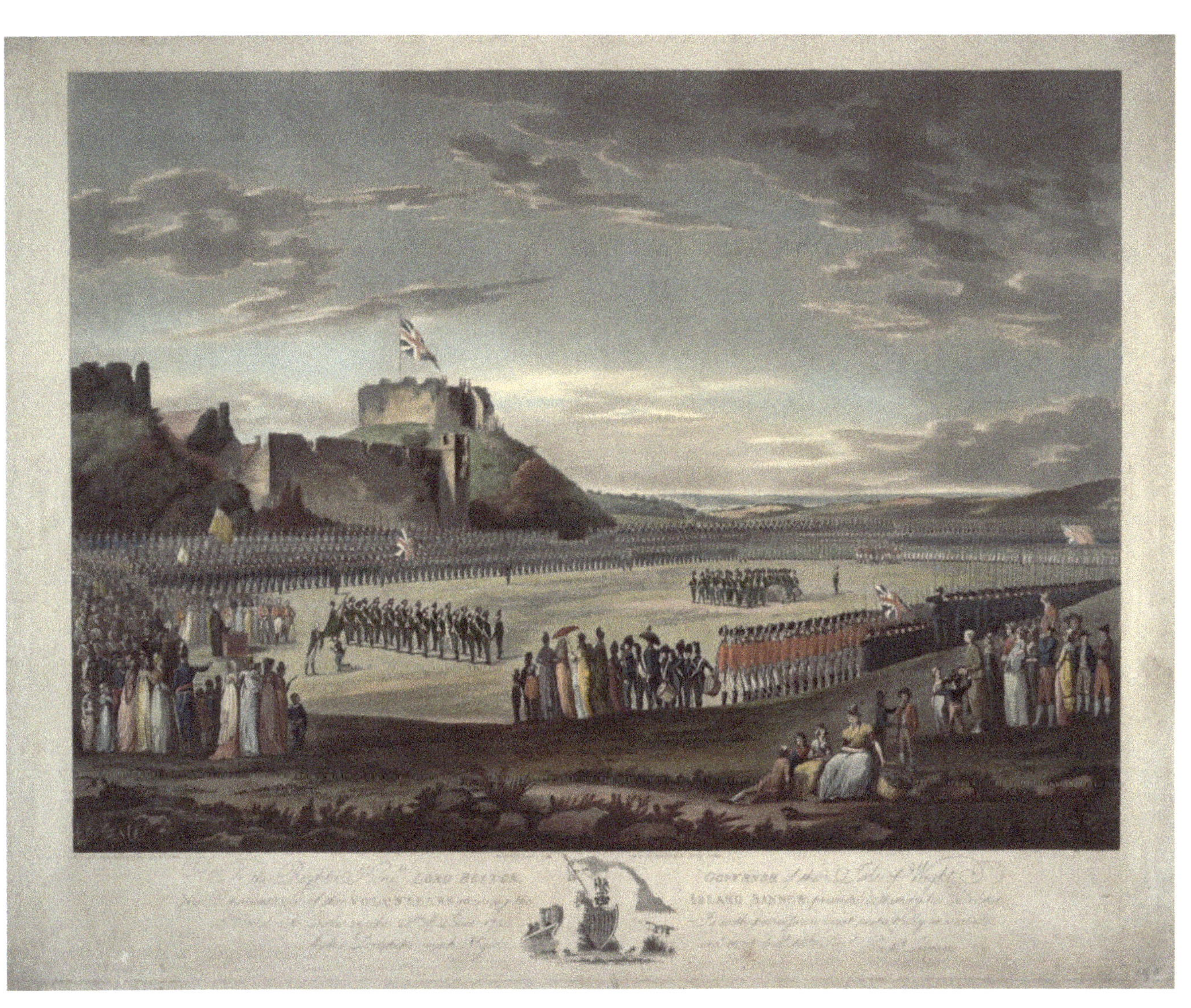
LORD BOLTON
GOVERNOR of the Isle of Wight
VOLUNTEERS
ISLAND BANNER

67 – SERGEANT MAJOR PATRICK GOULD

Mezzotint after George Watson engraved by John Young and published by P Garof, print seller of South Hanover Street, Edinburgh in December 1810 with the following printed dedication: 'Sergeant Major Patrick Gould, / Royal Regt. Edinr. Volunteers (Blue) 1794.' A single figure wearing a fur-crested helmet with feather plume appears as though pointing his cane towards a party of volunteers drilling.

Patrick Gould was a native of Alva in Clackmannanshire, being born there on 31 January 1749. After a short time as an apprentice tailor, Gould joined the army. In 1793 he was appointed as drill sergeant to the Argyllshire Fencibles, transferring in the following year to the 1st Edinburgh Volunteers. Of his ability as a drill sergeant, John Kay wrote of him, 'He was accurate, attentive, and active; and as a drill none could surpass him.' After his death on 22 September 1815, Sergeant Major Gould's remains were interred in Greyfriars Kirk churchyard.

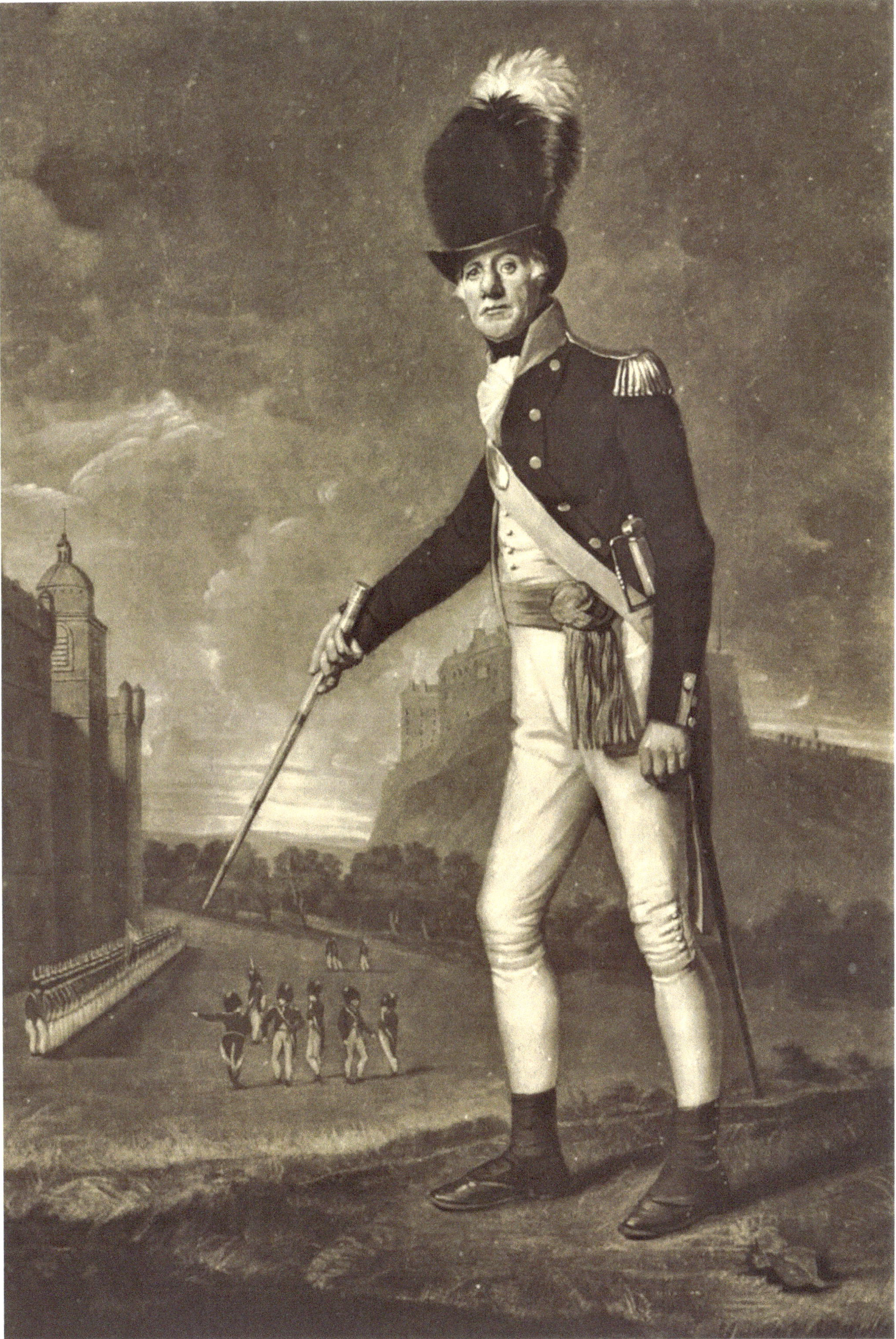

68 – EDINBURGH ROYAL VOLUNTEERS

A partly-coloured etching by and after John Kay dated 1794. An officer stands with his right arm raised, his index finger pointing to a party of marching volunteers. There are more men drilling in the background, also a stout man holding a sword.

The Anne SK Brown Military Collection at Brown University Library include notes with this image that give the officer in the foreground as Partick Creighton, the adjutant of the Edinburgh Volunteers, and the stout man as a Captain Coulter. A William Coulter had been commissioned as lieutenant with the corps on 20 October 1794. (*Image courtesy of the Anne SK Brown Military Collection, Brown University Library*)

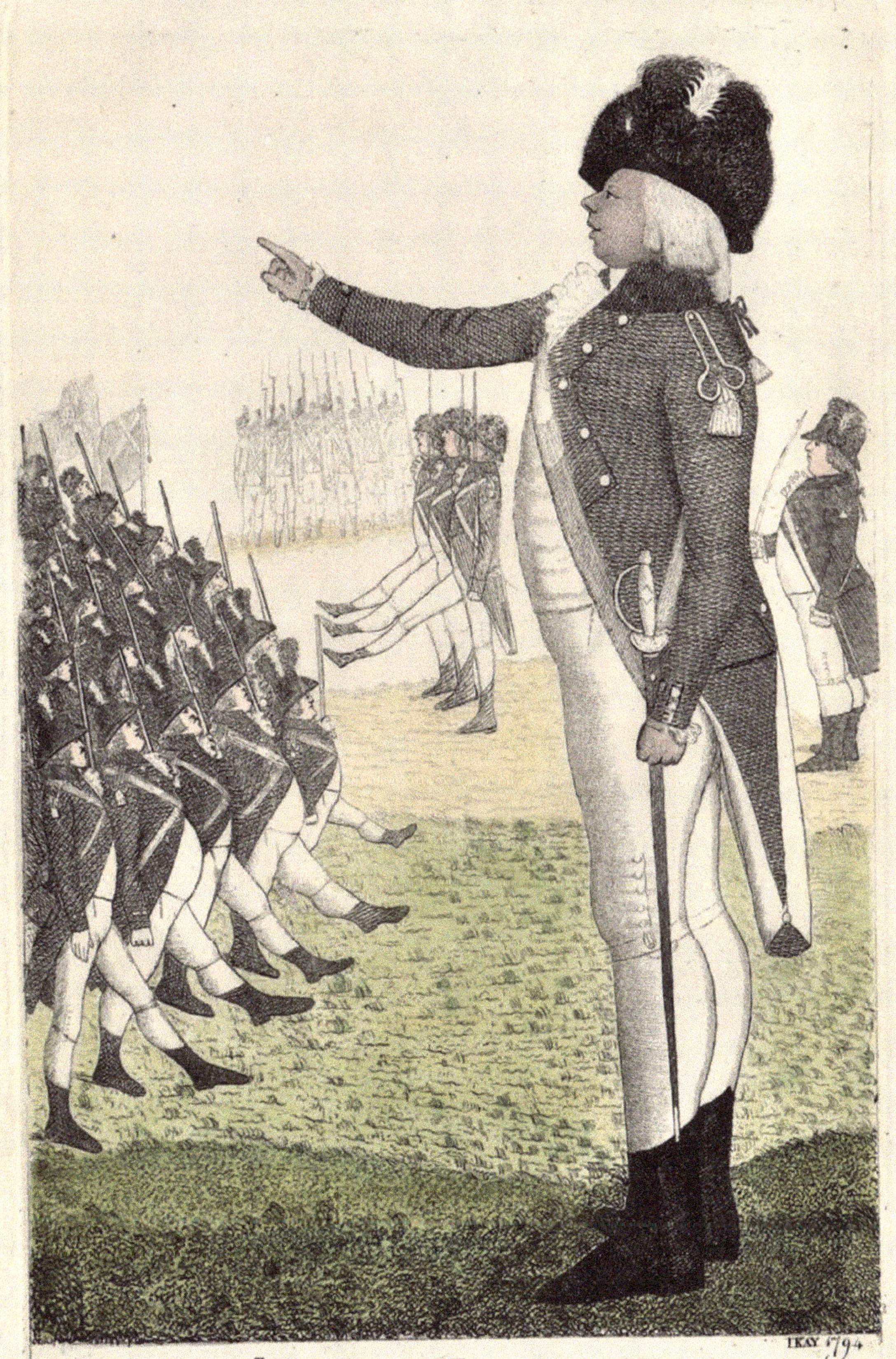

EDIN.R ROYAL VOLUNTEERS.

69 – LOYAL NORTH BRITONS ASSOCIATION

Coloured aquatint by Meyer and Frederick Christian Lewis after James Green, published by John Wallis, Jun of 16 Ludgate Street, City of London on 7 March 1804 with the following dedication: 'To the Right Honourable Lord Reay, Lieutenant Colonel Commandant the Officers and Gentlemen of the Loyal North Britons Association / This Print representing a Private of that Corps in the New Method of Charging the Bayonet is most respectfully dedicated / by their most obedt Servant John Wallis Jun.' A single figure wearing a red coat with white collar, shoulder straps and cuffs, white breeches, black gaiters, a fur-crested helmet with diced turban and tall feather plume and a tartan plaid. He holds his firelock high, his right hand clenching the butt. In the right distance, a party of soldiers pass by carrying a large white flag.

Details of this corps were included in the *Letters and Papers of Andrew Robertson*. He had been the prime mover in the formation of a corps of volunteers at the Royal Academy, but having failed to gain recognition by the Government, the Scottish-born miniaturist quickly associated himself with the Loyal North Britons. Robertson's portrait of the commanding officer, the Duke of Sussex, wearing the uniform of the corps was exhibited at the Royal Academy in 1806. Well known for his military-associated pictures, Robertson wrote in August 1804 how he was busy painting the Colonels of the City Regiments, which were to be engraved and published by subscription. The Loyal North Britons was disbanded in 1814.

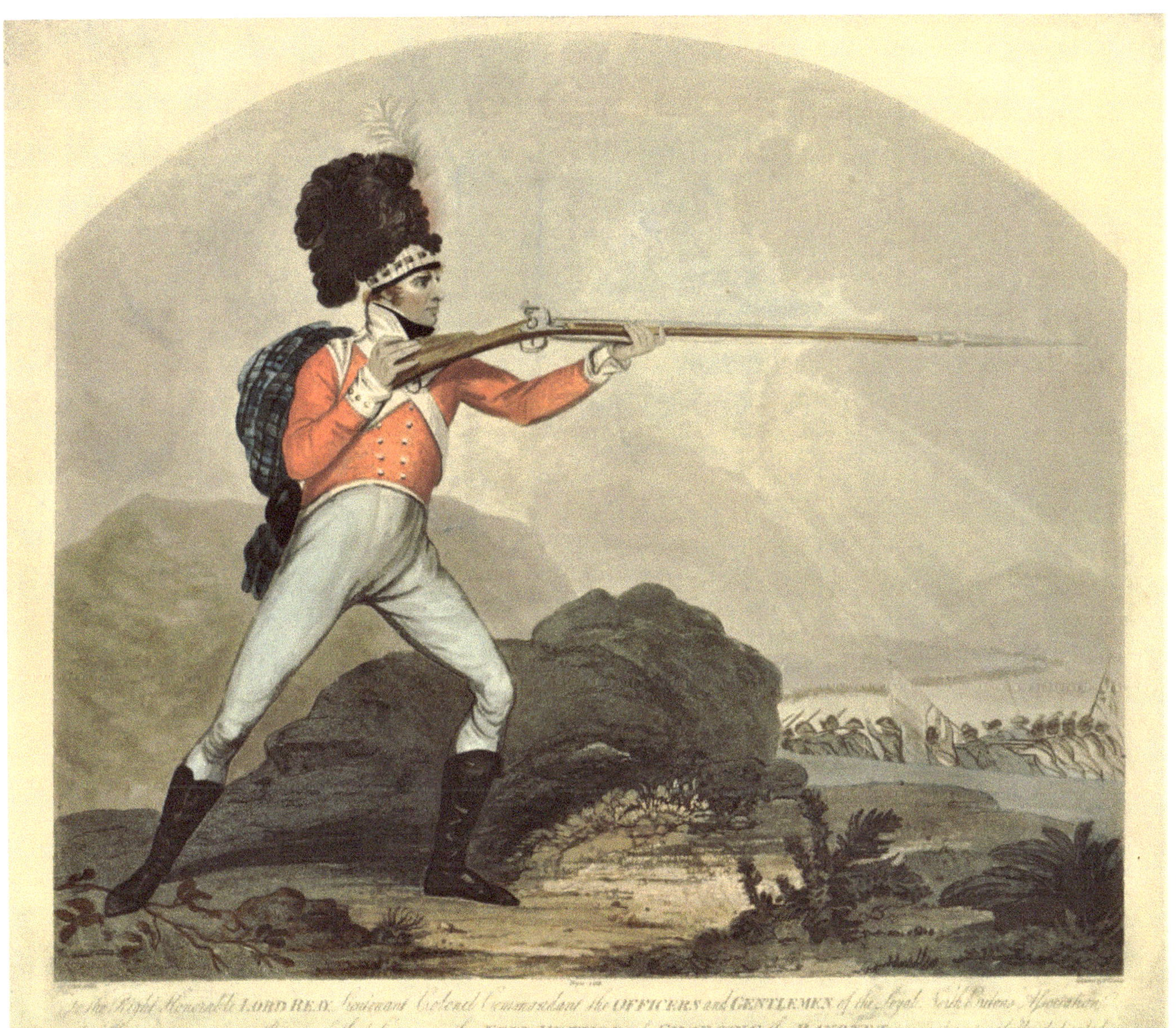
To the Right Honorable LORD REAY Lieutenant Colonel Commandant the OFFICERS and GENTLEMEN of the Royal North Britons Association
this Print representing a Private of that Corps in the NEW METHOD of CHARGING the BAYONET is most respectfully dedicated

70 – THE HIGHLAND ARMED ASSOCIATION

Plate LXX after Thomas Rowlandson and published by Rudolph Ackermann on 1 January 1799 as part of his *Loyal Volunteers of London and Environs*. A single figure against a plain background wearing a red coat with yellow collar, lapels and cuffs, a tartan kilt, black feather bonnet with green feather plume and diced band, diced hose and black shoes.

The following text accompanies the image: 'The Highland Association was formed in July, 1798, when it was resolved, that before a Candidate become a Member he should be recommended, and his address be given the Secretary, who is to inquire his Character and Station in Life….' Also noted is that 'This Corps at present consists of two Companies, but mean (if possible) to extend to 800 Privates, to be all Battalion men.'

Dress: 'A scarlet Jacket with yellow Facings; silver Lace on the Button-holes; Buttons white, with Crown and Thistle; a belted Plaid and Hose; a Highland Bonnet, smartly mounted with Ostrich Feathers; a green hackle Feather fixed under the Cockade with silver Loop over it, and Button of the Corps; an ornamental hair Purse in front of the kilt; the Shoe to be tied with a leather Latchet; the Plaid to be made of the Tartan, similar to that worn by the 42nd Regiment.'

Arms: 'Officers and Sergeants shall wear Broad Swords, and Privates the Firelock and Bayonet; Belts of white leather; the Breast-plate of tutanag, with Crown and Thistle in centre.'

The corps held drill in a field belonging to a Mr Burton and at Plant's Riding House in Moor Place.

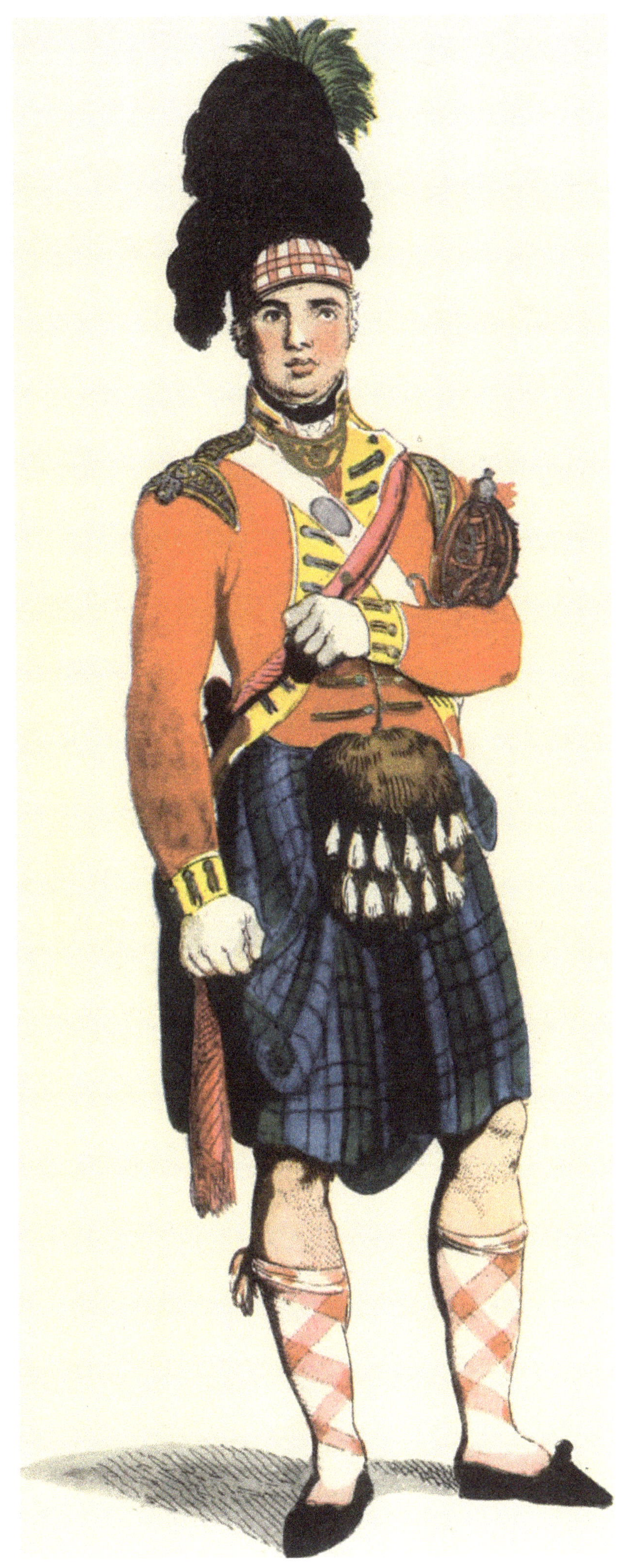

71 – 3rd LONDON VOLUNTEERS

Hand-coloured aquatint drawn and etched by Peltro William Tomkins and published by Elizabeth Walker. Single figure wearing a blue coat with red collar, lapels, cuffs and turnbacks, white breeches, black gaiters and a fur-crested helmet with white over red plume. There are two shoulder-belts, one of which has an oval gold plate. The volunteer stands with one hand on his hip, the other holding a firelock by his side. Two other men, one with blue breeches, talk in the background.

The War Office publication, *A List of the Officers of the Militia, The Gentlemen & Yeomanry Cavalry and Volunteer Infantry* for 1805 reveals that Lieutenant-Colonel John Pooley Kensington commanded this corps of ten companies.

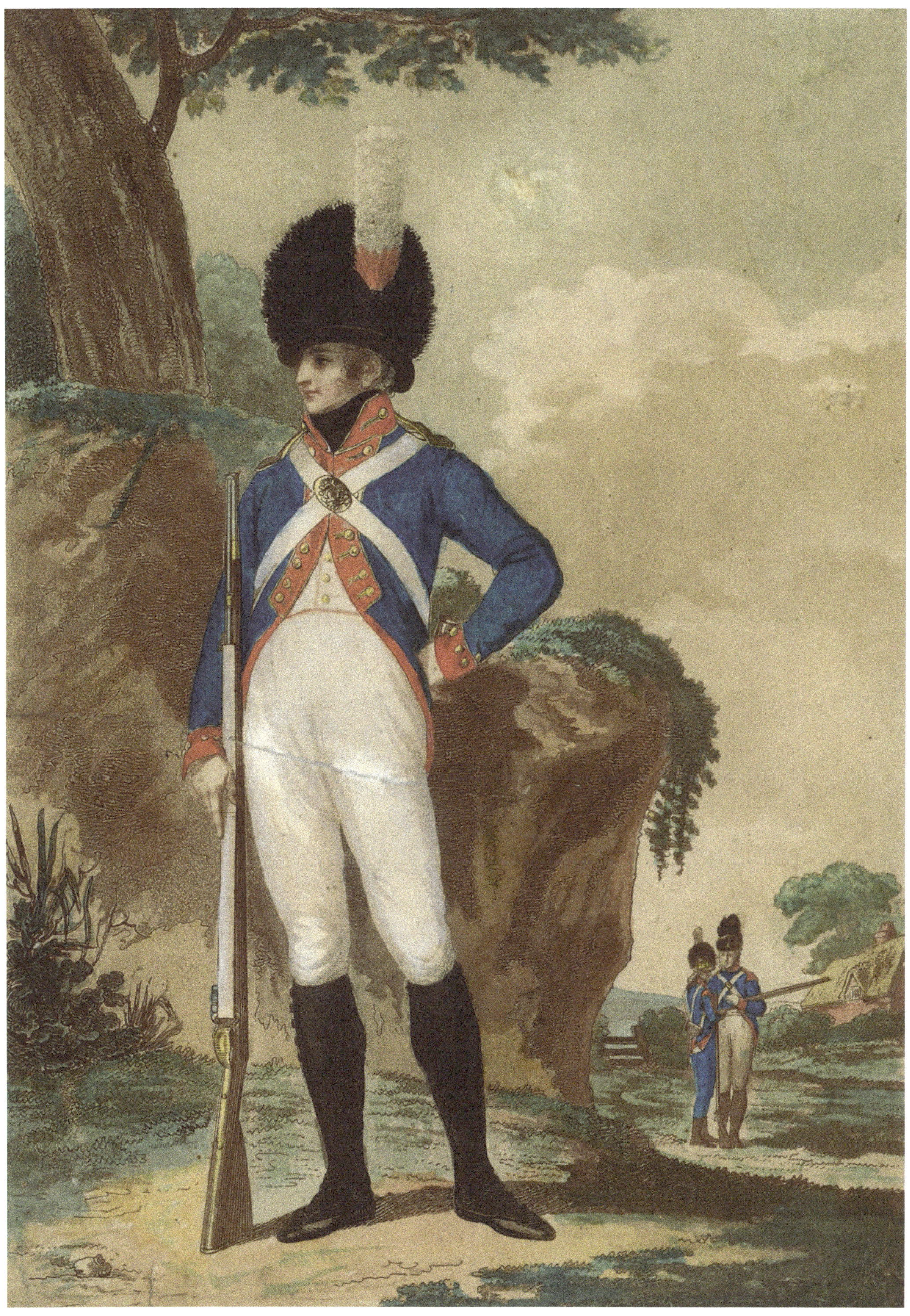

72 – MONTGOMERYSHIRE VOLUNTEER CAVALRY

Colour chromolith by Woodall, Minshall, Thomas & Co after Richard Simkin, one of the plates from *The Historical Records of the Yeomanry and Volunteers of Montgomeryshire* compiled by Lieutenant-Colonel RW Williams and Benson Freeman and published by Woodall, Minshall, Thomas & Co, Oswestry, 1909. Two figures standing in open country, one mounted and one standing. The coats are red with silver lace and black facings, the breeches white, boots black, helmets fur-crested with white plumes.

The services of three troops of cavalry in Montgomeryshire, each of forty rank and file, were accepted on 2 November 1803 and with the county's volunteer infantry were known collectively as the Montgomeryshire Volunteer Legion. The three troops were located one in Montgomery, one in Welshpool and a third in Newtown and Abermule. The regimental history records the following uniform detail: '...but the uniform selected was not grey as originally proposed, but scarlet, the facings being black, the infantry officers wearing gold lace, and those of the Cavalry silver. The Cavalry headdress was a black bearskin-crested light Cavalry helmet of black leather, with black moleskin turban or band, ornamented with silver chain and the Regimental badge in silver on the right side, a white hackle feather being worn on the left side. The jacket was of scarlet cloth with black collar and cuffs, being braided with rows of white cord across the breast and up the back, similar to the Horse Gunners, the collars being edged with white cord, the cuffs having a simple knot of the same material. Three rows of silver ball buttons were displayed on the front of the jacket. The breeches were of white leather, and worn with black, military boots, the belts and gloves were white. And the pouches black. The Officers' dress was much the same as that of the men, with the exception that silver lace replaced the white cords; they also wore crimson silk waist sashes. The headstall was of black and white leather, and the saddle holsters were covered with bearskin flounces, the cloak case being blue, edged with scarlet.'

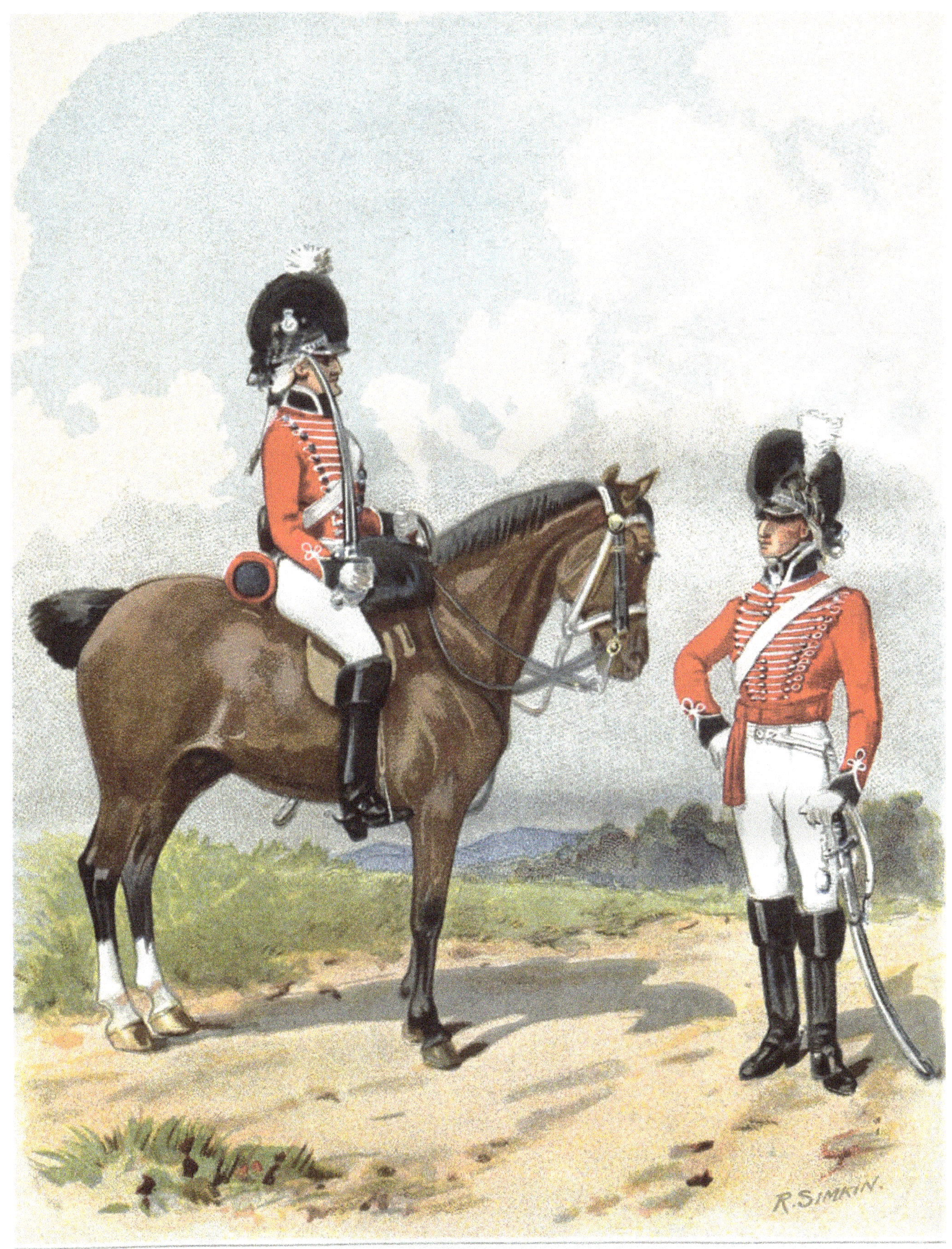

1803.

73 – PIMLICO VOLUNTEER ASSOCIATION

Plate 21 from Rudolph Ackermann's *Loyal Volunteers of London and Environs*, published 10 July 1798 after Thomas Rowlandson. A single figure against plain background wears a red coat with blue collar, shoulder straps, lapels and cuffs and gold buttons. The breeches are dark blue, the half gaiters black, the helmet fur-crested with white over red plume. The volunteer holds his firelock at his right side.

The Pimlico Volunteer Association was formed on 23 April 1798 under Stephen Rolleston who became Major Commandant. The text accompanying the image records how members of the corps had agreed to serve within their own parish without pay. They were also expected to provided their own uniforms and equipment. 'This Association', notes the text, 'consists of two Companies, of upwards of 60 each.... There is also an Auxiliary Corps, or Body of Reserve, consisting of about 200 Artificers, who have agreed to serve in case of any Tumult or Invasion.' Colours were received from the hand of the Right Hon the Countess of Carlisle in the Rotunda at Ranelagh on 20 May 1799. The gold oval breast plate seen being worn in the image was engraved with the letter P within the Garter and the words Loyal Infantry over the crown. The buttons were of the same design.

N

PIMLICO
VOLUNTEER

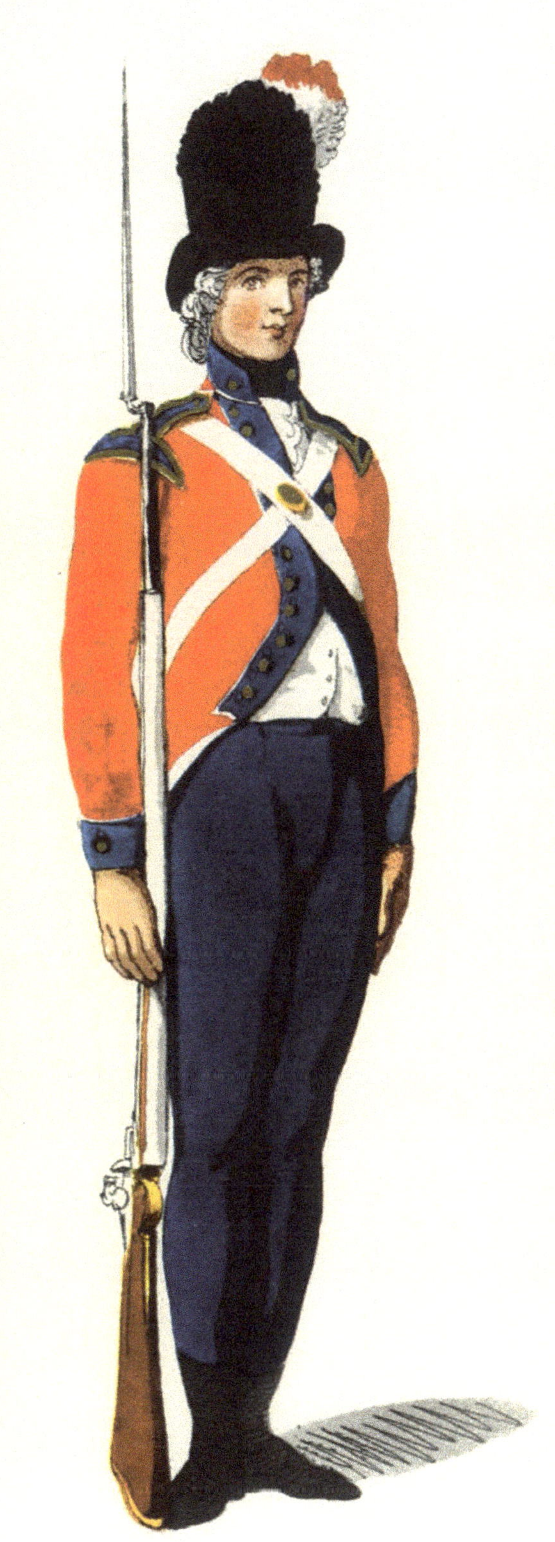

Rowlandson Delin

UNFIX BAYONET 1.st Motion

At the word Unfix *the right thumb is slip'd behind the Barrel, the same as* N.º 6

74 – St MARGARET AND St JOHN WESTMINSTER VOLUNTEER ASSOCIATION

Plate 40 from Rudolph Ackermann's *Loyal Volunteers of London and Environs*, published 20 August 1798 after Thomas Rowlandson. A single figure against a plain background wearing a long dark blue coat with red epaulettes, a white waistcoat, white breeches, black half gaiters and a fur-crested helmet with red plume. A firelock is being held in the prime and load 2nd position.

The corps was formed in May 1798 under the command of Major Commandant Lord Viscount Belgrave. Members had agreed to serve within the Cities of London and Westminster and to assist the civil magistrates of the district when called upon to protect property and preserve public order. There were three companies under the command of Captains John Jones, Griffin and Fernside. Colours were received from the hand of Lady Belgrave in grounds at Millbank.

The breast oval yellow plate seen in the illustration bore the arms of Westminster within the Garter and the title St Margaret and St John Association.

No. 40

St. MARGARET. & St. JOHN. Westr. VOLUNTEER

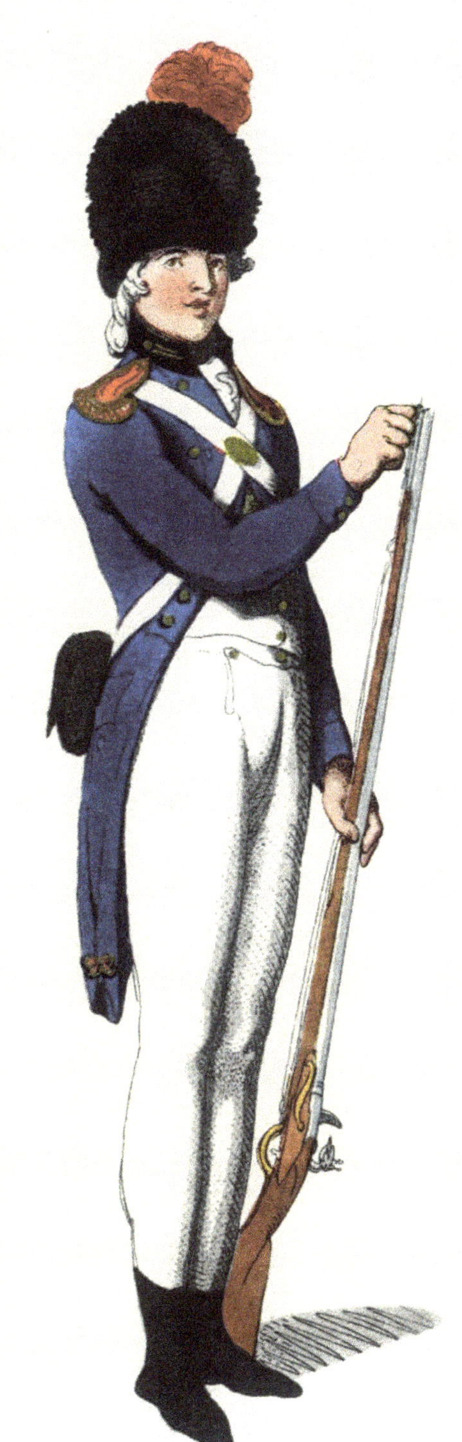

Rowlandson Delin

PRIME & LOAD 2d loading motion

The right hand strikes the muzzle & Immediately seizes the ramrod between the joint of the forefinger & thumb.

75 – A LONDON VOLUNTEER

Print drawn and engraved by Peltro William Tomkins and noted in the Index To British Military Costume Prints as possible part of a set published by Elizabeth Walker of Loyal London Volunteers. The subject, one of the 3rd Regiment of London Volunteers. A single figure wearing a red coat with dark facings, dark grey breeches, black gaiters and a fur-crested helmet with tall white plume. He stands with a firelock in his hand by an open tent. In the background, more tents with several uniformed figures. (*Image courtesy of the Anne SK Brown Military Collection, Brown University Library*)

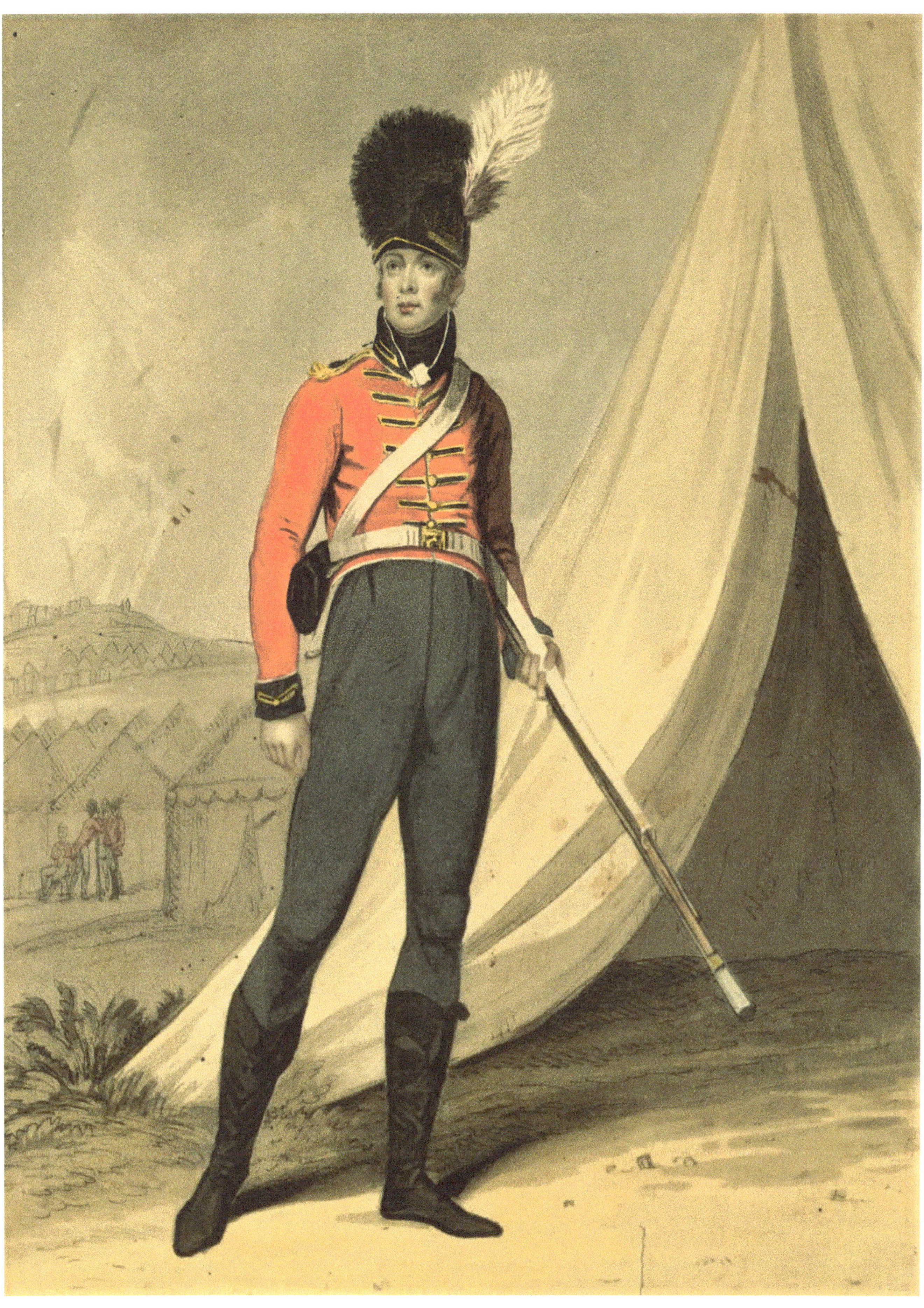

76 – DUKE OF GLOUCESTER'S LOYAL VOLUNTEER

Drawn by Ann Wadsworth, engraved by T Richards and published as part of a series of fourteen colour aquatints by John Wallis of 16 Ludgate Street, City of London on 9 November 1804 with the following inscription below the image: 'Duke of Gloucester's / Loyal Volunteer / Dedicated by permission to Colonel the Rt Honble Lord Viscount Chetwynd.' Against a quiet country scene with trees and a lake is a single figure dressed in a red coat with blue collar, lapels and cuffs, gold epaulettes, white waistcoat, dark blue breeches, black boots and a fur-crested helmet with white plume. He has white cross-belts with gold oval plate attached and holds a firelock with fixed bayonet to his left side. His right index finger is placed over the muzzle.

Colonel Chetwynd's commission was dated 30 July 1803, the corps numbering seven companies.

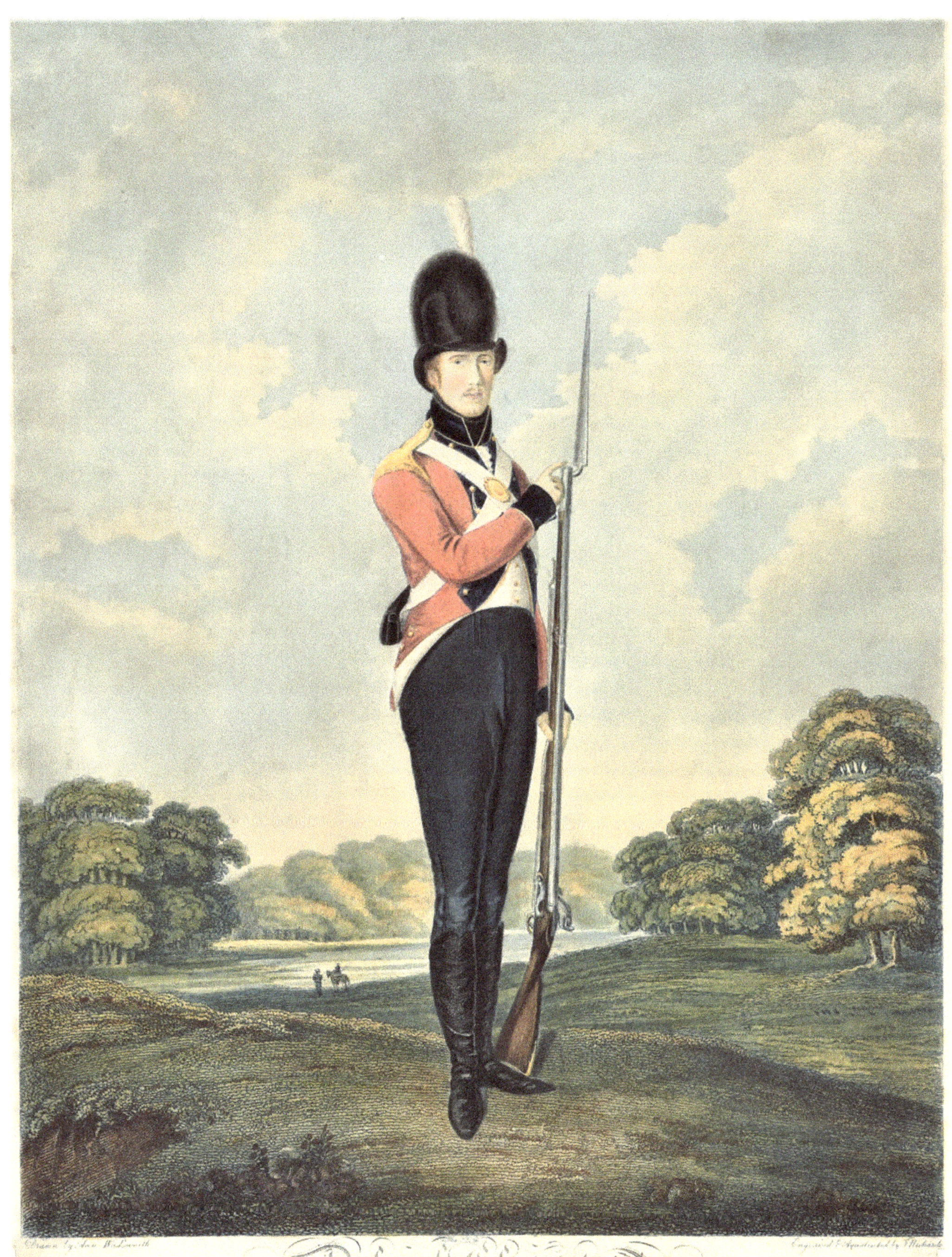

Duke of Gloucester's

LOYAL VOLUNTEER.

77 – 1st REGIMENT OF LOYAL LONDON VOLUNTEERS

Partly-coloured aquatint engraved by Frederick Christian Lewis after James Green and published by John Wallis of 16 Ludgate Street, City of London on 4 June 1804 with the following dedication printed below the image: 'To Samuel Birch Esqr. Lieutenant Colonel Commandant, / The Officers and Gentlemen of the first Regiment of / Loyal London Volunteers / This print representing their Uniforms is most respectfully dedicated by their / obliged humble Servant John Wallis Junior'. Between the wording are the foliated letters RED in script and the date 1797. A single figure holds his left hand up, his right grasping a firelock. The background shows a tented camp to the right and hills to the left.

The print was issued coloured, the coat red with blue facings, the breeches blue. Samuel Birch's commission as Lieutenant-Colonel Commandant was dated 17 September 1803, the services of the regiment having been accepted on the previous 4 August. (*Image courtesy of the Anne SK Brown Military Collection, Brown University Library*)

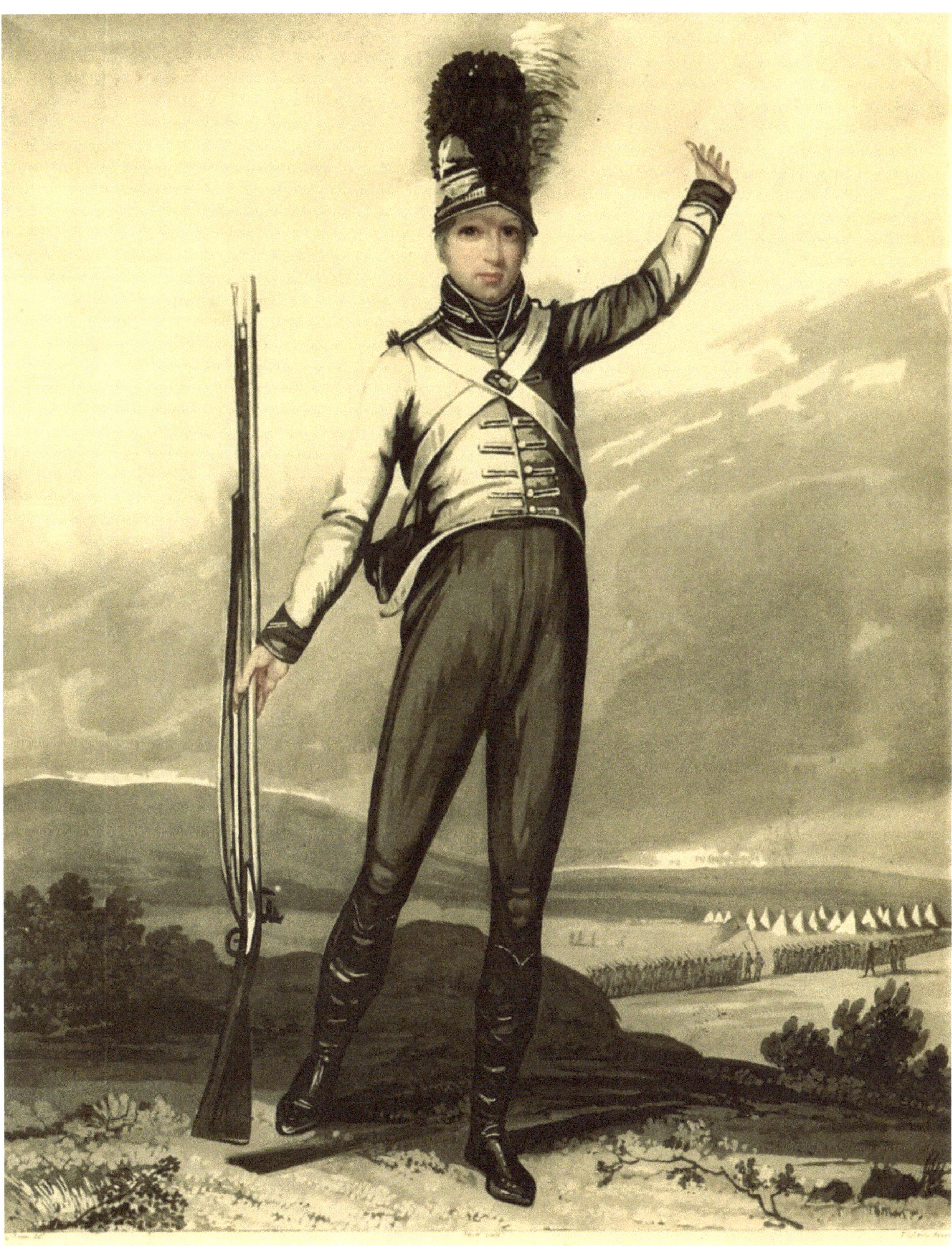

78 – ROYAL YORK MARYLEBONE VOLUNTEERS

Colour aquatint drawn and engraved by Ann Wadsworth, aquatinted by Frederic Christian Lewis and published John Wallis of 16 Ludgate Street, City of London on 21 December 1803 with the following dedication: 'Royal York / Marylebone Volunteer. / Dedicated by permission to the Right Honble Lord Viscount Duncannon Lieut Col Commandant.' A single figure holding a firelock and wearing a red coat with blue facings, blue breeches and a black shako with tall white over red plume and gold plate with star design engraving. The buttons are gold with gold cord decorating the buttonholes, the waist-belt is white with a lion mask locket.

Frederick Viscount Duncannon was commissioned as Lieutenant-Colonel Commandant on 25 January 1803. (*Image courtesy of the Anne SK Brown Military Collection, Brown University Library*)

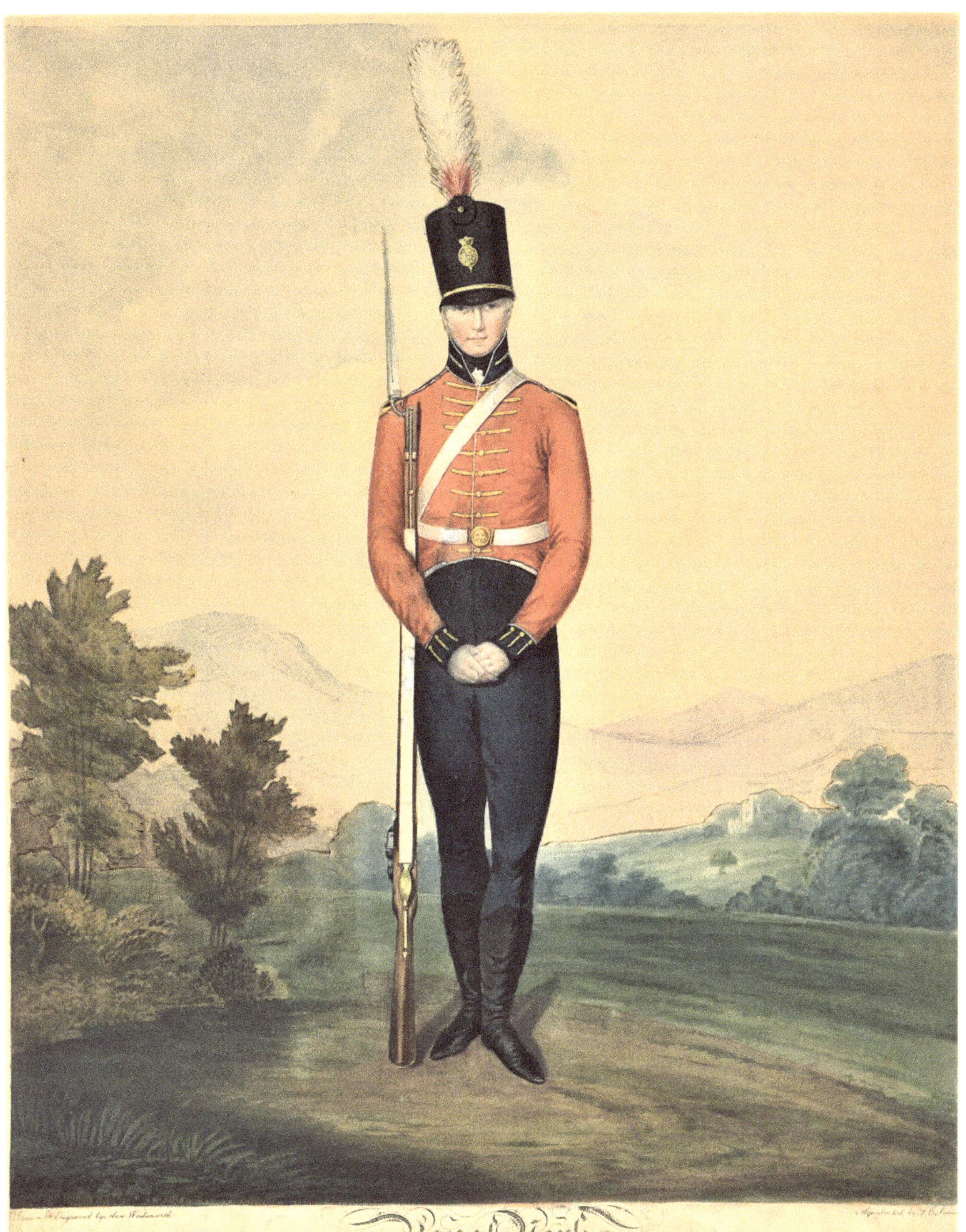
Royal York
MARYLEBONE VOLUNTEER..
Dedicated by permission to the Right Hon.ble Lord Viscount Duncannon Lieu.t Col.l Commandant

79 – MILITARY PORTRAITS – OR A BRACE OF HEROES

Hand-coloured engraved caricature published on 30 July 1798 by Samuel William Fores with the caption 'Military Portraits – or a Brace of Heroes. / Sarjeant I desire you will back upon that Old / Woman facing the front rank the glare of her / red cloak will put the Gentlemen out.' The words are those of a mounted volunteer wearing a red coat with blue facings, gold epaulettes and blue breeches. To the right is a line of civilian spectators behind a fence, to the left are others, one waving a large red flag, in a marquee. A caption below reads, 'Major Sturgeon O Such Marchings and Counter-marchings! From St James's to Tottenham Court,! From Tottenham Court to St James!!!'

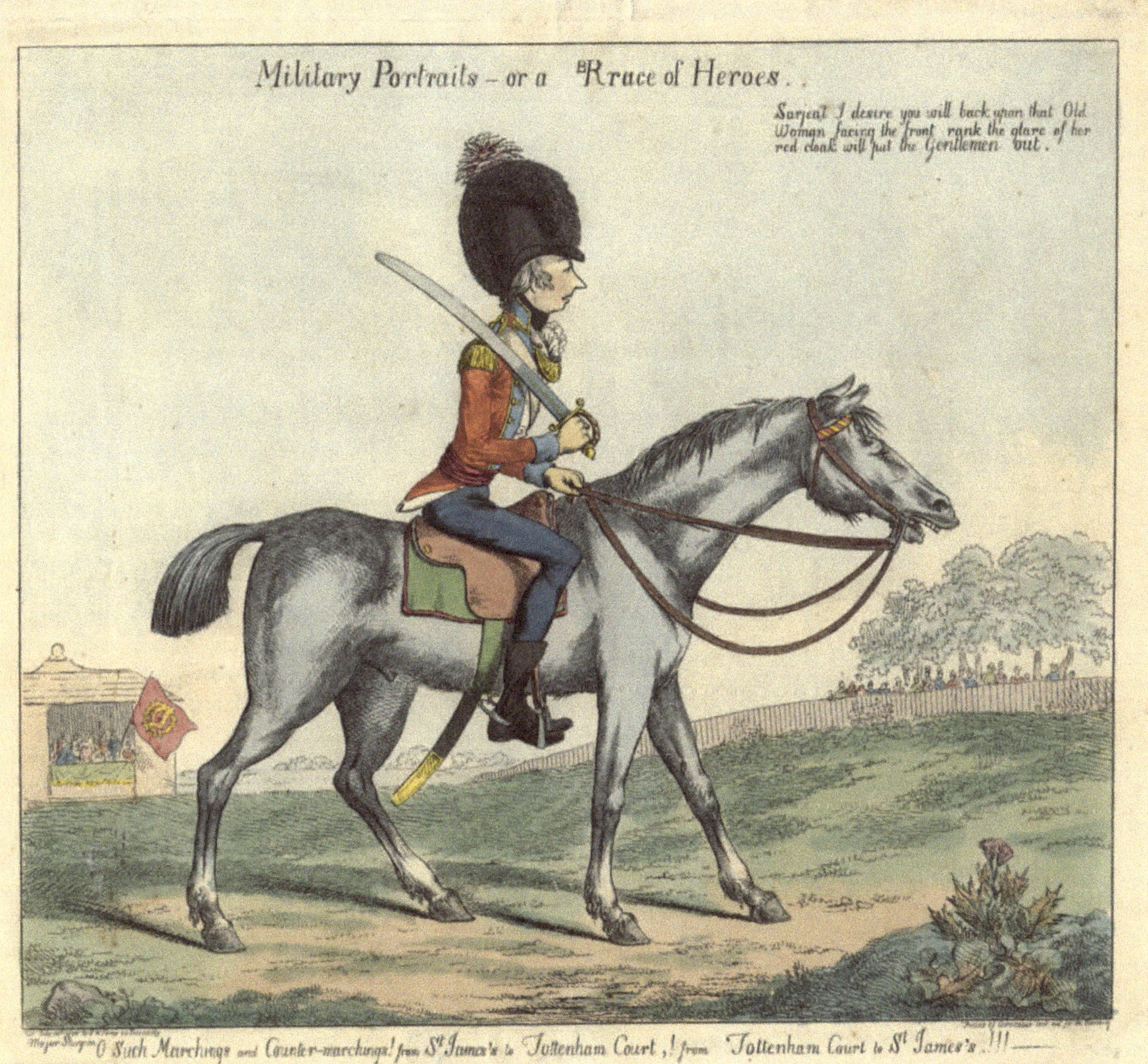
Military Portraits – or a BRrace of Heroes. .
Sarjeat I desire you will back upon that Old Woman facing the front rank the glare of her red cloak will put the Gentlemen out.
Major Sturgeon O Such Marchings and Counter-marchings! from St James's to Tottenham Court,! from Tottenham Court to St James's.!!!——

80 – DUDLEY LOYAL ASSOCIATION

Coloured aquatint engraved by T Cartwright after Thomas Phillips and published by T Philips of 5 Leicester Square, London on 1 May 1799 with the following caption printed below the image: 'To the Right Honble Lord Viscount Dudley and Ward ' This Plate representing the Interior View of Dudley Castle with the Loyal Association of the Town and Neighbourhood as assembled on the 9th of Augt. 1798. / to celebrate the Birth Day of the Honble Mr Ward is with Permission humbly dedicated / by his Lordships obliged & devoted Servt ' Thomas Phillips.' A vast crown is gathered all over a mound leading to a ruined tower flying a Union flag. Below mounted and dismounted volunteers pass by wearing blue coats and white breeches as others in red stand in conversation in the middle ground.

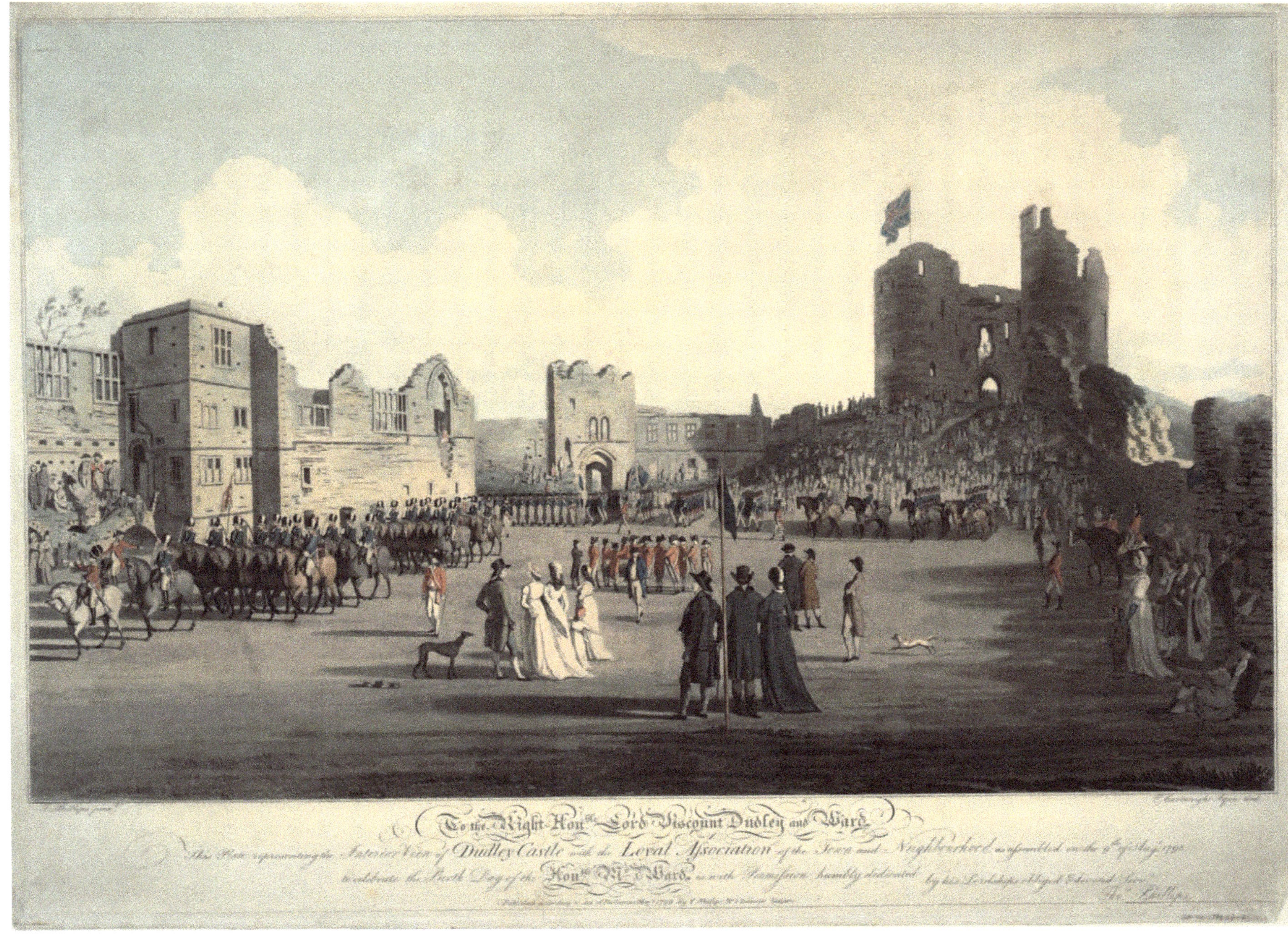

To the Right Hon.ble Lord Viscount Dudley and Ward

This Plate representing the Interior View of Dudley Castle with the Loyal Association of the Town and Neighbourhood as assembled on the

to celebrate the Birth Day of the Hon.ble M.r Ward, is with Permission humbly dedicated by his Lordships obliged & devoted Serv.t

Tho.s Phillips

81 – ATTENTION GENTLEMEN

Original ink and watercolour caricature signed by GM Woodward [George Moutard Woodward] showing an officer addressing two volunteer recruits - 'Attention Gentlemen heads up if you please'. With his firelock on his left shoulder, the man in the centre replies, 'Ah & legs out of the way too; this is the fourth time that fellow has trod my shoes down at heel in marching round the Skittle Ground.' (*Image courtesy of the Anne SK Brown Military Collection, Brown University Library*)

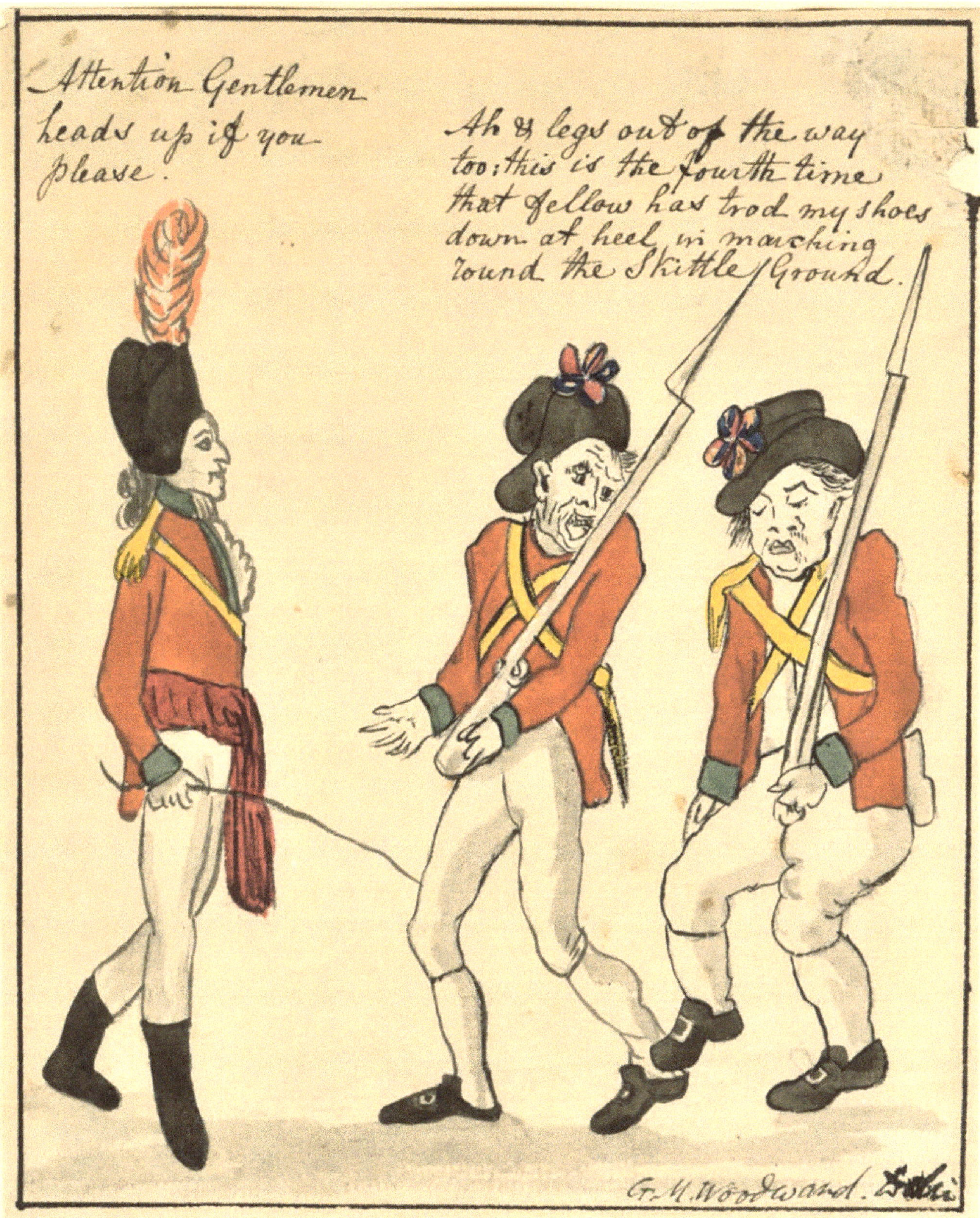
Attention Gentlemen heads up if you please.
Ah & legs out of the way too: this is the fourth time that fellow has trod my shoes down at heel in marching round the Skittle Ground.
G. M. Woodward. Delin

82 – JOHN POOLEY KENSINGTON, 3RD LONDON VOLUNTEERS

Proof stipple engraving by Edward Bumford after Archibald Robertson, published on 3 April 1805 by Edward Bumford of 10 Barnsbury Place, Islington and John Wallis Junior of 16 Ludgate Street, London with the following dedication: 'John Pooley Kensington, Esqr. / Lieut. Colonel Commandant / of the Third Regiment of London Volunteers. / To the Officers, non commissioned Officers & Privates of the 3rd Regt. / This Print is most respectfully Inscribed / by their obedient Servants, / Edwd Bumford & John Wallis Junr.' (*Image courtesy of the Anne SK Brown Military Collection, Brown University Library*)

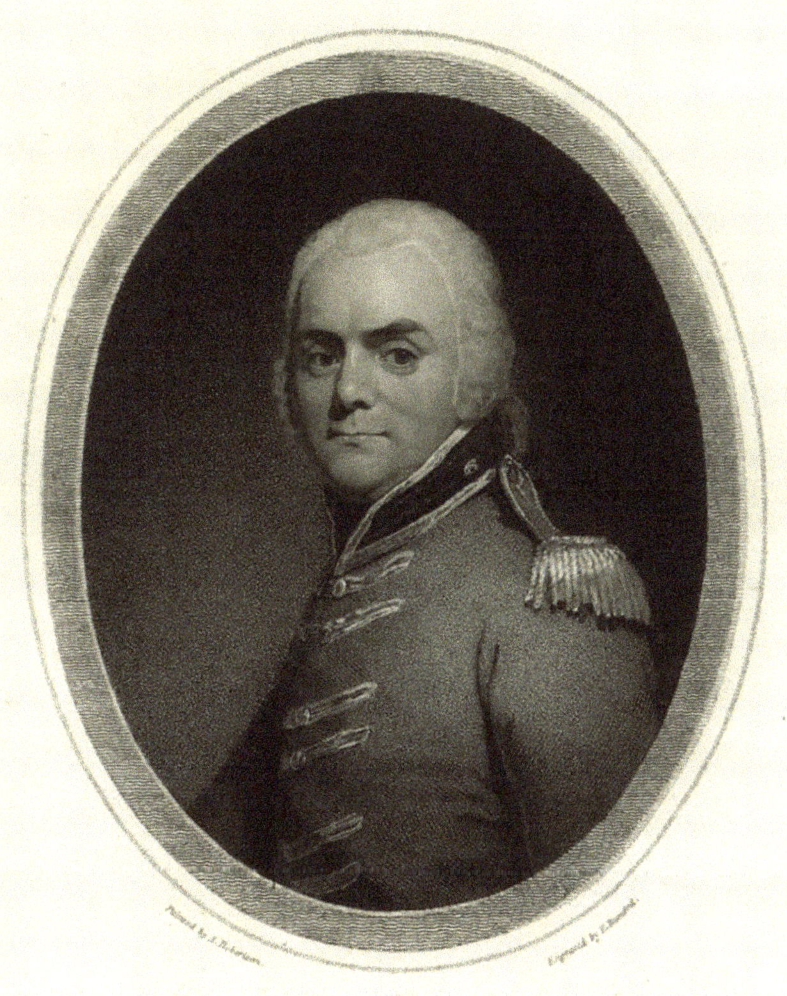

Painted by A. Robertson — Engraved by E. Bumford

JOHN POOLEY KENSINGTON, ESQ.[r]

Lieut. Colonel Commandant

of the THIRD REGIMENT of LOYAL LONDON VOLUNTEERS.

To the Officers, non commission'd Officers, & Privates, of the 3.[d] Reg.[t]
This Print is most respectfully Inscribed
by their obedient Servants,
Edw.[d] Bumford & John Wallis, Jun.[r]

Published [illegible] by Edward Bumford [illegible] & John Wallis Jun. [illegible] Ludgate Street London.

Proof

83 – JOHN PETER HANKEY, 9TH LONDON VOLUNTEERS

Proof stipple engraving by Edward Bumford after Archibald Robertson, published on 5 November 1804 by Edward Bumford of 10 Barnsbury Place, Islington with the following dedication: 'John Peter Hankey, Esqr. / Lieutenant Colonel Commandant / of the Ninth Regiment of Loyal London Volunteers. / To the Officers, non commissioned Officers & Privates of the 9th Regt. / This Print is most respectfully Inscribed / by their obedient Servant / Edward Bumford 'Private in the 7th Compy.'

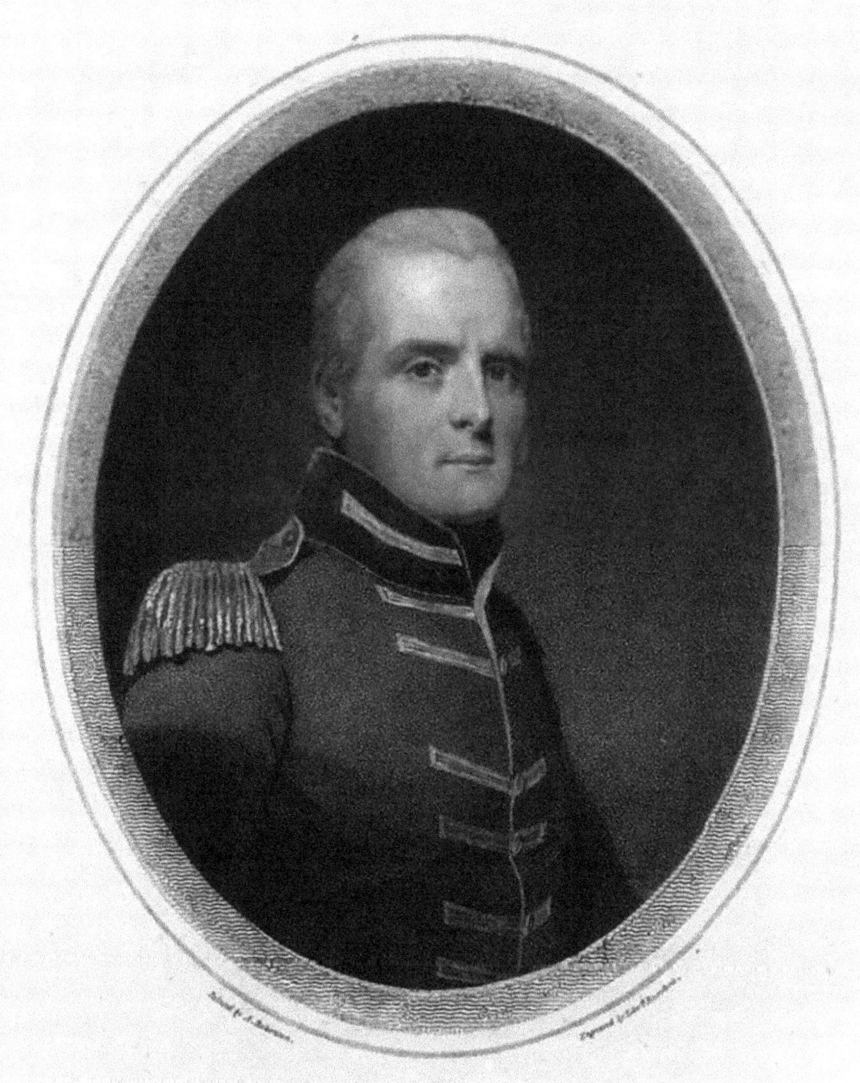

JOHN PETER HANKEY, ESQ.r

Lieut. Colonel Commandant

of the NINTH REGIMENT of LOYAL LONDON VOLUNTEERS.

To the Officers, non commission'd Officers, & Privates, of the 9.th Reg.t

This Print is most respectfully Inscribed.

by their obedient Servant

Edward Bumford.

Private in the 7.th Comp.y

Published Nov. 3. 1804 by Edward Bumford N.o 10 Barnsbury Place Islington.

Proof

84 – THE FREEMAN'S OATH

Hand-coloured engraving accompanying a poem entitled 'The Freeman's Oath', drawn and etched by William Nelson Gardiner of Corpus Christi College Cambridge, Bachelor of Arts and member of the St James Loyal Volunteers. Published by WN Gardiner of 48 Pall Mall, London on 10 August 1803 and printed by W Bulmer & Co of Cleveland Row. A group of volunteers wearing various uniforms and waving swords stand before a background of Britannia and a lion. To the side the barrel of a cannon faces out to sea. To the left a woman holding a young child sits in a chair and a boy dances, raising his arms. On the right of the image, a young man wearing a sword-belt holds a girl in his arms.

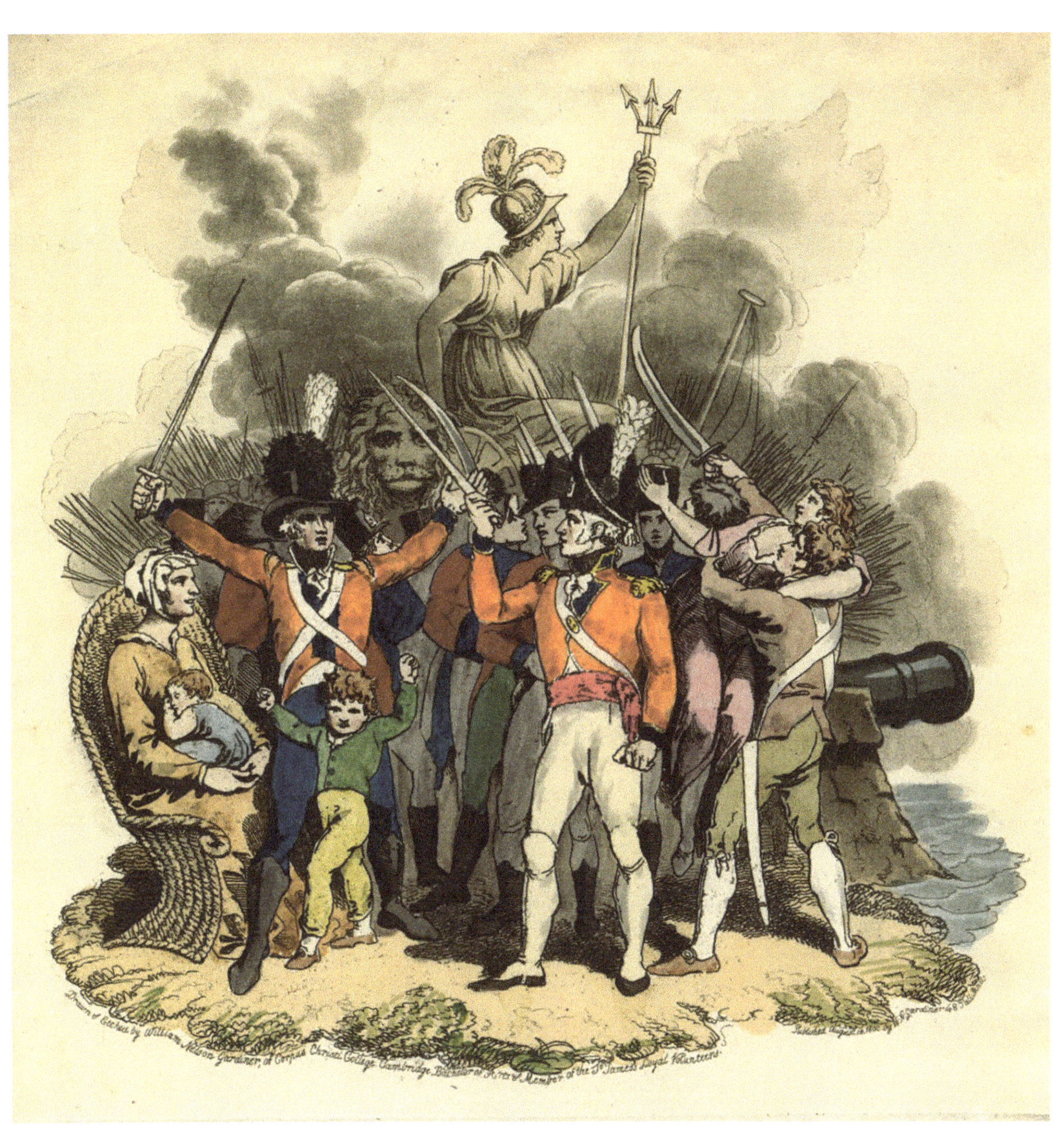
Drawn & Etched by William Nelson Gardiner, of Corpus Christi College Cambridge Bachelor of Arts & Member of the St. James's Loyal Volunteers.

85 – ELEGANT ATTITUDES FOR FUGAL MEN

Hand-coloured caricature by JB Gearing and published by Samuel William Fores of 50 Piccadilly, London on 13 February 1804 with the following title: 'Elegant Attitudes for Fugal Men.' Below this, 'Dedicated to the Volunteer Associations of Great Britain by their Obedient Humble Servant JB Gearing.' Five volunteers in various uniforms depicted carrying out drill positions in a dance style. (*Image courtesy of the Anne SK Brown Military Collection, Brown University Library*)

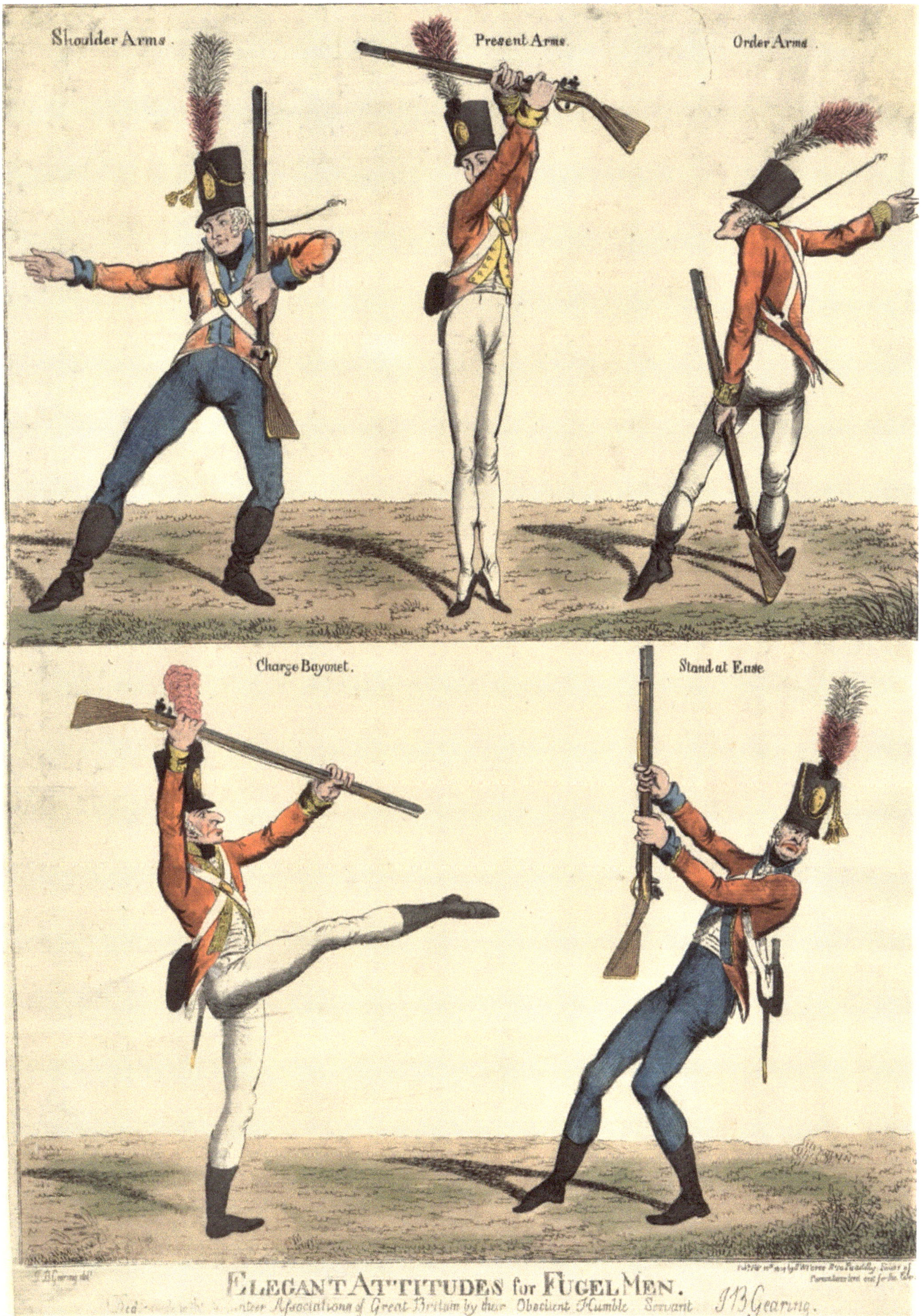

Shoulder Arms.

Present Arms.

Order Arms.

Charge Bayonet.

Stand at Ease

ELEGANT ATTITUDES for FUGEL MEN.

[illegible] unteer Afsociations of Great Britain by their Obedient Humble Servant J B Gearing.

86 – A MEMORIAL FOR POSTERITY

Poster published by John Wallis of 16 Ludgate Street, City of London in memory of two volunteer reviews held in Hyde Park. A representation of a volunteer holding the Royal Standard and a firelock standing on ground close to the sea and with a tented camp in the distance. Below this, the caption: 'Copy of His Majesty's gracious Approbation of the Appearance of the several Volunteer / and Associated Corps which were reviewed in Hyde Park, on Wednesday the 26th and Friday / the 28th of October, 1803.....Respectfully Inscribed to the Volunteers of London and Westminster, / By their obedient humble Servant, John Wallis.' Following is a representation of General Order of 29 October 1803, and a General Return of the several corps, with their named commanders, that were reviewed. (*Image courtesy of the Anne SK Brown Military Collection, Brown University Library*)

A MEMORIAL *for* POSTERITY.

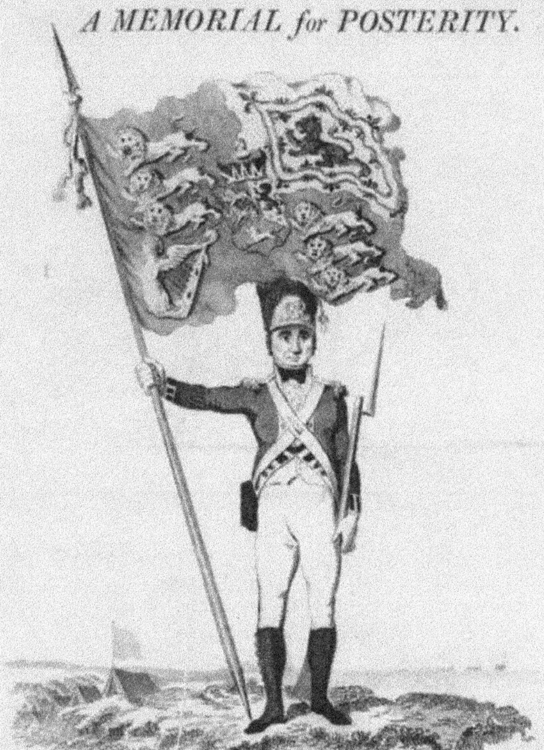

COPY of His MAJESTY's gracious APPROBATION of the Appearance of the several VOLUNTEER and ASSOCIATED CORPS which were reviewed in *Hyde-Park*, on *Wednesday* the 26th and *Friday* the 28th of October, 1803......Respectfully Inscribed to the VOLUNTEERS of *London* and *Westminster*,

By their obedient humble Servant, JOHN WALLIS.

GENERAL ORDERS.

Horse-Guards, Oct. 29, 1803.

HIS Royal Highness the Commander in Chief has received the King's command to convey to the several Volunteer and Associated Corps which were reviewed in Hyde-Park on the 26th and 28th inst. his Majesty's highest approbation of their appearance, which has equalled his Majesty's utmost expectation.

His Majesty perceives, with heartfelt satisfaction, that the spirit of loyalty and patriotism, on which the system of the armed Volunteers throughout the kingdom was originally founded, has risen with the exigencies of the times, and at this moment forms such a bulwark to the Constitution and Liberties of the Country, as will enable us, under the protection of Providence, to bid defiance to the unprovoked malice of our enemies, and to hurl back, with becoming indignation, the threats which they have presumed to vent against our independence, and even our existence as a nation.

His Majesty has observed with peculiar pleasure, that, amongst the unprecedented exertions which the present circumstances of the country have called forth, those of the Capital of his United Kingdom have been eminently conspicuous. The appearance of its numerous and well-regulated Volunteer Corps, which were reviewed on the 26th and 28th instant, indicates a degree of attention and emulation, both in officers and men, which can proceed only from a deep sense of the important objects for which they have enrolled themselves, a just estimation of the blessings we have so long enjoyed, and a firm and manly determination to defend them like Britons, and transmit them, unimpaired, to our posterity.

The Commander in Chief has the highest satisfaction in discharging his duty, by communicating these his Majesty's most gracious sentiments, and requests that the Commanding Officers will have recourse to the readiest means of making the same known to their respective corps.

FREDERICK, Commander in Chief.

General Return of the Volunteer Corps reviewed by his Majesty in Hyde-Park, on the 26th and 28th of October, 1803.

On WEDNESDAY the 26th of October.

CORPS.	COMMANDERS.	Effective in the Field.
Loyal London Vol. Cavalry	*Lieut. Col. Anderson*	217
Hon. Artillery Company	*Colonel Le Mesurier*	604
1st. Reg. Royal East-India Vol.	*Colonel Sir L. Darell*	640
2d Do. Do. Do.	*Colonel Sir H. Inglis*	636
3d Do. Do. Do.	*Colonel J. Roberts*	583
1st Do. Loyal London Vol. Inf.	*Lieut. Col. Birch*	737
2d Do. Do. Do.	*Lieut. Col. J. Smith*	657
3d Do. Do. Do.	—— *Kensington*	804
4th Do. Do. Do.	—— *Price*	790
5th Do. Do. Do.	—— *T. Smith*	501
6th Do. Do. Do.	—— *Wigston*	647
7th Do. Do. Do.	—— *Shaw*	464
8th Do. Do. Do.	—— *Canning*	777
9th Do. Do. Do.	—— *Sir W. Curtis*	651
10th Do. Do. Do.	—— *Combe*	587
11th Do. Do. Do.	*Major Sabine*	293
1st Reg. Tower Hamlets Do.	*Lieut. Col. Mellish*	550
Whitechapel Do.	—— *Craven*	445
Mile End Do.	*Major Liptrap*	333
St. George in the East Do.	—— *Sploit*	330
Radcliffe Do.	—— *Boulcot*	109
Shoreditch Do.	—— *Marshall*	394
Bromley St. Leonard Do.	—— *Stannard*	173
Bethnal Green Do.	—— *Carrick*	166
St. Catharine Do.	*Captain Jenkins*	121
Christ Church Volunteers Do.	*Major Stevens*	184
		12,401

On FRIDAY the 28th October.

CORPS.	COMMANDERS.	Effective in the Field.
London and Westminster Light Horse Volunteers	*Colonel Herries*	727
Westminster Reg. Vol. Cavalry	*Lieut. Col. Elliott*	223
Southwark Troop of Yeomanry	*Captain Collingdon*	69
Clerkenwell Cavalry	—— *Selton*	46
Lambeth Do.	—— *Watson*	40
St. George's Reg. Vol. Infantry	*Colonel Earl of Chesterfield*	663
St. James's Do. Do.	—— *Lord Amherst*	934
Bloomsb. and Inns of Court Do.	—— *Cox*	929
Royal Westminster Do.	—— *Robertson*	991
Prince of Wales's Do.	—— *M. P. Andrewes*	640
St. Margaret's and St. John's	*Hon. Lieut. Col. Eden*	623
Loyal North Britons	*Lieut. Col. Lord Reay*	280
Marylebone	*Colonel Lord Dunmmon.*	908
Law Association	*Lieut. Col. Hon. T. Erskine*	335
Duke of Gloucester's	*Colonel Lord Chetwynd*	402
The Somerset-Place	—— *Tierney*	380
St. Giles's & St. George's Do.	*Lieut. Col. Sir J. Nicholl*	605
The Clerkenwell	*Major Magnise*	701
Loyal British Artificers	*Lieut. Col. Burton*	342
The Loyal Britons	—— *Davison*	127
St. Andrew and St. George's	—— *Bosnier*	514
1st and 2d Batt. Queen's Royal	*Colonel Lord Hobart*	926
The Knightsbridge	*Major Eyre*	124
The St. Clement's Danes	—— *Bicke*	243
1st Surry	*Lieut. Col. Gaitskill*	515
The St. Sepulchre	*Major Ford*	174
The St. Saviour's	—— *Potts*	154
The Loyal Southwark	*Colonel Tierney*	543
Lambeth	*Lieut. Col. Edwards*	553
Christchurch	*Major Toulmin*	171
St. John's	—— *King*	138
St. Olave's	*Captain Shaw*	110
Rotherhithe	*Major Wells*	153
Duke of Cumberland's Corps of Volunteer Sharp Shooters	*Captain Barber*	84
Gray's Inn Corps of Vol. Riflemen	*Captain J. K. Cooke*	38
		14,676

HARRY CALVERT, Adj. Gen.

LONDON: Printed for JOHN WALLIS, No. 16, Ludgate-Street.
BY [illegible] CRANE-COURT, FLEET-STREET.

87 – THE RIGHT HON THOMAS LORD ERSKINE

Hand-coloured stipple engraving by James Hopwood after an original picture by Archibald Robinson which was exhibited at Somerset House in 1805. Below the image the following printed caption: 'The Right Honble. Thomas Lord Erskine. / Lord High Chancellor of Great Britain. / Late Lieut. Col. Commandant of the Law Association.' The colonel wears a scarlet jacket with gold epaulettes, gold lace edging to the collar, gold buttons, a gold gorget and a shoulder-belt plate bearing the Cross of St George.

Colonel Erskine's commission as lieutenant-colonel commandant of the Law Association Volunteers was dated 28 July 1803. He had been called to the Bar in the summer of 1778 and went on to feature in many famous criminal cases, including the defence of Lord George Gordon in his 1781 trial for treason and that of ex-soldier James Hadfield who had fired a shot at the King in the Drury Lane Theatre. (*Image courtesy of the Anne SK Brown Military Collection, Brown University Library*)

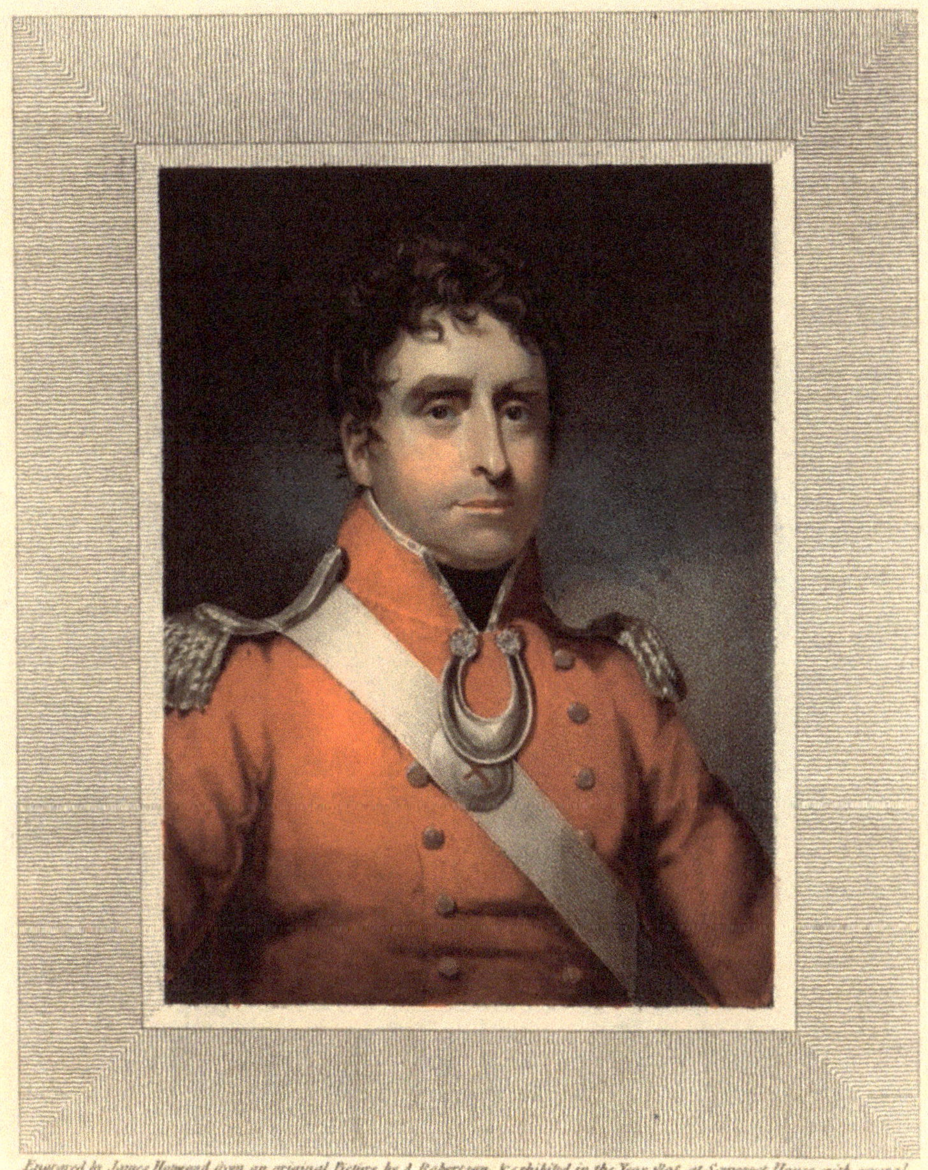

Engraved by James Hopwood from an original Picture by A. Robertson, & exhibited in the Year 1805 at Somerset House, with several other Commandants of the London District.

The Right Hon.ble Thomas Lord Erskine,

LORD HIGH CHANCELLOR OF GREAT BRITAIN,

late Lieu.t Col. Commandant of the Law Association.

88 – CORNHILL MILITARY ASSOCIATION

Hand-coloured engraving by Charles Grignion after Edward Dayes and published by Robert Wilkinson of 58 Cornhill, City of London on 7 August 1799. A parade of volunteers wear red coats and white breeches before an audience of civilians gathered in front of a building.

The building on the right is the former Leathersellers' Hall, that on the left St Helen's Church, Bishopsgate. The Cornhill Association was first organised on 10 June 1797 under the command of Major Commandant Robert Williams. (*Image courtesy of the Anne SK Brown Military Collection, Brown University Library*)

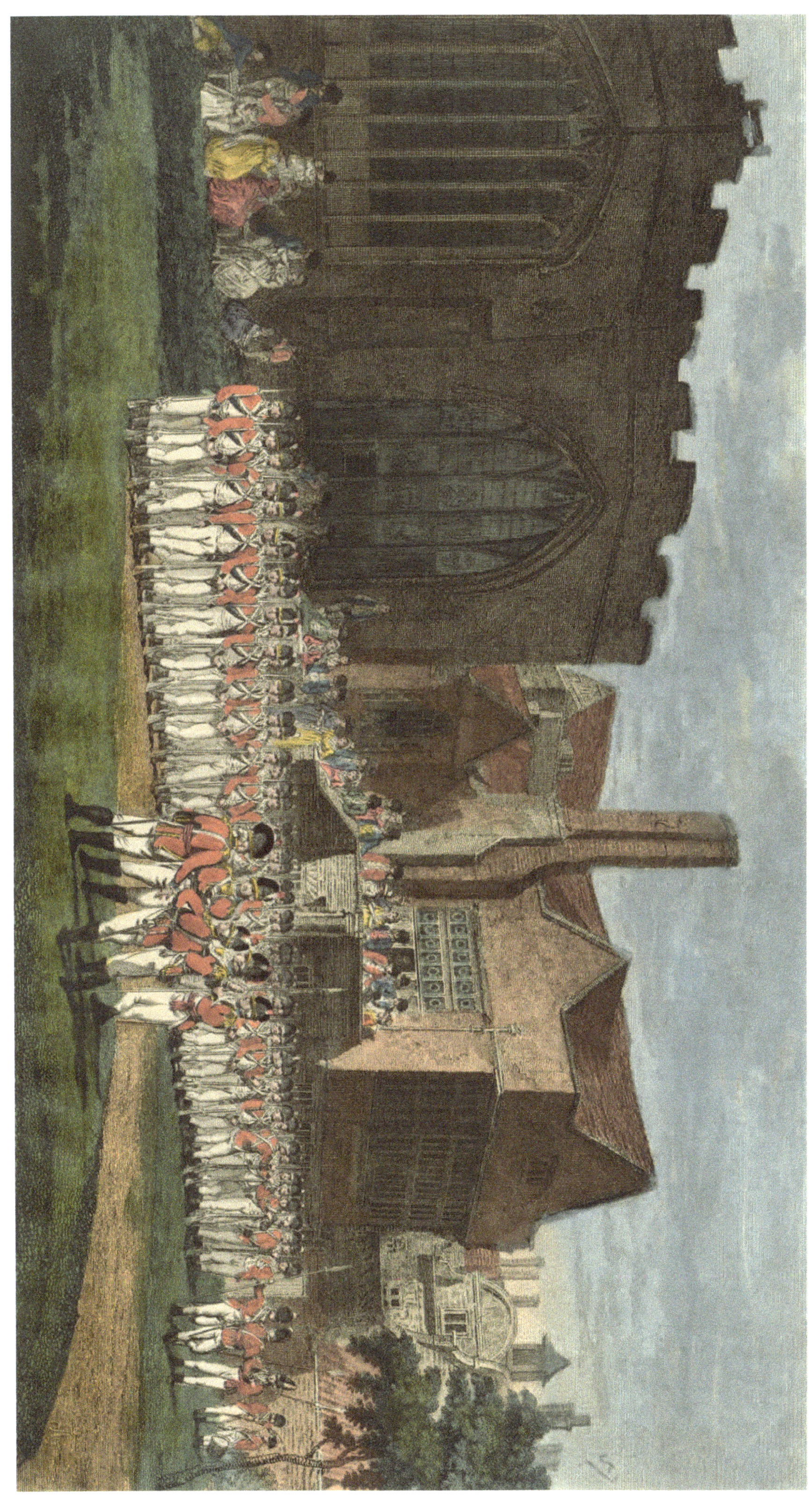

89 – ALDGATE WARD ASSOCIATION

Plate 56 from Rudolph Ackermann's *Loyal Volunteers of London* painted by Thomas Rowlandson and published 1 November 1798. A single figure against a plain background wears a red coat with blue facings, white breeches, black gaiters and a fur-crested helmet with white-over-red plume. He holds his firelock in the 'Make Ready' as a rear rank position.

The Aldgate Ward Association Volunteers was formed on 4 May 1798 under the command of Captain Harvey Christian Combe, Alderman of London and Member of Parliament for the City of London. At the time of Rowlandson's print the corps consisted of one company of some seventy privates, the officers, in addition to Captain Combe, being Lieutenant Charles Chambers and Ensign Richard Radford. The gold oval cross-belt plate worn in the picture was engraved with the letters AWV, as were the buttons.

ALDGATE WARD ASSOCIATION.

No. 56.

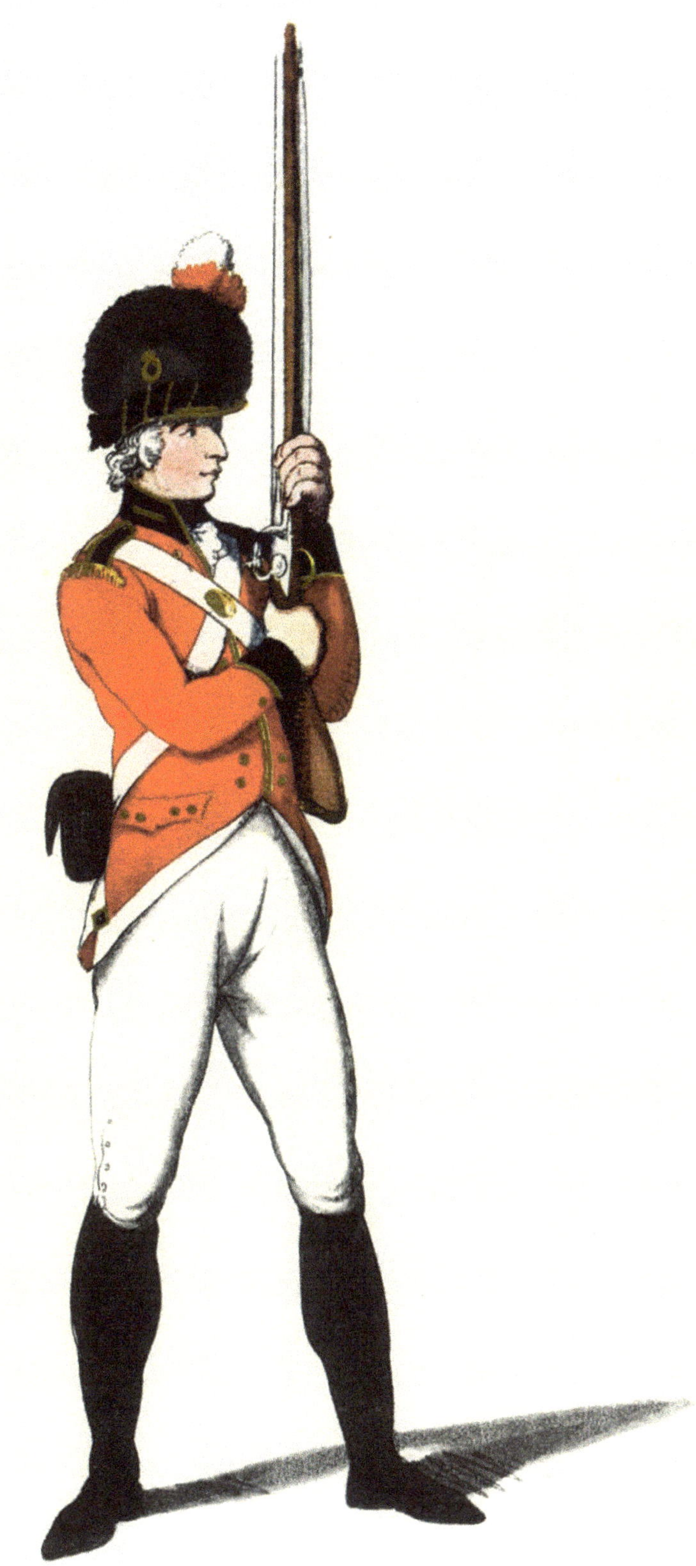

Rowlandson Delin.

MAKE READY (as a Rear Rank)

The same as a front rank the feet excepted, the right foot steps out to the right & the left steps forward.

London Pub. Nov. 1 1798 at Ackermann's Gallery 101 Strand.

90 – FARRINGDON WARD WITHIN VOLUNTEERS

Plate 55 from Rudolph Ackermann's *Loyal Volunteers of London* painted by Thomas Rowlandson and published 25 October 1798. A single figure against a plain background wears a blue coat with red facings and gold braid. The waistcoat and breeches are white and the fur-crested helmet has a white plume. He holds his firelock in the 'Prime and Load' as a rear rank position.

Major Commandant Price, a City of London alderman, commanded the corps which was raised in May 1798. At time of Rowlandson's painting the Farringdon Ward Within Volunteers were made up of two companies.

FARRINGTON WARD within. N° 5

VOLUNTEER.

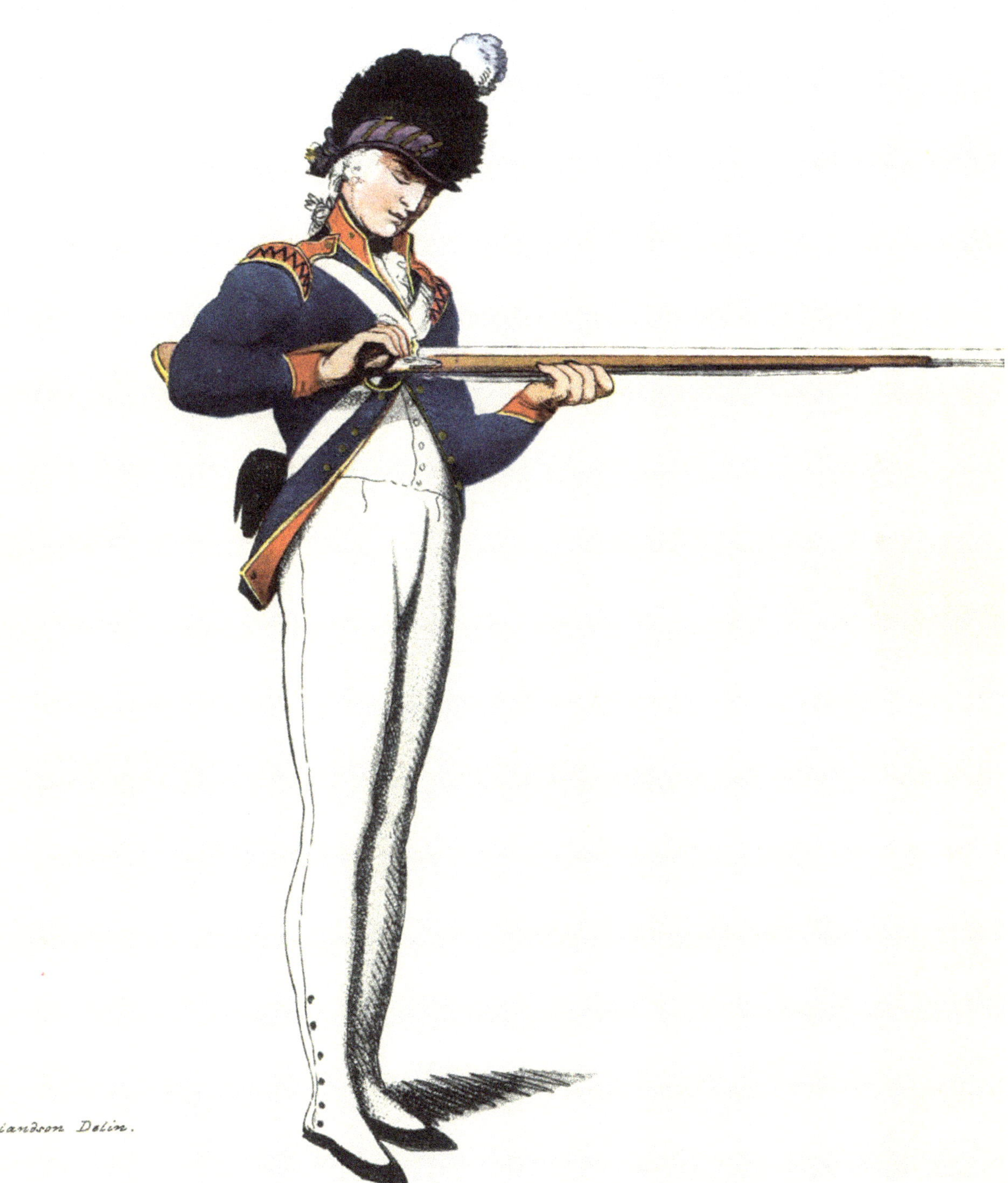

PRIME & LOAD *(as a Rear Rank.)*

The same as a front rank, excepting the Firelock which is held close under the Arm.

London Pub. Oct 25, 1798. at Ackermann's Gallery. 101 Strand.

91 – TOES OUT! STAND EASY

Hand-coloured song sheet illustration published by Laurie & Whittle of 54 Fleet Street, London on 12 May 1800, the first verse of which runs: 'Will Buckram. A Taylor, play'd Soldier so bad, / The Adjutant placed him in the awkward squad, / Attention! Good Buckram (the serjeant bawls out), / Do stand like a Soldier, and turn your toes out.'

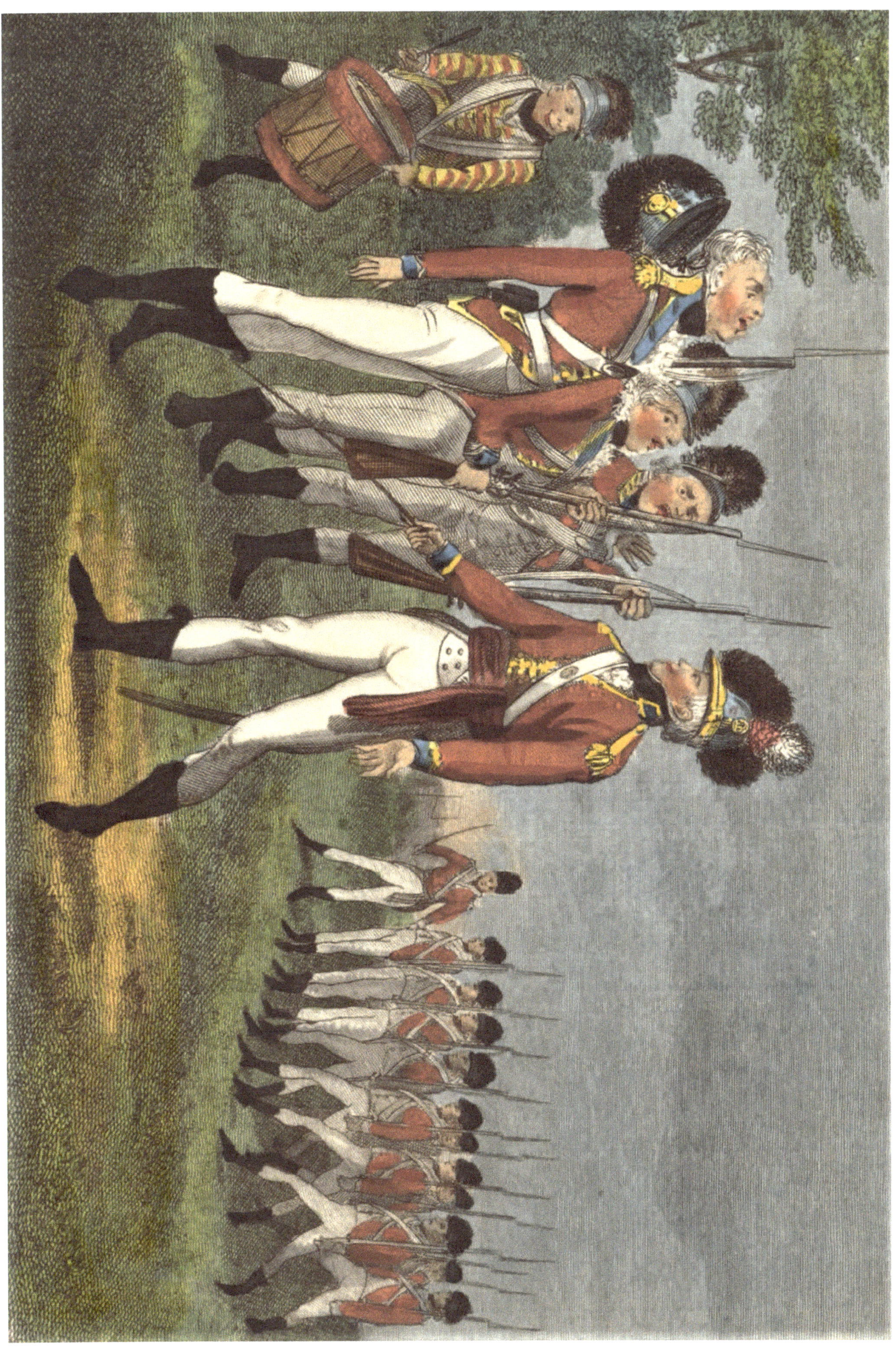

92 – PREPARATIONS FOR THE SPRING CAMPAIGN!

Hand-coloured engraved caricature after George Moutard Woodward published by W Holland of 50 Oxford Street, London on 20 April 1800 with the caption, 'Preparations for the Spring Campaign!'

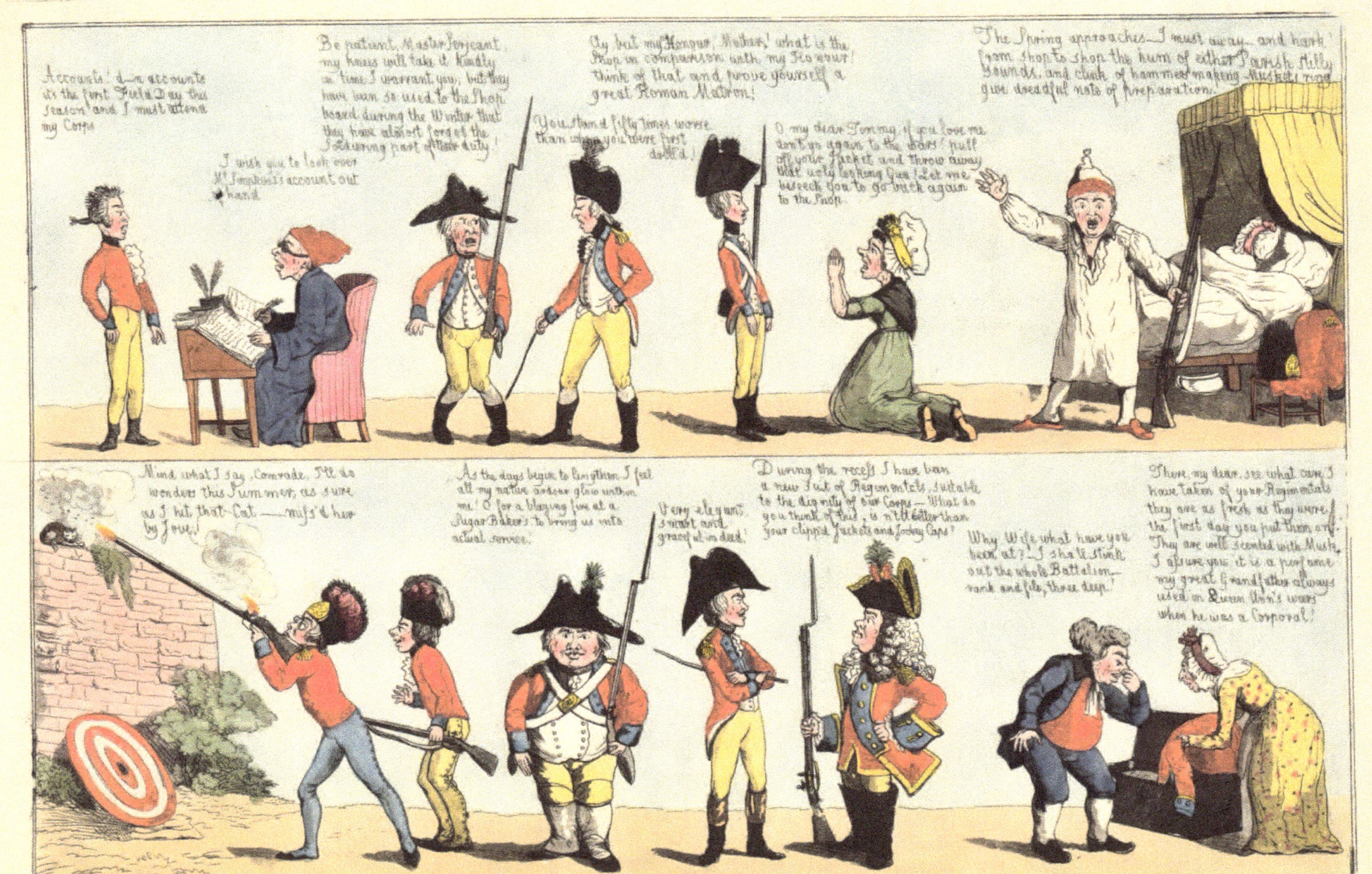

PREPARATIONS for the SPRING CAMPAIGN!

93 – DOWGATE WARD VOLUNTEERS

Plate 76 after Thomas Rowlandson from Rudolph Ackermann's *Loyal London Volunteers*, published on 20 April 1799. A single figure against a plain background stands with his firelock in the 'Order Arms' (from advance 2nd motion) position. He wears a red coat with dark facings, a white waistcoat, white breeches and black gaiters. The helmet is fur-crested with a white-over-red plume.

The corps consisted of one company of seventy-six privates, the commanding officer being Captain Joseph Fitzwilliam Vandercom, a haberdasher of Dowgate Street.

DOWGATE WARD
VOLUNTEER

No. 76

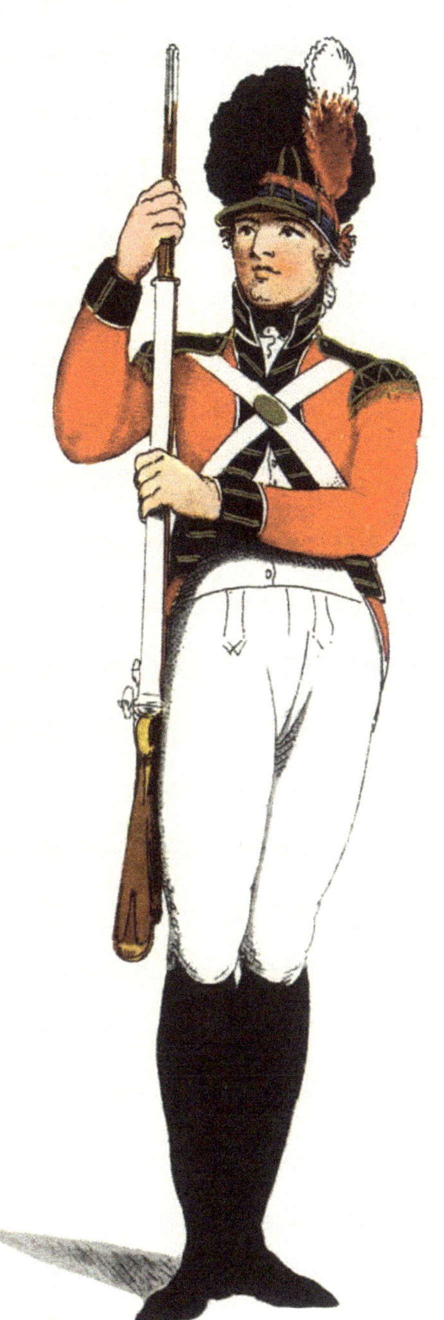

Rowlandson Delin.

ORDER ARMS *(from Advance 2d Motion.)*

At the Motion the right hand quits the Lock & smartley lays hold of the Firelock near the Trumpet pipe at the 3d motion the fire lock is forced to the Ground the left hand quitting it & right is extended along the sling the same as attention.

London Pub April 20. 1799. at Ackermann's Gallery, 101 Strand.

94 – LOYAL BERMONDSEY VOLUNTEER ASSOCIATION

Plate 68 after Thomas Rowlandson from Rudolph Ackermann's *Loyal London Volunteers*, published 10 December 1798. A single figure against a plain background wears a red coat with dark green facings, white breeches and a fur-crested helmet sporting a red plume. He hold his firelock in the 'Present Arms' (1st motion from mourn arms) position.

This corps was enrolled in May 1798, records the notes accompanying the plate, under Robert Rich Esq, 'to serve in Southwark and Rotherhithe.' Of one company, the Loyal Bermondsey Volunteer Association's place of arms was in the Jamaica House near Rotherhithe. Colours were presented on 1 May 1799. The cross-belt plate just visible in the image was engraved with the letter LBV and a crown.

LOYAL BERMONDSEY VOLUNTEER

No. 68

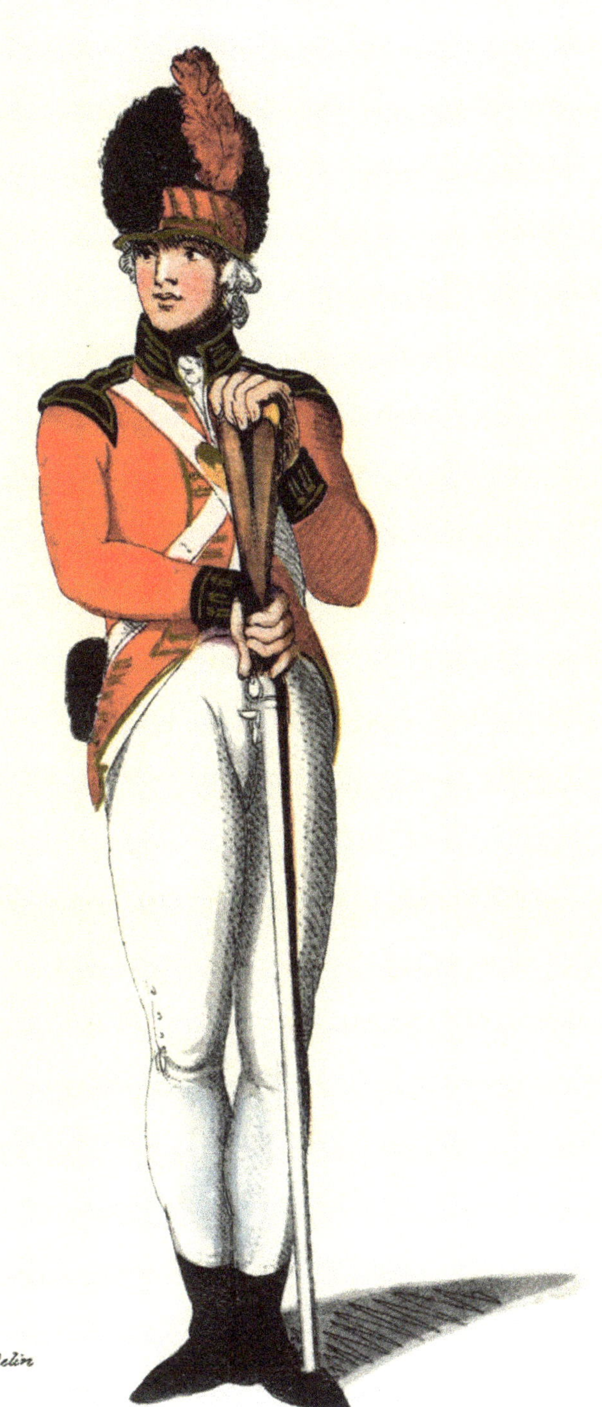

Rowlandson Delin

PRESENT ARMS 1st Motion from Mourn Arms

At the word Arms. the hollow of the right foot is brought against the left heel. at the same instant; the right hand takes hold of the small of the butt: with the back of the hand inwards

London Pub Dec 1 1798 at Ackermanns Gallery 101 Strand

95 – JOHN GILPIN THE SECOND OR CITY LIGHT HORSE VOLUNTEERS

Hand-coloured caricature after Isaac Cruikshank, published by Samuel William Fores of 3 Piccadilly on 17 July 1794 with the caption, 'John Gilpin the Second or City Light Horse Volunteers Performing their Evolutions.' As a riding master stands, whip in hand, on the left, several volunteers are experiencing problems keeping their mount in check.

John Gilpin was said to have been a wealthy City of London draper and was a feature of a poem by William Cowper which told how he became separated from his wife and children when he lost control of his horse.

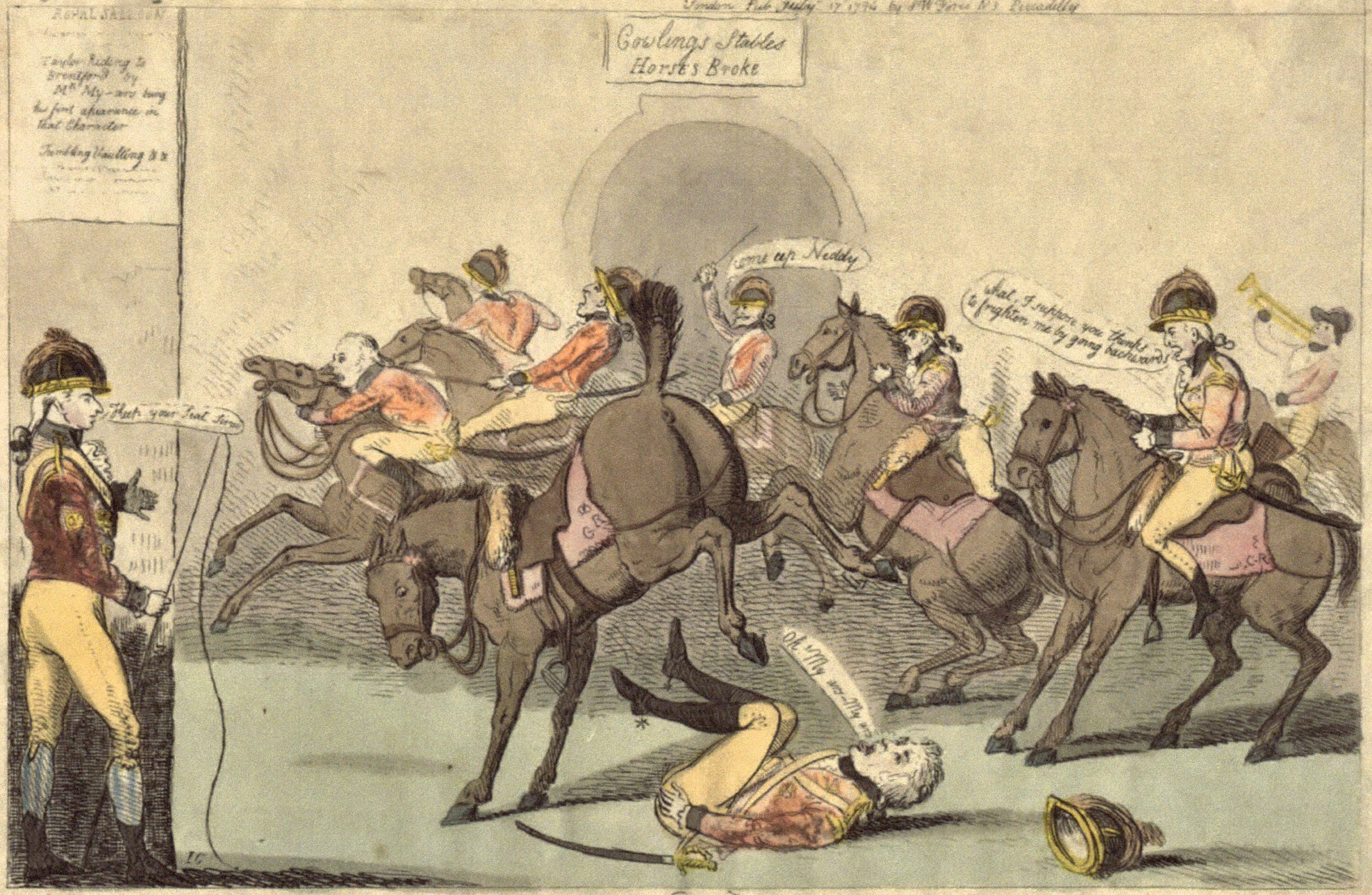

London Pub. July 17 1794 by S.W. Fores No 3 Piccadilly

John Gilpin the Second, or City Light Horse Volunteers Performing their Evolutions.

96 – MR JOHN GOLDHAM

Hand-coloured mezzotint engraved by Samuel William Reynolds after Dean Wolstenholme and published by P & D Colnaghi & Co with the following caption below the image: 'This Print representing Mr John Goldham field Adjutant of the London Volunteer Cavalry, executing the six Divisions of the Austrian Broad Sword Exchange at speed with a sabre in each hand, / and with the utmost effect and precision is Dedicated to Lieut, Col Anderson [sic] and the other Officers and Members of the Regiment by their most obedient and very humble Servant Dan Wolstenholme.' A single mounted figure in a blue coat, white breeches and crimson sash standing in his stirrups wielding a sabre in each hand.

Misspelt in the caption, the commander of the London Volunteer Cavalry was Lieutenant-Colonel John Proctor Anderdon. (*Image courtesy of the Anne SK Brown Military Collection, Brown University Library*)

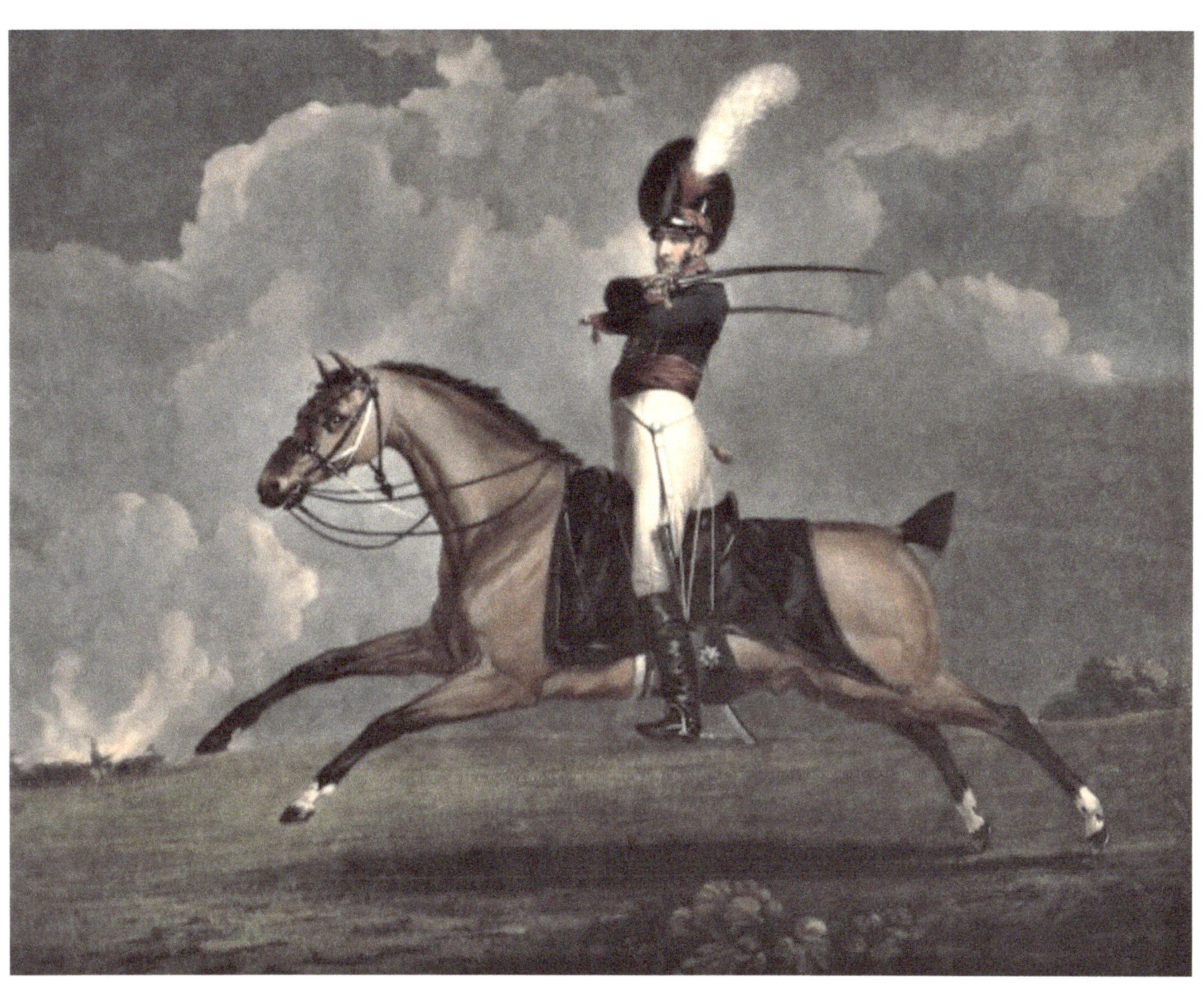

97 – THE RT HON JOHN LORD SOMERVILLE

Mezzotint engraving by James Ward after Samuel Woodforde and published by Antonio Cesare de Poggi of 91 New Bond Street, London on 15 March 1800 with the following caption: 'The Rt. Honble. John Lord Somerville / One of the Sixteen Peers for Scotland, President of the Board of Agriculture / And Colonel of the West Somerset Yeomanry'. A full length figure against a country scene that includes a man leading two oxen.

David J Knight includes a copy of this print in his book *Directory of Yeomanry Cavalry 1794-1828* (the 2013 Special Number issued by the Military Historical Society) together with the following uniform description: 'He wears the uniform adopted in 1797, which comprises a Tarleton [helmet] with a red turban, white plume and gilt fittings; a blue-grey jacket with scarlet facings and gold braid and buttons; and white breeches.'

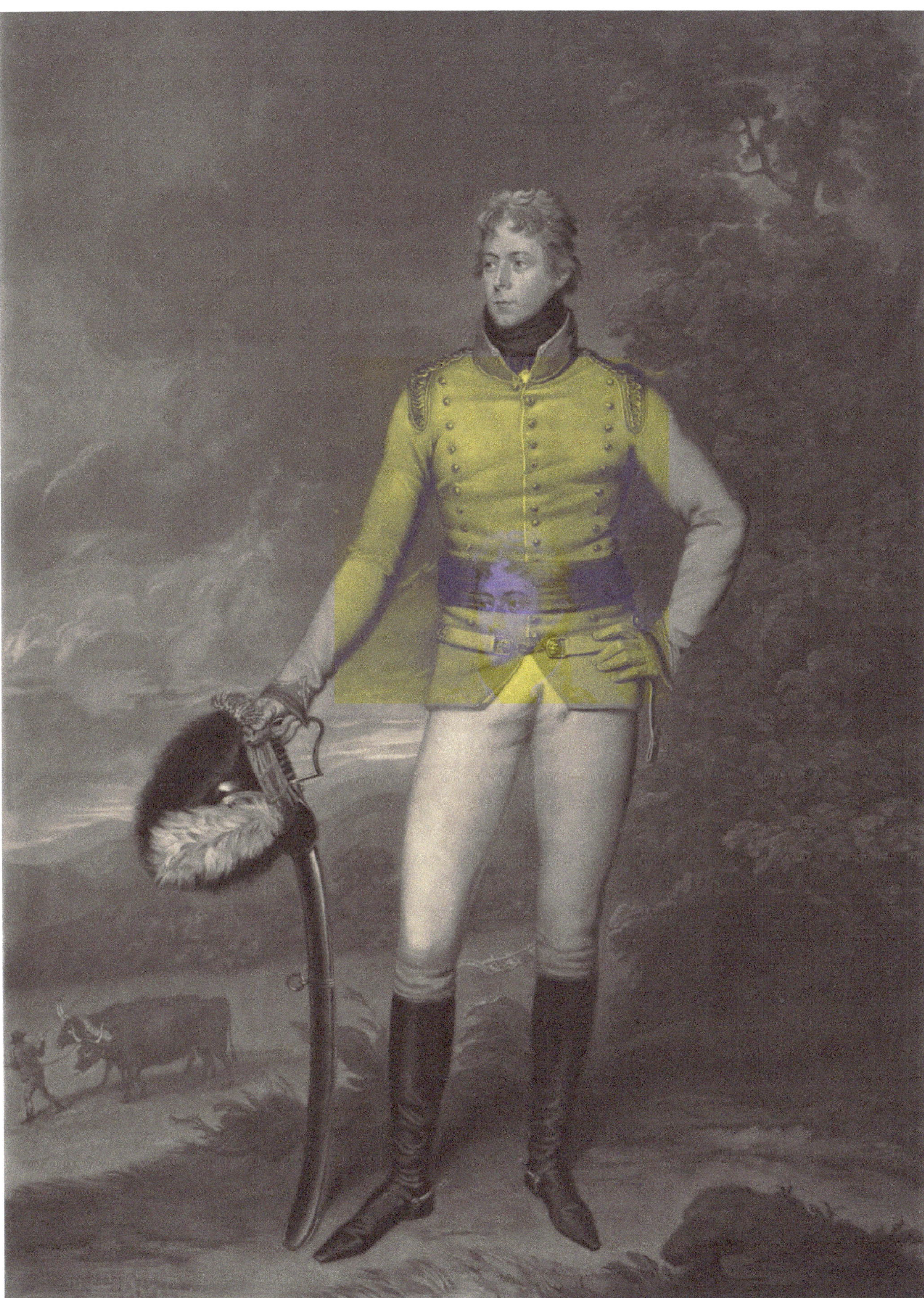

98 – VOLUNTEERS OF THE BRITISH EMPIRE

Broadside drawn and etched by William Nelson Gardiner and published by him on 10 September 1803 and featuring the words of a song or poem, 'Dedicated to the Volunteers of the British Empire'. The printing by W Bulmer & Co of Cleveland Row, London. Below a large monument inscribed with the words 'Defending his King & Country Coll James Gardiner fell at the Battle of Preston Pans 1745', group of volunteers are gathered, one mounted, the rest on foot.

William Nelson Gardiner of Corpus College Cambridge was a Bachelor of Arts and member of the St James's Loyal Volunteers. Colonel James Gardiner, mentioned on the monument, had joined the army at fourteen and was mortally wounded during the Battle of Prestonpans as mentioned. (*Image courtesy of the Anne SK Brown Military Collection, Brown University Library*)

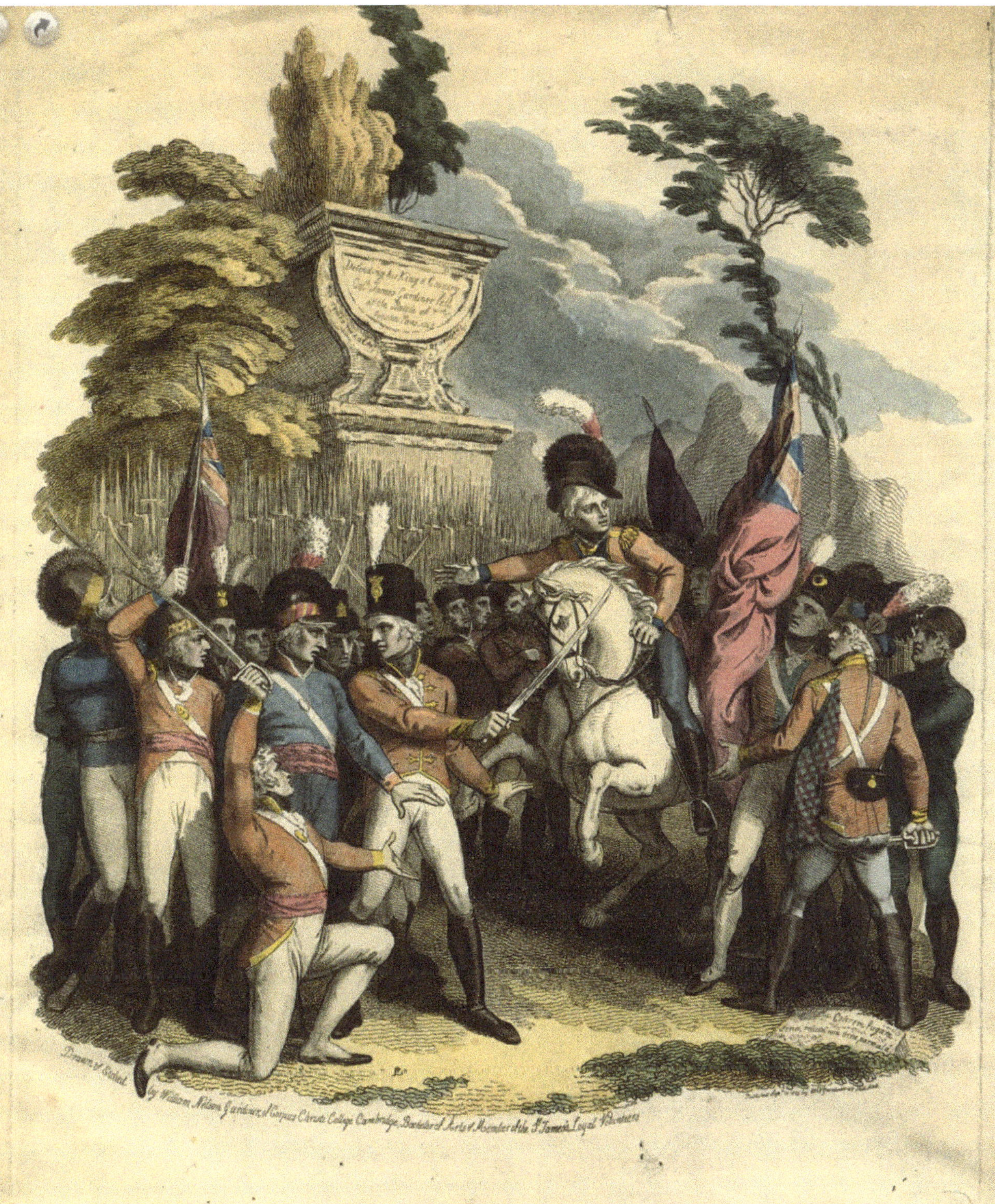

DEDICATED to the VOLUNTEERS of the BRITISH EMPIRE,

By their Comrade, WILLIAM NELSON GARDINER.

Volunteers, by glory led,
Sons of Heroes who have bled,
Welcome to your gory bed,
Or to glorious victory.

Now's the day, and now's the hour;
See the front of battle lour;
See approach false Gallia's power,
Gallia! chains, and slavery!

Who will be a traitor knave?
Who can fill a coward's grave?
Who so base as be a slave!
Traitor! coward! turn and flee!

For Britain's King, for Freedom's shore,
Who will urge the faulchion's power?
Freeman live—or live no more,
Volunteer! march on with me!

By oppression's woes and pains!
By our scorn of servile chains!
We will drain our dearest veins,
But we shall be, shall be free!

Lay the proud invaders low!
Tyrants fall in every foe;
Liberty's in every blow!
Forward! let us do, or die!

Printed by W. Bulmer and Co. Cleveland Row;
for W. N. Gardiner, No. 48, Pall-Mall.

99 – St CATHERINE'S ASSOCIATION

Plate 63 after Thomas Rowlandson from Rudolph Ackermann's *Loyal London Volunteers*, published on 20 December 1798 at Ackermann's Gallery, 101 Strand, London. A single figure against a plain background is shown demonstrating the 'Club Arms' (3rd motion) position. The supporting text that accompanies the image records that the corps had been formed on 20 June 1798 under the direction of Robert Jenkins, Esq. The dress of the corps is also described: 'Helmets, elegantly decorated, with Label inscribed St Catharine's Association; on right side, a Garter, Crown, and GR in cypher; and round it, a handsome Trophy, with St Catharine's Wheel at the bottom.' The same device also appeared on the oval shoulder-belt plate and on the buttons.

St. CATHERINE'S. ASSOCIATION

No. 63

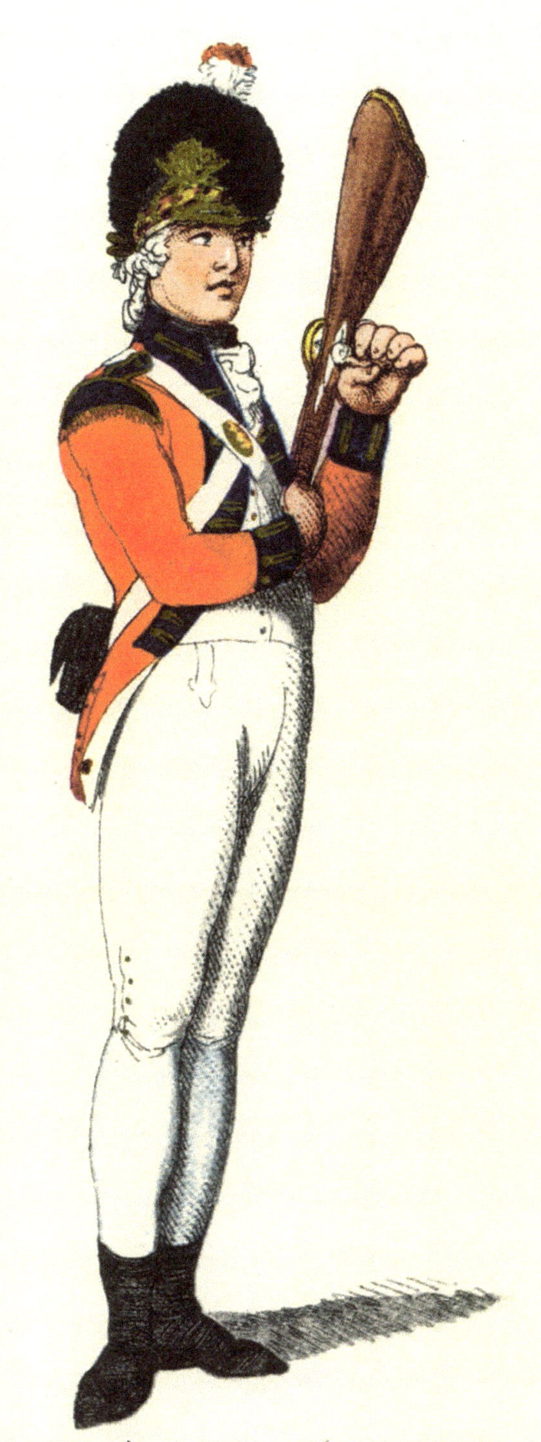

Rowlandson Delin

CLUB ARMS (3d Motion)

The left Elbow is sunk close to the side: & the left hand seizes the cock & hammer between the forefinger & thumb.

London Pub. Dec 20 1798. at Ackermanns Gallery 101 Strand

100 – LONDON AND WESTMINSTER LIGHT HORSE VOLUNTEERS

Plate 1 of nine after Thomas Rowlandson from the cavalry section of Rudolph Ackermann's *Loyal London Volunteers*, published 24 June 1798. A single mounted figure in the act discharging a pistol. Accompanying the image, the text includes 'This very respectable and brilliant Association, consisting of six Troops, was first formed in the year 1780, and takes Precedency of all other Volunteer Military Associations. They have been frequently reviewed, and as often received the warmest testimonies of approbation from the highest authorities.'

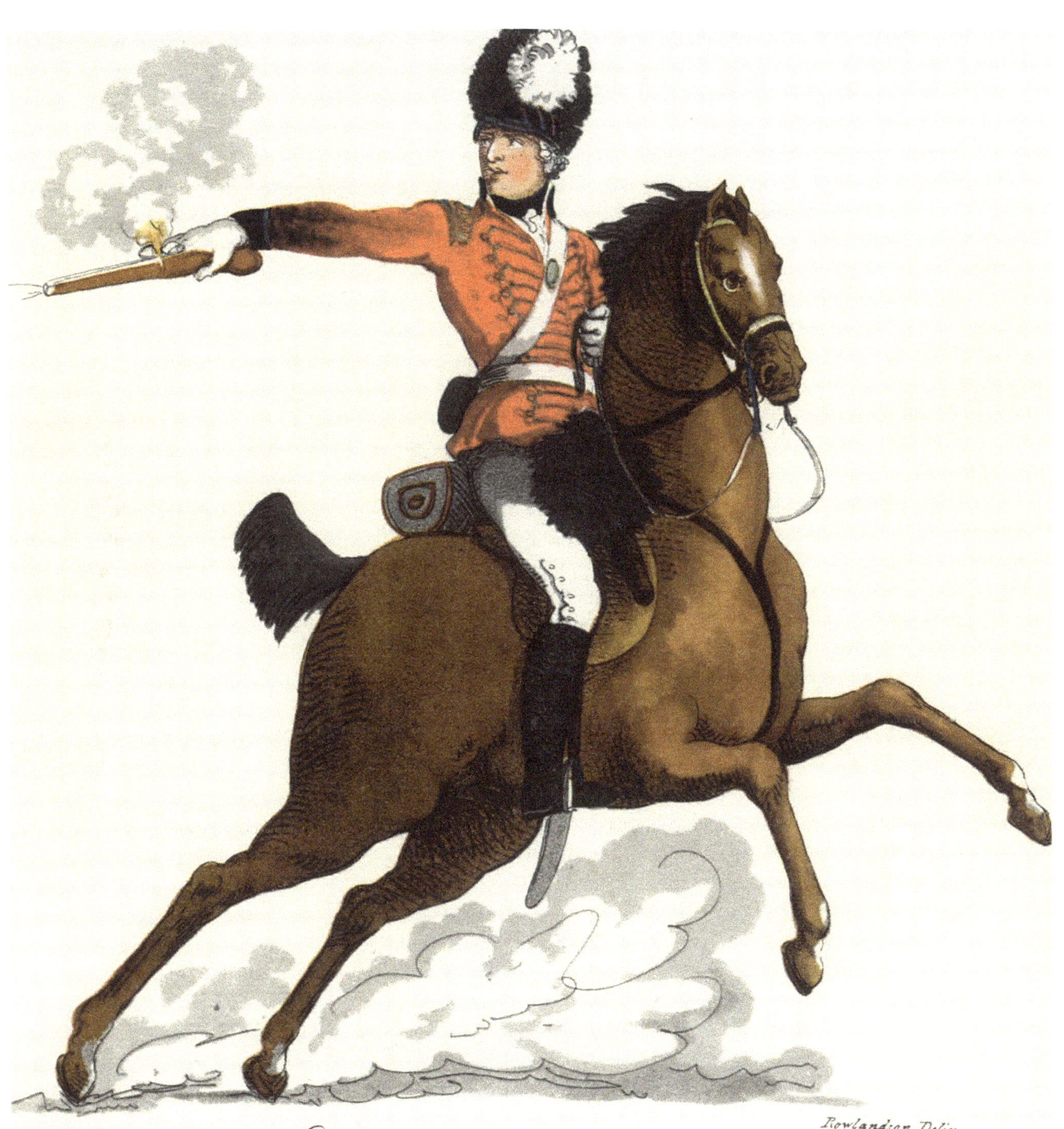
Rowlandson Delin

101 – BRIDGE WARD ASSOCIATION

Plate 65 after Thomas Rowlandson from Rudolph Ackermann's *Loyal London Volunteers*, published on 4 January 1799 at Ackermann's Gallery, 101 Strand, London. A single figure illustrates the 'Mouen Arms' (1st motion) and wearing a red coat with light blue facings and light blue breeches decorated with red braid.

As one company of sixty-six infantry, the corps was formed under the command of Captain John Boddy on 10 May 1798. Headquarters were at the Fishmongers' Hall close to London Bridge. The cross-belt plate seen in the illustration was a silver oval inscribed with the letters BWA.

BRIDGE WARD
VOLUNTEER.

No. 65

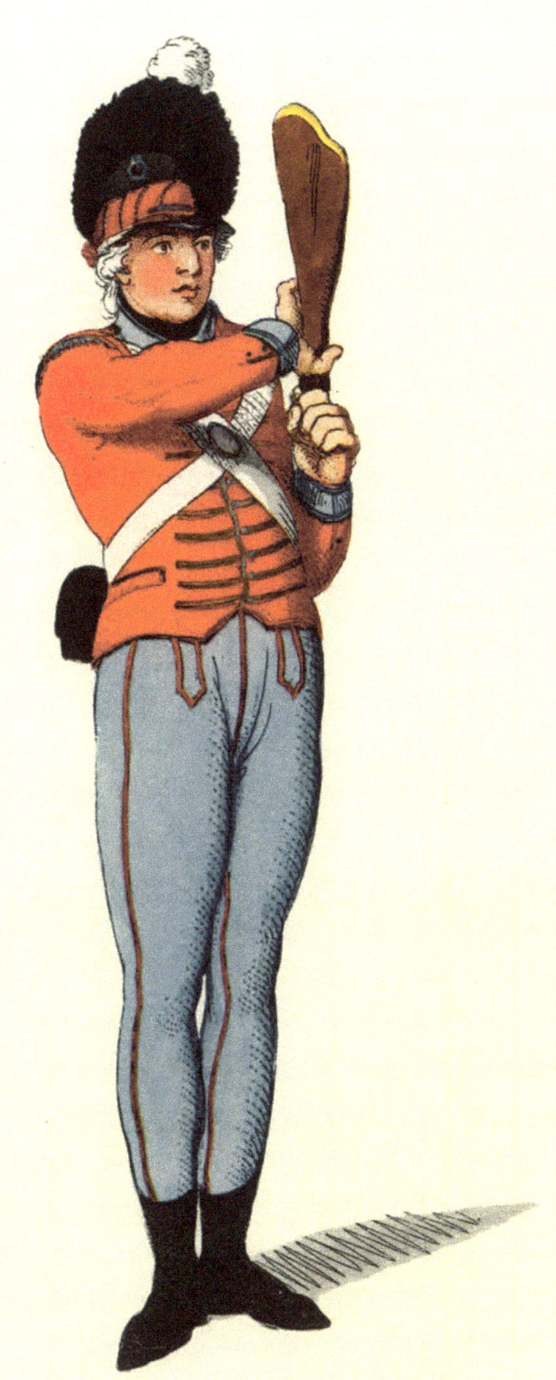

Rowlandson Delin.

MOURN ARMS (1st Motion)

At the word Arms the right hand quits the firelock behind, & takes hold of the small of the Butt.

London Pub. Jan. 1. 1799. at Ackermann's Gallery. 101 Strand.

BIBLIOGRAPHY

Many books of reference have been consulted for this 'Guide', most importantly the *Index To British Military Costume Prints 1500-1914* which was compiled and published by the Army Museums Ogilby Trust in 1972.

TITLES FOR THE MILITARY UNIFORMOLOGIST

Uniformologist: one who studies uniforms – especially military uniforms – through ages and civilisations.

We have a developing range of books dedicated to uniformology, drawing on seminal works from the 18th and 19th century. N&MP have used state-of-the-art printing technology to provide facsimile editions of these hitherto almost unattainable collections and series of military uniform plates.

The artists who illustrated these works customarily painted uniforms that were contemporary, or near contemporary, to them and had most commonly restricted their subjects to the uniforms either of their own nation or those that they had personally seen.

Some contain lively commentary from expert Ray Westlake and in some we have let the plates talk for themselves – but all, without exaggeration, are both masterpieces of military art, and important historical reference works.

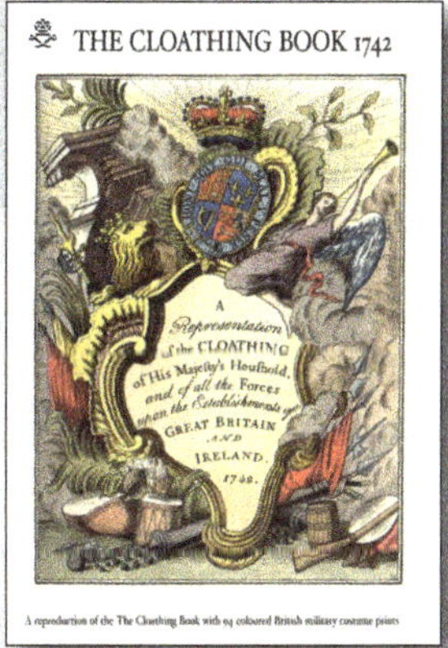

REPRESENTATION OF THE CLOATHING OF HIS MAJESTY'S HOUSEHOLD 1742 – THE CLOATHING BOOK 1742

The uniforms of the whole British Army of 1742 in 94 superb colour plates. Reprint of an original and rare book commissioned by the Duke of Cumberland, victor of Culloden, and presented to King George II.

9781843428305

CAPTAIN MACDONALD'S ARTILLERY DRESS ALBUM 1625-1897

A series of watercolour sketches illustrating the dress of the Regiment.
A beautifully illustrated definitive history of the Royal Regiment of Artillery's uniforms, produced at the end of the 19th century with full colour plates.

9781783310227

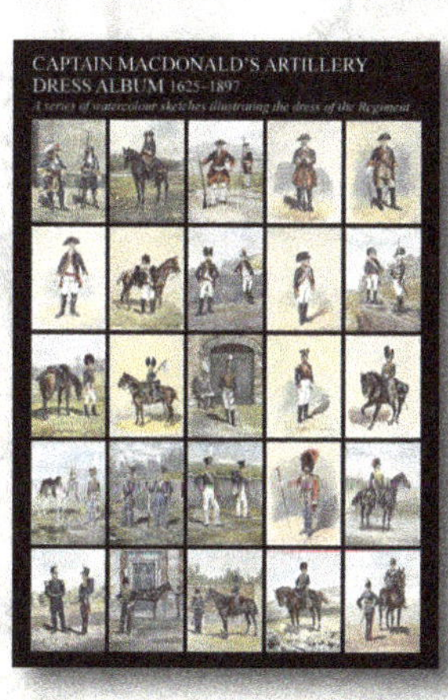

www.naval-military-press.com

BELLANGÉS'S SOLDIERS OF THE FRENCH REPUBLIC AND THE EMPIRE 1795-1814

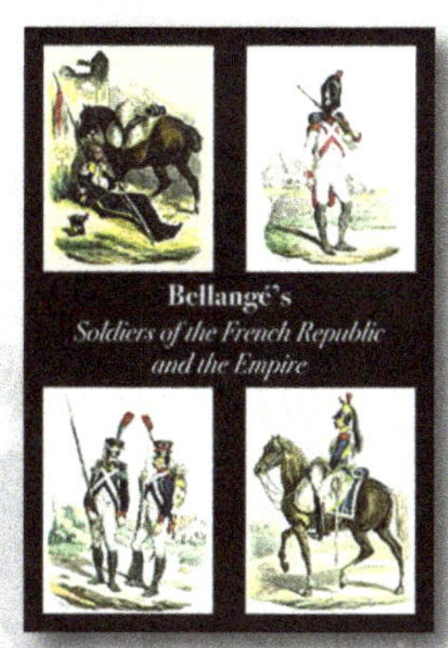

Taken from the first German translation of 'Histoire de l'empereur Napoleon' (1840), that was enlarged for this edition with six new illustrations.

Bellangés's fifty detailed and brightly coloured uniform plates present the soldiers of the different regiments of the French Republic and the Empire in their respective costumes.

9781783318414

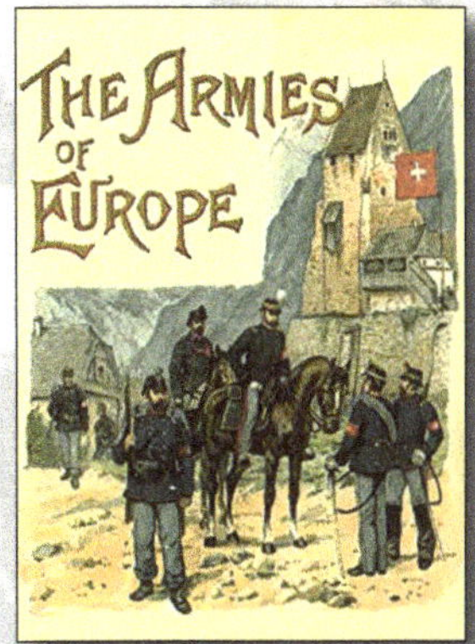

Richard Knötel's ARMIES OF EUROPE ILLUSTRATED (1890)

Classic descriptions complete with colour plates and vignettes by the renowned military artist and pioneer of the study of military uniform Richard Knötel, covering the armies of: The British Empire – The German Army – Austria-Hungary – Italy – France – Russia – Denmark, Sweden and Norway – Spain and Portugal – Switzerland – Holland and Belgium – Turkey and the States of the Balkan Peninsula.

9781783311750

CHARLES HAMILTON SMITH'S COSTUME OF THE ARMY OF THE BRITISH EMPIRE – ACCORDING TO THE 1814 REGULATIONS

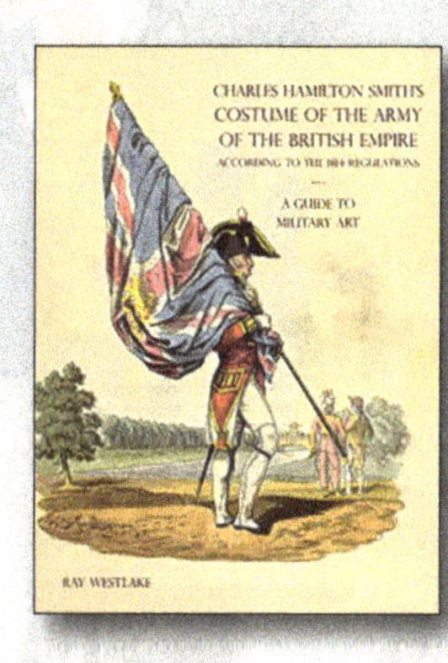

This is a full reissuing of the 60 hand-coloured aquatint plates by I.C. Stadler, after drawings by Smith, originally produced in 1815 for the oldest commercial art gallery in the world, Colnaghi and Co. Paul Colnaghi became the official print-seller to the Prince Regent, and he was asked to organise the Royal Collection, receiving a Royal Warrant when the Prince Regent became George IV. Uniquely, many of Smith's uncoloured original drawings are also included in this edition.

9781783319916

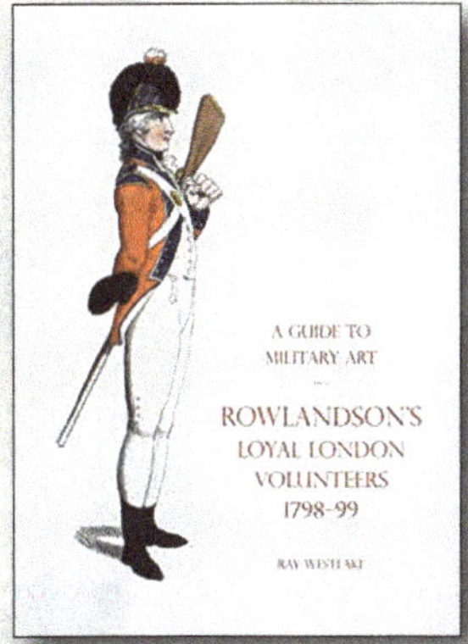

ROWLANDSON'S LOYAL LONDON VOLUNTEERS

The most original set of English military plates from the Napoleonic period – The Loyal Volunteers of London & Environs, Infantry & Cavalry, in their respective uniforms. Representing the whole of the Manual, Platoon & Funeral Exercise in 89 plates. Designed and etched by T. Rowlandson and originally published in London during 1798-99 by Ackermann. Reproduced here from high from an original volume is a full set of Rowlandson's 87 plates, together with an additional two that were to be included in some (even scarcer) bound volumes by the publisher. To accompany each plate, Ackermann prepared a page of letterpress which included details of when the corps had been formed, its uniform and names of officers. That text has been reproduced in full, together with additional notes prepared by Ray Westlake.

9781783318889

www.naval-military-press.com

MAJOR LOVETT'S MILITARY DRESS AND FIELD UNIFORMS OF THE RAJ

During the Years Leading up to the Great War

Classic representation of the British Indian Army at the height of the English Age of Empire, in 72 superb uniform plates. This is an invaluable work for anyone interested in the Indian armies and their military uniforms.

9781474536363

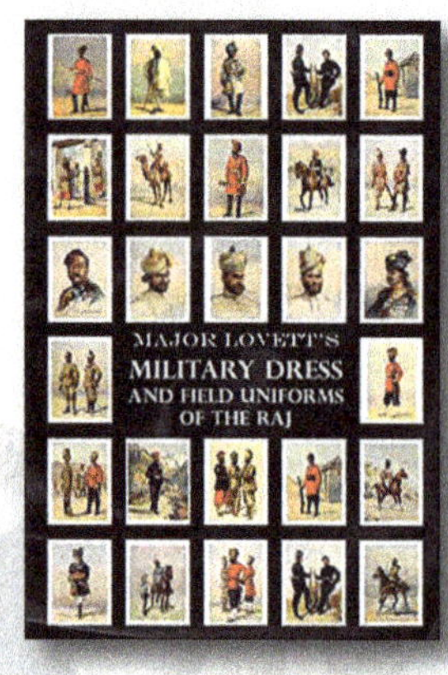

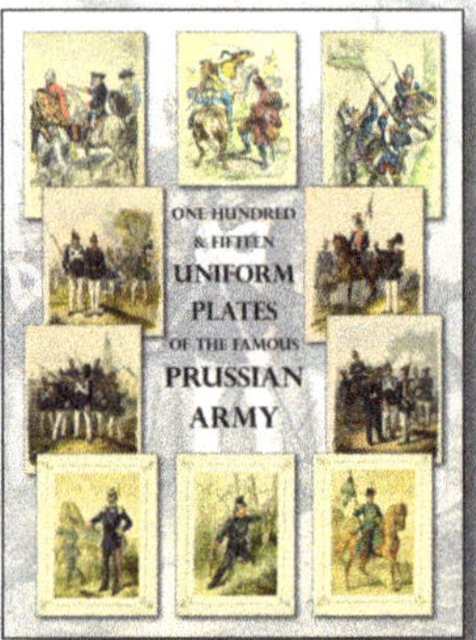

ONE HUNDRED AND FIFTEEN UNIFORM PLATES OF THE FAMOUS PRUSSIAN ARMY UNDER FREDERICK THE GREAT, FREDERICK WILLIAM IV AND PRINCE REGENT WILHELM: OMNIBUS EDITION

This is a compilation omnibus edition of three colourful 19th century military costume plate editions, detailing the Pre-Unification Prussian Army 1751-1855 in accurately hand-coloured facsimile images. Lively commentary from expert Ray Westlake on each plate enhances their historical usefulness.

9781474537551

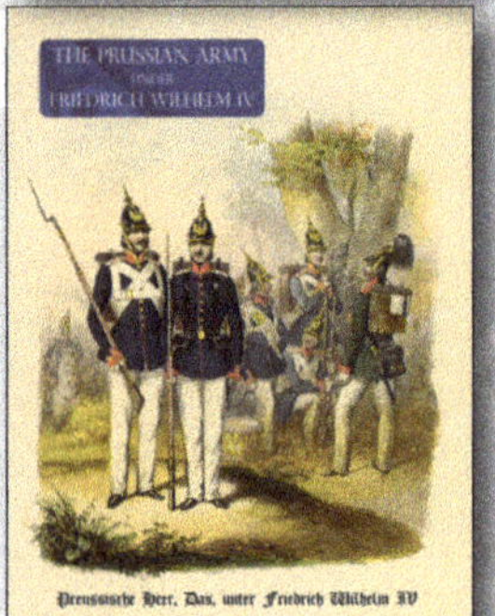

PRUSSIAN ARMY (UNIFORM) UNDER FREDRICH WIHELM IV

PREUSSISCHE HEER, DAS, UNTER FRIEDRICH WILHELM IV

An excellent visual presentation of the Prussian Army and their uniforms under the Kaiser Friedrich Wilhelm IV. Series of 36 facsimile numbered contemporary hand-coloured lithographs. This is a colourful series of military costume plates with over 200 military figures in their 'natural surroundings': camping, in battle, on horseback, on the march, etc.

9781474537582

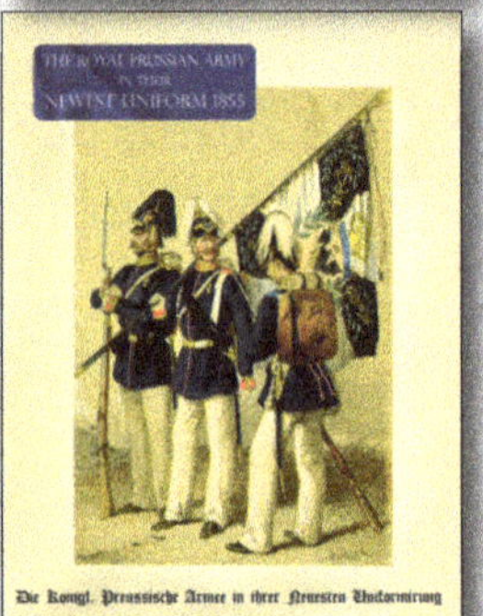

ROYAL PRUSSIAN ARMY IN THEIR NEWEST UNIFORM 1855

DIE KÖNIGL. PREUSSISCHE ARMEE IN IHRER NEUESTEN UNIFORMIRUNG

The beautiful plates depict the various uniforms of the Prussian Army as defined by the 1855 regiment. The work comprises 48 facsimile hand-coloured tinted lithographic plates of military uniforms, each mounted within a lithographed border incorporating the crowned initials of the Prussian king. A small title strip is at the bottom of each leaf, identifying the plate. Mitscher & Röstell, 1859.

9781474537582

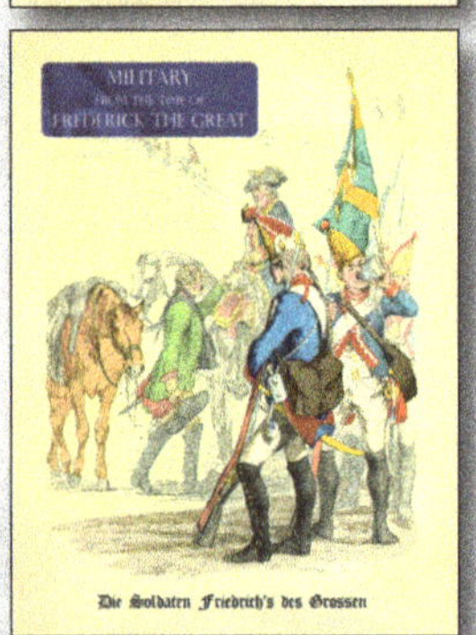

MILITARY (UNIFORM) FROM THE TIME OF FREDERICK THE GREAT

DIE SOLDATEN FRIEDRICH'S DES GROSSEN

Thirty excellent and accurately coloured plates of the uniforms of different Prussian regiments under Frederick the Great by wood engraver Eduard Kretzschmar (1807-1858) and illustrator Adolf von Menzel (1815-1905).

9781474537575

www.naval-military-press.com

www.ingramcontent.com/pod-product-compliance
Lightning Source LLC
LaVergne TN
LVHW070532110826
845147LV00017BA/975
9781474538305